Maurice Evans
1901 —

MACBETH

THE FALCON

SHAKESPEARE

. . . and for his crest or cognizance a falcoun, his wings displayed argent, standing on a wreath of his colours, supporting a speare gould steeled as aforesaid. . . .

So in part reads the confirmation of the Grant of Arms made by the Heralds' office to John Shakespeare in 1599 as described by Garter King of Arms.

Edited by BETTY BEALEY, *Head of the English Department, North Toronto Collegiate Institute, Toronto*

LONGMANS CANADA LIMITED, DON MILLS (TORONTO)

MACBETH

by *William Shakespeare*

The photographs appearing on the end-papers are reproduced with the permission of the Victoria and Albert Museum, London; Angus McBean, London; and the National Film Archive, London.

© 1965 BY LONGMANS CANADA LIMITED,
55 BARBER GREENE ROAD, DON MILLS (TORONTO), ONTARIO
PRINTED AND BOUND IN CANADA BY THE HUNTER ROSE CO. LIMITED

3 4 5 6 7 8 9 10 11   74 73 72 71 70 69 68 67 66

To my friends and colleagues, and especially
to my sister Barbara

So thanks to all at once, and to each one. . . .

CONTENTS

SHAKESPEARE'S GREATNESS: A CAPSULE

> A thousand poets pried at life,
> But only one amid the strife
> Rose to be Shakespeare.
>
> *Robert Browning*

IN AN oversimplified analysis of the genius of Shakespeare, it may be said that he was a great poet, a great playwright, a great patriot, and a psychologist who had an unerring insight into human nature.

As a poet, he used words with unforgettable magic; the felicity of his phrases echoes all the way from Macbeth's:

> I have liv'd long enough: my way of life
> Is fall'n into the sear, the yellow leaf,

to Horatio's:

> Good night, sweet prince,
> And flights of angels sing thee to thy rest.

It ranges from Antony's "I am dying, Egypt dying" to Prospero's

> We are such stuff
> As dreams are made on; and our little life
> Is rounded with a sleep.

It extends from lyric sweetness to tragic splendour.

As a playwright, Shakespeare was a master of his art; he understood and practised with consummate success all the theatrical devices required for low comedy and high tragedy. Memorable scenes spring to mind: the quarrel of Brutus and Cassius in *Julius Caesar*, the blinding of Gloucester in *King Lear*, the trial in *The Merchant of Venice*, the play extempore in *Henry IV, Part I*, the great duel in *Hamlet*.

Shakespeare was a great patriot; his love for England shines through the lines of "time-honour'd Lancaster" in *Richard II*:

This blessed plot, this earth, this realm, this England,
This land of such dear souls, this dear dear land.

It speaks in the proud words of Philip Faulconbridge at the end of *King John*:

This England never did, nor never shall,
Lie at the proud foot of a conqueror.

But Shakespeare's chief glory lies in the creation of characters. Although Hamlet is the supreme example, on his heels tread Falstaff, Lear, Macbeth, Shylock, Rosalind, and a host of others. Browning's comment does indeed go to the heart of the matter.

BIOGRAPHY OF SHAKESPEARE

(This sketch does not pretend to be a definitive life; it is inserted only as a guide to the Multiple Choice Quiz, p. 205, which presents some miscellaneous facts about Shakespeare's life.)

Birth, Parents, Education

With regard to Shakespeare's birth, we know only that the baptismal register for the parish church of the Holy Trinity, Stratford, bears the following entry for April 26, 1564: *Gulielmus, filius Johannes Shakespeare*. The house on Henley Street is assumed to have been the place of his birth. Neither Shakespeare's father nor his mother could write; the former, a man of civic importance who later fell on evil days, signed documents with his mark, a pair of glovers' compasses. Shakespeare's mother, born Mary Arden, used a running horse as her "signature". Ben Jonson said of his friend Will that he had "small Latin and less Greek", but others have brushed aside his lack of a classical education by saying that he was "naturally learned". His knowledge of the work of the poet Ovid is evident in his writings. It is probable that he left the Stratford Grammar School at the age of thirteen; later in his youth, he may have been a schoolmaster in the country, according to a tradition reported by John Aubrey.

Family

Married at eighteen to Anne Hathaway, who was eight years older than he, Shakespeare was the father of three children: Susanna, and the twins, Hamnet and Judith, the latter named after a young couple who were friends of the Shakespeares. One of the great tragedies of Shakespeare's life was the death of his son in 1596 at the age of eleven. It has been suggested that the many precocious small boys in his plays owe their existence to Shakespeare's memories of Hamnet. Although both his daughters married, Shakespeare's own family became extinct with the death of his granddaughter Elizabeth in 1670. The three sons of his daughter Judith (Mrs. Thomas Quiney) died young: one in infancy, the other two in 1639.

The Years Between

A tradition, which cannot be substantiated, states that Shakespeare left Stratford in the late 1580's because he had been accused of poaching on the estate of Sir Thomas Lucy. For a number of years, we lose sight of him. Some critics maintain that he must have been a soldier in the Low Countries; others that he was a sailor. These convictions are based on his sound knowledge of both these occupations, the military and the sea-faring. Another tradition has it that he first made a living holding horses at the playhouse door. In 1592, however, a jealous playwright referred to him as "this upstart crow, beautified with our feathers". Shakespeare was already on the high road to fame and fortune.

Later Years

In 1596, Shakespeare's father applied for and in 1599 received a coat of arms: "Gould on a bend sable, a speare of the first, the point steeled proper" with the proud motto *Non sans droit*. In the year 1597, Shakespeare purchased the largest dwelling in Stratford, New Place, for the sum of sixty pounds; it was described as "a pretty house of brick and timber" with two barns and two gardens. A mulberry tree, reputed to have been planted by Shakespeare in his garden, was cut down in 1758. Shakespeare died at New Place on April 23, 1616, and was buried in the chancel of the parish church; he lies there still, since no one has apparently been bold enough to invoke the curse mentioned in his epitaph. In an elaborate will, which contained bequests to the poor of Stratford and to his friends for the purchase of "mourning rings", Shakespeare provided carefully for his family, leaving his wife specific items of furniture.

Achievements and Interests

In a period of about twenty years, Shakespeare wrote 37 plays, 154 sonnets, and 2 long poems: a record that indicates matchless energy and inspired industry. The great majority of his plays were acted at the Globe Theatre, which burned down in 1613 during a performance of what may have been Shakespeare's final play, *Henry VIII*. About half of his plays were published separately during his lifetime in quarto form, including the longest one, *Hamlet*. The shortest of the tragedies, *Macbeth*, was first published in the Folio of 1623.

Shakespeare's interests must have been wide and varied; it appears that he was keenly interested in sports, particularly bowling. He must have read widely, though the only book that we know he owned was a copy of Florio's translation of the writings of Montaigne, the French essayist. (Even the authenticity of his signature in it has been challenged.)

Certain American scholars have tried to discredit Shakespeare as the author of the plays, maintaining that Francis Bacon (or perhaps Christopher Marlowe) wrote them. The most distinguished and eminent critics, however, have no doubt that William Shakespeare wrote the mighty works attributed to him. "Any other assumption about the authorship of these works shows a wanton and reckless disregard of unimpeachable evidence" (Wilfred J. Osborne).

SHAKESPEARE AND HOLINSHED

Shakespeare's main source for the historical incidents in *Macbeth* was the second edition of Raphael (Ralph) Holinshed's *Chronicles*,[1] which appeared in 1587. Two separate sections of the *Chronicles* provided the raw material: the "Historie of Makbeth" and the murder of King Duff by Donwald, who was Captain of the Castle of Forres. The outline of Shakespeare's plot is mainly that presented by Holinshed. In the *Chronicles*, Shakespeare discovered that Macbeth played a heroic part in putting down King Duncan's enemies. He also found the Witches' prophecies to Macbeth and Banquo in Holinshed.[2] From the *Chronicles*, he also obtained the idea that Lady Macbeth incited her husband to the murder, but the part played by Lady Macbeth merges with that played by Donwald's wife in the murder of King Duff, as reported by Holinshed. Certain details of the murder were also borrowed from that portion of the *Chronicles*.[3]

[1] *Holinshed's Chronicle as Used in Shakespeare's Plays*, Allardyce and Josephine Nicoll, ed. (Everyman's Library; Toronto, J. M. Dent & Sons, (Canada) Limited, 1927).
[2] *Ibid*, p. 210.
[3] *Ibid*, pp. 212-13.

Examples of pathetic fallacy on the night of the murder as reported by Lennox, Ross, and the Old Man also occur in Holinshed,[1] as do the plans for the murder of Banquo, his death, and the escape of Fleance.[2] Macbeth's distrust of Macduff, the escape of the Thane of Fife, the murder of Lady Macduff and her children "with all other whom he found in that castell" also have their origin in the *Chronicles*.[3] The second series of prophecies appeared in Holinshed,[4] but of all the episodes in the play, the interview between Malcolm and Macduff in Act IV, Scene 3, follows the original most closely.[5] Details of the final overthrow of Macbeth are also to be found in the *Chronicles*.[6]

It is, however, more interesting to consider the changes Shakespeare made and the episodes that sprang from his own lively imagination, all of which reveal his consummate skill in stagecraft and the art of the theatre.

Shakespeare was well aware of the dramatic value of compression; he adds immeasurably to the power of *Macbeth* by giving the impression that the events happened in a period of several months, whereas Macbeth actually reigned for seventeen years. Nevertheless, there are moments when we feel that years have indeed passed. Macbeth implies as much in his lines: "my way of life/Is fall'n into the sear, the yellow leaf." And when we meet Malcolm in Act IV, Scene 3, he appears to have become much older and wiser in the ways of the world.

At the beginning of the play, Shakespeare telescopes the rebellion of Macdonwald, the invasion of Sweno, and a later attack by King Canute into one episode, chiefly to add to the prowess and stature of Macbeth. Another significant change occurs with regard to the death of Macdonwald. In the original, he slays himself; Shakespeare has him killed by Macbeth in

[1]Holinshed, *op. cit.*, p. 215.
[2]*Ibid*, p. 216.
[3]*Ibid*, pp. 217-18.
[4]*Ibid*, p. 218.
[5]*Ibid*, pp. 219-21.
[6]*Ibid*, pp. 222-3.

order to bring out Macbeth's fierce valour on the field of battle.

The murder of King Duff is carried out in the *Chronicles*, not by his host, Donwald, but by four of the latter's hired servants. The corresponding murder of Duncan is carried out by Macbeth with the result that the horror of the crime is emphasized, and Macbeth's shattered remorse can be conveyed in a scene of great power.

In Holinshed, Banquo is murdered after the banquet, not before, as in *Macbeth*. This change in timing provides Shakespeare with the dramatic opportunities afforded by the Ghost, the frantic behaviour of Macbeth, and the presence of mind of Lady Macbeth.

To measure the greatness of Shakespeare's art, we need only note that the brief, significant opening scene, the dagger scene, the banquet scene, and the sleep-walking scene have no counterpart in the *Chronicles*.

Shakespeare's skill in the creation of characters is seen to advantage in his treatment of the shadowy figures of the *Chronicles*; to Duncan, Macbeth, Lady Macbeth, and Banquo, he adds breadth and depth; in short, humanity.

Duncan in Holinshed is presented as a man of "softness" who "had too much of clemencie" and "overmuch slacknesse in punishing offendors". Shakespeare, it is true, implies an element of weakness in him, but causes even his murderer to speak of one who

> . . . hath been
> So clear in his great office, that his virtues
> Will plead like angels, trumpet-tongu'd against
> The deep damnation of his taking-off.

In this way, the great wickedness of the crime is emphasized.

Macbeth, historically, was "a valiant gentleman", "the sure defence and buckler of innocent people", who at the outset of his reign "used great liberalitie towards the nobles of the realme" and "set his whole intention to maintain justice". In the *Chronicles*, also, his character degenerates, but never does he reveal the imagination and depth of conscience shown by Shakespeare's Macbeth; never do we sense the great impression of waste that makes the tragedy moving.

Lady Macbeth was said to be "verie ambitious, burning in unquenchable desire to beare the name of a queene"; her behaviour, as recorded in the *Chronicles*, is not motivated by love for her husband. Donwald's wife, like Lady Macbeth, urged her husband to commit the murder of his King, and he "determined to follow hir advise in the execution of so heinous an act". The touch of humanity in Lady Macbeth's inability to murder Duncan, her faint after the discovery of the body, the growing estrangement between her and her husband, the pathos of her breakdown, and the hint at suicide are all Shakespeare's own inventions.

Since Banquo was regarded as the (legendary) founder of the Stewart line, Shakespeare lessened his guilt in the matter of Duncan's murder. The *Chronicles* specifically state that Macbeth, "communicating his purposed intent with his trustie friends, amongst whom Banquo was the chiefest, upon confidence of their promised aid, . . . slue the king at Enverns". Shakespeare presents him as resisting temptation:

> Merciful powers,
> Restrain in me the cursed thoughts that nature
> Gives way to in repose!

(Nevertheless, he was tempted to the extent that he never accused Macbeth.) It was fitting, too, that an ancestor of James's should be described as possessing "royalty of nature": the reigning monarch must have listened with great satisfaction to this praise of his forbear:

> 'tis much he dares,
> And, to that dauntless temper of his mind,
> He hath a wisdom that doth guide his valour
> To act in safety.

To compare the *Chronicles* with *Macbeth* is to be convinced of the genius of Shakespeare.

THE SOLILOQUIES

A soliloquy is a speech made by an actor when he is alone on the stage. (It has been defined as a "thought projection".) The soliloquy has a threefold purpose: to reveal character, to advance the plot, and to create atmosphere. (In *Macbeth*, the first soliloquy is labelled "aside", because it is spoken in the presence of Banquo, Ross, and Angus.)

Of the 1,993 lines in *Macbeth*, approximately 91.5 per cent are in verse (as compared with 69.37 per cent in *Hamlet*). Macbeth's six major soliloquies make up approximately 122 lines, or nearly 7 per cent of the verse in the play.

An examination of the main soliloquies delivered by Macbeth gives us a deep insight into his character, and also throws light on the events of the plot. Through them, we see all that is best and worst in this tragic hero, who thought he had gained the whole world, but discovered that he had lost his own soul; a man who sowed the wind and reaped the whirlwind; a man who came to realize the truth of the bitter and inexorable dictum: "The wages of sin is death." Three of the soliloquies have to do with the murder of Duncan: I. iii. 128-42, I. vii. 1-28, and II. i. 33-64. One precedes the murder of Banquo, III. i. 48-72, and the last two reveal how Macbeth's achievements have turned to dust and ashes in his mouth, V. iii. 19-29 and V. v. 17-28.

The keynote of the soliloquy "Two truths are told" (I. iii. 128-42) is bewilderment. It reveals that Macbeth has entertained the thought of achieving the crown by murder, but at this stage his whole being is in revolt against the idea. In a revealing comment, he indicates that he is a prey to terrors of the imagination, although he is not alarmed by a human antagonist: "Present fears/Are less than horrible imaginings." The soliloquy reveals that the seeds of temptation are already germinating within him.

Of Macbeth's second soliloquy, "If it were done" (I. vii. 1-28),

Professor G. B. Harrison writes, "This speech is the most important in the play, for only here can Macbeth claim our moral sympathy. He is so clear sighted about the foul business. It will bring retribution even in this world; and his only motive is an ambition which knows itself to be futile."[1] It is not, however, merely fear of retribution that restrains him, but the sheer horror of the crime towards which his ambition drives him. "What really holds him back is the hideous vileness of the deed."[2] The mood is one of indecision, and Macbeth reveals in his vivid figures of speech the poetic imagination that is one of his prominent characteristics.

The Dagger Soliloquy (II. i. 33-64), with all its eerie flashes of brilliance, adds immeasurably to the atmosphere of the play. In Macbeth, there is a definite relationship between conscience and imagination; he is impelled towards the deed but filled with apprehension concerning it. Having dismissed the hallucination by an act of will, he nerves himself to proceed with the crime and moves towards the deed as if it were "an appalling duty".[3] The soliloquy advances the plot in that we feel the murder to be inevitable:

> the bell invites me.
> Hear it not, Duncan, for it is a knell
> That summons thee to heaven, or to hell.

The Banquo Soliloquy (III. i. 48-72) resembles the Duncan Soliloquy (I. vii. 1-28), because both present Macbeth's analysis of the character of his victim, who in each case is an admirable figure standing in the hero's way. In both, Macbeth implies a motive; in the first, it is his ambition to gain the throne; in the second, it is his ambition to retain it and pass it on to his heirs. He works himself up into a rage against Banquo, and the soliloquy

---

[1]G. B. Harrison, *Shakespeare's Tragedies* (London, Routledge & Kegan Paul, Ltd., 1952), p. 193.
[2]A. C. Bradley, *Shakespearean Tragedy* (Toronto, The Macmillan Company of Canada Ltd.; London, Macmillan & Co. Ltd., 1958), p. 355.
[3]*Ibid*, p. 358.

ends on a note of defiance as he challenges fate itself. We see that Macbeth's character is degenerating; there is no bewilderment or hesitation, no dagger to give evidence of subconscious insecurity. Here, there are only resentment and fury, which lead directly to the second great crime.

In nine deeply moving lines (V. iii. 19-29), Macbeth sums up the tragedy of his existence. He sees clearly the price he has paid for his crown; the tone is one of bleak despair. He has sacrificed to the god of his fierce ambition all that made life worthwhile:

> And that which should accompany old age,
> As honour, love, obedience, troops of friends,
> I must not look to have.

His isolation is complete.

When the death of his wife is announced to him, Macbeth seems numb and drained of all emotion. His soliloquy beginning "She should have died hereafter" (V. v. 17-28) brings out the emptiness of life and the littleness of man. It is her death that prompts these bitter reflections; existence is without substance and without meaning:

> It is a tale
> Told by an idiot, full of sound and fury,
> Signifying nothing.

In each of the last two soliloquies, with all their brilliant imagery, we see the withering of the hero's soul.

Lady Macbeth delivers two soliloquies, the powerful lines beginning "Glamis thou art" (II. v. 15-30), and the four lines uttered in disillusionment as she waits for Macbeth in III. ii. 4-7. The first passage is memorable for the picture it gives of her inflexible will, as she expresses her determination that her husband shall be king. Her analysis of Macbeth is valid in its references to his ambition, but it has been argued that had she really understood him she would never have set her course to help him win the crown. Nowhere in the soliloquy does this single-minded woman express any selfish desire to be queen; her steely will-power is directed only towards making her husband king. Her fixed resolution, "Glamis thou art, and Cawdor, and shalt be/What thou art promis'd" makes her seem almost inhuman in her glittering confidence.

How different are the brief lines in which she expresses her realization that nothing has been gained if peace of mind has been forfeited (III. ii. 4-7)! This little speech, fraught with deep significance, is almost a premonitory hint of the horrors of the sleep-walking scene. How ironic it is that she who urged her husband with diabolical intensity to commit the murder of Duncan already senses that retribution has begun to exact its toll.

Banquo's soliloquy (III. i. 1-10) shows a brave man tempted. It is evident that he suspects Macbeth: "and I fear/Thou play'dst most foully for't." He also looks to the fulfilment of the prophecies made to him: "Why, by the verities on thee made good,/May they not be my oracles as well." Troubled and tempted, he takes no action and is struck down by the forces of evil.

The Porter's Soliloquy (II. iii. 1-21) is grimly grotesque; it comes at a tense moment in the play, just as Macbeth and Lady Macbeth have left the stage after the murder of Duncan. It thus relieves the pent-up emotions of the audience and also provides a short interval during which Macbeth and Lady Macbeth can prepare to meet whoever is knocking at the gate. In a sense, the speech might be said to represent a parody on the Dagger Soliloquy, for it, too, contains hallucinations as the Porter welcomes the farmer, the equivocator, and the tailor. It is in a much lower key, of course, and is expressed in prose partly for that reason. With its topical allusions, its euphemism (the everlasting bonfire), and its satire, it has a sombre humour, but it is chiefly impressive for its dramatic irony. Little does the Porter realize in his drunken rambling that he is truly the porter of hell, a hell created by Macbeth and Lady Macbeth.

Although the soliloquies of the play are spread among four characters and range from high tragedy to low comedy, those of Macbeth are undoubtedly the most powerful and the most poetic.

IMAGERY AND ATMOSPHERE

An image is "the little-word picture used by a poet or prose writer to illustrate, illuminate and embellish his thought".[1] Of the imagery in *Macbeth*, Miss Spurgeon says that it appears "to be more rich and varied, more highly imaginative, more unapproachable by any other writer, than that of any other single play."[2]

The play seems shrouded in an atmosphere of fear; the very word "fear" occurs forty-two times, more often than in any other Shakespearian play. It is summed up in Ross's words to Lady Macduff:

> But cruel are the times, when we are traitors
> And do not know ourselves; when we hold rumour
> From what we fear, yet know not what we fear.

Macbeth, too, speaks of the fear that will haunt him through the play: "I am afraid to think what I have done." Contributing to this all-pervading fear are the frequent references to what is strange and unnatural, from the murder of Duncan, an abnormal deed, to the passage in which Macbeth is prepared to see the whole universe in convulsion as long as he can get his own way.

It is fitting that darkness should envelop the play, since Shakespeare equates evil with absence of light: "Evil is in the air."[3] Both Macbeth and Lady Macbeth utter invocations to darkness to cloak their wicked deeds. Many of the memorable scenes occur at night: the murder of Duncan, the murder of Banquo, the sleep-walking of Lady Macbeth. Among these nega-

---

[1]Caroline Spurgeon, *Shakespeare's Imagery* (London, Cambridge University Press), p. 9.
[2]*Ibid*, p. 324.
[3]A. L. Rowse, *William Shakespeare* (London, Macmillan & Co. Ltd. and Toronto, The Macmillan Company of Canada Ltd., 1963), p. 381.

tive emotions and symbols, we find also numerous images dealing with disease and the longing for health and wholeness:

> Canst thou not minister to a mind diseas'd,
> Pluck from the memory a rooted sorrow,
> Raze out the written troubles of the brain,
> And with some sweet oblivious antidote
> Cleanse the stuff'd bosom of that perilous stuff
> Which weighs upon the heart?

> What rhubarb, senna, or what purgative drug,
> Would scour these English hence?

> Meet we the medicine of the sickly weal,
> And with him pour we, in our country's purge,
> Each drop of us.

Another dominant image is that of garments, frequently ill-fitting; Professor Cleanth Brooks sees in the clothing imagery a symbol of hypocrisy.[1] Macbeth refers to "borrow'd robes", to "golden opinions . . . worn now in their newest gloss". Angus speaks of Macbeth's royal title, which now hangs "loose about him, like a giant's robe/Upon a dwarfish thief".

References to sleep and sleeplessness abound. Macbeth has murdered sleep, another unnatural deed, and in so doing has destroyed forever his own peace of mind. The series of metaphors used to describe sleep (II. ii. 36-40) shows the intensity of his awareness of its restorative, soothing powers, and also acts as a premonitory hint of the suffering he will endure when deprived of its healing benediction. Throughout the play, Macbeth's inability to sleep reveals his tormented conscience; the strange irony with which he envies his victim is brought out in his cry: "Duncan is in his grave:/After life's fitful fever, he sleeps well." Macbeth yearns to "sleep in spite of thunder", the thunder of his own conscience. It is fitting too that Lady Mac-

[1]Cleanth Brooks, *The Well-Wrought Urn* (A Harvest Book; New York, Harcourt, Brace and World, Inc., 1956), p. 34.

beth's punishment should take the form of sleep-walking, evidence of her spiritual anguish.

Perhaps the most dramatic symbol in the play is the blood-stained hand. From the moment that Macbeth fears that his hand:

> will rather
> The multitudinous seas incarnadine,
> Making the green one red.

to the moment when Lady Macbeth seeks vainly to wash the indelible stain from her hand (and soul), blood dominates the play. Duncan's first words in the play as he sees the bleeding Sergeant are ominous: "What bloody man is that?" Aware of the degree to which he has committed himself to evil, Macbeth, at the end of the banquet scene, declares with a savage bitterness:

> I am in blood
> Stepp'd in so far, that should I wade no more,
> Returning were as tedious as go o'er.

When Macbeth and Macduff eventually meet, their exchange is spoken in words of blood:

Macbeth.   But get thee back, my soul is too much charg'd
With blood of thine already.

Macduff.   I have no words;
My voice is in my sword, thou bloodier villain
Than terms can give thee out!

And the last reference made by Malcolm to "this dead butcher" shows how Macbeth's image has become identified with violence, brutality, and bloodshed.

On the other hand, the image of the newly born infant is found at frequent intervals during the play; it has been suggested that it symbolizes the triumph of life over death. Macbeth refers to "pity, like a naked new-born babe,/Striding the blast", and longs for an heir to establish his dynasty. The most appalling image Lady Macbeth can think of is that which entails

striking out her child's brains on the battlements. Banquo is told
that he will beget kings. As the Witches make their second series
of pronouncements to Macbeth, the babe image is again brought
out in the Second Apparition, a bloody child (the infant Macduff) and in the Third, the child with a tree in his hand who
"wears upon his baby-brow the round/And top of sovereignty".
Life, symbolized also in the tree, is triumphant.

"*Macbeth* is above all a triumph of atmosphere: a sombre
realm of guilt, guilt for murder suggested, premeditated, accomplished, multiplied, and at length expiated."[1]

THE TEXT

Although a number of Shakespeare's plays were printed in six-
penny quartos during his lifetime, our only text for *Macbeth* is
that of the First Folio of 1623. This text is extremely defective[2]
and may have been printed from a prompt copy, since the stage
directions are unusually full. This prompt copy may have been
a cut version of the original manuscript; in any case, *Macbeth*
is the shortest of Shakespeare's tragedies (1,993 lines); of all the
plays, only *The Comedy of Errors* is shorter. Editors have argued about the authenticity of various scenes, but most agree
that Act III, Scene 5 is spurious, along with lines 39-43 of Act
IV, Scene 1. The character of Hecate seems both unnecessary
and un-Shakespearian when compared with the haglike Weird

---

[1]A. L. Rowse, *op. cit.*, p. 381.
[2]"Except that it is divided into scenes, as well as acts, it is one of the worst
printed of all the plays, especially as regards the metre, and not a few
passages are hopelessly corrupt" (Cambridge Editors).

Sisters; and the lines of the First Witch (IV. i. 125-32) do not seem to resemble the trochaic earthiness with which the Witches normally speak. Since the two songs found in these scenes appear also in a play entitled *The Witch* by Thomas Middleton (1570-1627), it has been conjectured that he was responsible for the interpolations.

THE DATE

Since *Macbeth* appears to be a compliment written for the approval of James I, who was crowned in March, 1603, it can hardly have been written before that date. One critic, Greg, states that it was "obviously designed to flatter King James". There are several factors that connect it with the King: Banquo, his ancestor, is described by Macbeth as being royal by nature; the "two-fold balls and treble sceptres" may be a reference to the coronation ceremony; the touching for the King's evil refers to an attribute on which James prided himself. One editor implies that the King actually commanded Shakespeare to write the play.[1] Malcolm's recipe for a good king may have been directed at James; perhaps, James thought he recognized himself in the description! Finally, James was keenly interested in demonology, having published a book on the subject himself.

As far as a terminal date is concerned, we have a reference to a production of the play seen by the celebrated physician and astrologer, Dr. Simon Forman, at the Globe on April 20, 1610. His summary of the plot contains some interesting details: "And when MackBeth had murdred the kinge, the blod on his handes could not be washed of by any means, nor from his

[1] *A New Variorum Edition of Shakespeare: Macbeth*, H. H. Furness, Jr., ed. (New York, Dover Publications, Inc., 1963), p. 361.

wives handes which handled the bloddi daggers in hiding them, By which means they became both much amazed and affronted. the murder being knowen, Dunkins 2 sonns fled, the on to England, the other to Walles, to save themselves."[1]

The weight of evidence, however, seems to point to 1606 as the year of composition. For one thing, the idea of equivocation is a recurrent one in the play and appears to be a reference to the trial of Henry Garnet, Superior of the Order of Jesuits in England, on March 28, 1606. Garnet had been implicated in the Gunpowder Plot and had flatly contradicted himself on oath; he defended himself by trying to justify the doctrine of equivocation, but was hanged nevertheless. Lady Macduff's reference to the hanging of traitors may be related to this incident.

References to the good harvest of 1606 have been seen in the line: "Here's a farmer, that hang'd himself on th' expectation of plenty." "The price of corn (wheat) was then, as now, the great criterion of plenty or scarcity. That in the summer and autumn of 1606 there was a prospect of plenty of corn appears from the audit-book of the College of Eton; for the price of wheat in that year was lower than it was for thirteen years afterwards. . . ." (Malone).

A third topical allusion found in the drunken Porter's soliloquy is the reference to the rascally tailor and his theft of his client's material. A volume called *The Black Year* by Anthony Nixon, published in 1606, contains the following item: "Gentlemen this year shall be much wronged by their taylors, for their consciences are now much larger than ever they were, for where they were wont to steale but half a yeard of brood cloth in making up a payre of breeches, now they do largely nick their customers in the lace too, and take more than enough for the new fashions sake, besides their old ones."

Some critics argue that all the topical allusions could be later interpolations; however, a number of them do seem to be closely woven into the fabric of the play.

[1]Furness, *op cit.*, p. 337.

SOME NOTES ON THE CHARACTERS

Macbeth

As the play ends, Malcolm dismisses Macbeth tersely as "this dead butcher"; Macduff calls him "an untitled tyrant, bloody-sceptr'd". He is the villain of the play and the source of evil. He shows himself weak in yielding to his wife's persuasions; cowardly in slaying the sleeping King, his kinsman, guest, and liege-lord; cruel in his hateful murder of Macduff's wife and children. But if this were all, he would not be a tragic figure. At the outset, Shakespeare shows him as a heroic character. The first words spoken of Macbeth by the bleeding Sergeant are "brave Macbeth"; Ross praises him as "Bellona's bridegroom"; Banquo calls him "noble partner". He is the man of the hour, the King's general, and the avenger of Duncan's enemies. At the end of the play, he displays this physical bravery again; it may be the courage of a cornered animal, but he dies fighting. His pride, too, is featured in his last crisis.

Macbeth is one of Shakespeare's triumphs in the art of character development; Macbeth plunges from the heights, where he is admired and respected, to the lowest depths, where he is cursed and execrated.

The key to Macbeth's character is his fierce, overmastering ambition. This quality is evident when we first meet him; as the Third Witch hails him "king hereafter", he *starts*. It is Banquo who notices this involuntary movement, which in Shakespeare suggests a guilty conscience. Lady Macbeth refers to this quality in her husband: "Thou wouldst be great,/ Art not without ambition." Macbeth himself admits that it is his besetting sin:

> I have no spur
> To prick the sides of my intent, but only
> Vaulting ambition.

He murders Duncan to gain the crown and Banquo to retain it. He is ambitious to found a line of kings, and this is a further reason for getting rid of Banquo, to whom the Witches had promised a royal dynasty.

At the beginning of the play, Macbeth lacks the ruthlessness to which he later falls prey. Lady Macbeth says of him that he is "without the illness", the unscrupulous attitude, that should attend ambition. He is "too full of the milk of human kindness". He is unwilling to "play false", but he is eager for victory, ill-gotten though it may be. There is a conflict in Macbeth between his desire for power and his standards of decency and moral behaviour. Because the seeds of ambition are deep within his soul, the Witches and his wife are able to influence him towards evil.

And yet to begin with, the man has a conscience. When he actually contemplates the murder of Duncan, he is repelled by the horrid image that makes his hair stand on end and his heart beat wildly. He is aware of the fact that:

> This even-handed justice
> Commends the ingredience of our poison'd chalice
> To our own lips.

True, he fears the consequences, but it is much more the sheer horror of the deed that holds him back. The supreme example of his conscience appears in the tortures he experiences after the murder of Duncan when he cannot pronounce "Amen". He has cut himself off from the goodness in the universe. As long as Macbeth's conscience is active, he is troubled by hallucinations, sleeplessness, and dreadful dreams. Once he has carried out the slaughter of Lady Macduff and her children, his conscience goes to sleep, and he is no longer tormented by ghosts and voices. Only when he meets Macduff at the end of his wretched life does he feel twinges of conscience again: "But get thee back, my soul is too much charg'd/With blood of thine already."

Macduff had once been Macbeth's friend; Malcolm says to Macbeth: "you have lov'd him well." Once Macbeth had pos-

sessed the highly valued approval of others: "I have bought/
Golden opinions from all sorts of people." At the end, in bitterness of spirit, he realizes that he has forfeited these high
opinions:

> And that which should accompany old age,
> As honour, love, obedience, troops of friends,
> I must not look to have.

This clarity of vision had always been part of him, and yet
he had defied it, bringing destruction on himself. This quality
enabled him to analyse the character of Duncan and later that
of Banquo; it inspired the great speech that followed Lady
Macbeth's death. These lines, with their emphasis on the littleness of man and the emptiness of life, have been used to prove
that there was no love left in his heart for his dead wife; however, it can be argued that her death has made him realize that
life holds nothing of value for him. In his heart, he loved her
still, although his selfish lust for power had driven them apart.

One further quality that keeps us from dismissing Macbeth as
nothing but a hardened villain is his gift for poetic speech. His
vivid imagination is shown in his brilliant use of figures of
speech, as in these metaphors describing life:

> Life's but a walking shadow, a poor player
> That struts and frets his hour upon the stage,
> And then is heard no more. It is a tale
> Told by an idiot, full of sound and fury,
> Signifying nothing.

It appears in Act V, Scene 3, as he looks with dreadful clarity
on his own tragedy:

> I have liv'd long enough; my way of life
> Is fall'n into the sear, the yellow leaf.

Macbeth is a tragic figure because he failed to live up to the
greatness within him; he was tempted, and he fell. He has been
compared with Milton's Satan, the once-proud Lucifer: "Angels

are bright still, though the brightest fell." Macbeth's fall from grace was indeed like that of a plunging meteor.

Banquo

"Banquho the thane of Lochquhaber, of whom the house of the Stewards is descended, the which by order of linage hath now for a long time inioied [enjoyed] the crowne of Scotland, even till these our daies . . . gathered the finances due to the king. . . ."[1] The fact that James I regarded Banquo as one of his forbears made it necessary for Shakespeare to make the Thane a worthy ancestor of the reigning monarch. In Holinshed, Banquo is an accessory to the murder of Duncan, a fact which the playwright deliberately suppresses.

We meet him as he and Macbeth journey towards Forres to meet the King; already, Banquo has been described by the Sergeant as a valiant warrior, who had played a notable part in the battle against the Norwegians (I. ii. 34-40). He is alert and observant; he notices Macbeth's abrupt start at the third prophecy. His own attitude towards the Witches, in contrast to Macbeth's, is that of an honest man: "Speak then to me, who neither beg, nor fear/Your favours, nor your hate." Untroubled, as yet, by temptation, he warns Macbeth:

> And oftentimes, to win us to our harm,
> The instruments of darkness tell us truths,
> Win us with honest trifles, to betray's
> In deepest consequence.

Duncan greets Banquo warmly and the latter responds with sincerity and loyalty; the King has a great affection for, and great confidence in, his less spectacular general.

Banquo's powers of observation and his appreciation of nature are shown in his comments when the royal party arrives at Inverness. His speech on the nesting habits of the "temple-haunting martlet" reflects Shakespeare's own interest in birds.

But the prophecies made to Banquo cannot be lightly for-

[1]Holinshed, *op. cit.*, pp. 207-8.

gotten. After the banquet following their arrival, we see that he is tormented by what has been prophesied to him. Nevertheless, although he dreams of the fulfilment of the prophecies, he fights off the temptation in his waking hours:

> A heavy summons lies like lead upon me,
> And yet I would not sleep. Merciful powers,
> Restrain in me the cursed thoughts that nature
> Gives way to in repose!

He parries Macbeth's hints about the future by asserting his loyalty to Duncan.

We do not see Banquo again until he appears in response to the summons that wakes the sleeping guests after the discovery of the murder of Duncan. Shocked, Banquo rebukes Lady Macbeth, but remains silent until Macbeth has reported his frenzied murder of the grooms. It is he who notices that Lady Macbeth is on the verge of fainting. Then he calls for an investigation:

> let us meet,
> And question this most bloody piece of work,
> To know it further.

and asserts his innocence.

Evidently, Banquo has kept his own counsel, however; Macbeth is crowned and the once-blameless Banquo has become a supporter of the new regime. Nevertheless, he suspects that Macbeth played "most foully" for the throne, and he wonders whether the prophecies made to him will not also come true— and so, he does nothing. This is fatal, for Macbeth, suspicious, watchful, and jealous, plots his former friend's murder.

The soliloquy beginning "To be thus is nothing" presents a glowing picture of Banquo, a man whom James would be proud to call his ancestor:

> and in his royalty of nature
> Reigns that which would be fear'd: 'tis much he dares,
> And, to that dauntless temper of his mind,

> He hath a wisdom that doth guide his valour
> To act in safety.

Macbeth acts swiftly, fearing possible assassination and wishing to thwart the fulfilment of the prophecies made to his friend and colleague. Banquo pays the penalty for his failure to pursue an honest course. He had omitted to challenge Macbeth's assumption of the throne, perhaps in the hope that it would come to his descendants if he let sleeping dogs lie.

But Banquo gets his revenge; his smile of triumph as he points at his descendants, the show of eight kings, must have been gratifying indeed to James. The modern audience is perhaps more interested in Banquo as a psychological study: the honest man who is tempted, struggles, falls, and is punished.

Lady Macbeth

Malcolm, having dismissed Macbeth as "this dead butcher", refers to Lady Macbeth as "his fiend-like queen". Dr. Johnson asserted that she was "merely detested"; another critic (Lee) calls her "the Clytemnestra of English tragedy". Is she merely, to use Shakespeare's words of another Queen, "a tiger's heart wrapped in a woman's hide"?

Lady Macbeth's first words in the play, after she has read her husband's letter about the Witches, reveal the iron determination and strength of will that are the keynotes of her character: "Glamis thou art, and Cawdor, and shalt be/What thou art promis'd." The soliloquy that follows reveals a partial understanding of her husband's character; she is aware of his ambition and his scruples. She is ambitious for him, not for herself, and because of her great love for him determines that he shall wear the crown.

Her invocation to the powers of evil and darkness may be interpreted as showing that normally she is not the fierce and cruel woman she seeks to be. She is unable to commit the murder herself because the elderly King resembles her father. Prior to the murder, she nerves herself with some of the drink she had prepared for the grooms.

In welcoming Duncan, she shows an icy self-possession; indeed, throughout the play she displays a strong social sense. She is always the competent hostess: "Be bright and jovial among your guests to-night"; "Your noble friends do lack you."

Entering at the end of Macbeth's great soliloquy of doubt, she lashes him with all the scorn she can command, seeking to force him to commit the deed that supposedly will bring happiness to them both. Had she understood her husband's true character, she might well have hesitated. And so, although she has been called the Fourth Witch, it may be said that she acted in an unselfish desire to make her husband King.

Once the murder of Duncan has been carried out, we cannot help admiring her presence of mind and resourcefulness; it is she who takes command of the situation. Her lack of imagination is shown in her inability to share her husband's tormented remorse: "What do you mean?" she cries desperately. Nevertheless, her courage is beyond question; it is she who returns the daggers to Duncan's chamber, at what cost is revealed in the sleep-walking scene: "Yet who would have thought the old man to have had so much blood in him?" It may also have been lack of imagination that made her utter the callous remark: "What, in our house?" when the murder was discovered. (It is, of course, possible that she had decided to play the part of the injured hostess.)

Lady Macbeth's faint has been the subject of much speculation, but we may accept it as genuine if we see it as a prelude to the sleep-walking scene. Even nerves of steel have their breaking-point, a point reached as Lady Macbeth listens, possibly in horror, to the account of the murder of the grooms and Macbeth's description of the murdered Duncan.

Her disillusionment sets in early:

> Nought's had, all's spent,
> Where our desire is got without content:
> 'Tis safer to be that which we destroy
> Than by destruction dwell in doubtful joy.

The growing separation between her and her husband is part of the great price she has paid for her part in the crime. He no longer needs her as he plans the murder of Banquo, and she can only ask dully, perhaps fearfully: "What's to be done?"

And yet in the banquet scene, her love for Macbeth enables her to make a final valiant and gallant effort to save him. Her social sense comes to her rescue once more:

> Question enrages him: at once, good night.
> Stand not upon the order of your going,
> But go at once.

Her exhaustion is evident in her final speech of the scene, as she says wearily, knowing that she has failed to save him: "You lack the season of all natures, sleep."

Lady Macbeth appears for the last time in the sleep-walking scene. The once-determined will is broken, but it is as yet only in her sleep that she is overcome by a tortured conscience. In her isolation and anguish, she speaks incoherently of the three great crimes and feverishly rubs her hands, fearful of discovery. But this indelible stain is on her conscience, and that which is done "cannot be undone". We cannot help feeling pity for this broken woman, now helpless, guilt-ridden, and frightened of the dark. Shakespeare's genius is shown nowhere more powerfully than in the contrast between the proud lady of the first act and the shattered being of the fifth. It is easy to believe that, unable to endure her sufferings, she committed suicide.

Macduff

"Candour is Macduff's keynote," according to Granville-Barker.[1] This frankness shows itself in the bluntness of speech that springs from a clear conscience, and is revealed in such terse lines as "Wherefore did you so?"; "No, cousin, I'll to Fife"; and "Turn, hell-hound, turn!" A man of the utmost integrity, he is described on several occasions as "the good Mac-

[1] H. Granville-Barker, *The Players' Shakespeare: The Tragedie of Macbeth* (London, Field Roscoe & Co., 1923), p. xlvi.

duff". Patriotism is another of his leading characteristics; when he hears Malcolm's recital of his supposed evil qualities, he can exclaim only: "O Scotland, Scotland!" His first question to Ross when the latter arrives bearing the tragic news of the slaughter of Macduff's household is: "Stands Scotland where it did?" It is only fitting that he should be the first to hail Malcolm as King of Scotland once Macbeth has been slain.

Although Macduff is probably among Duncan's retainers in the earlier scenes of the play, his first important appearance is his arrival at the gates of Macbeth's castle after the murder of the King. It is significant that he should be the one knocking at the gate, the symbol of the vengeance that is to overtake Macbeth. With clean hands and a clear conscience, he enters the castle, discovers, and announces, the murder of Duncan; unlike the other Scottish Thanes, he will have nothing to do with the new regime, and suspicious of Macbeth, withdraws to his own castle.

Only after the fateful banquet is over do Macbeth's thoughts turn to Macduff, who has defied the King by his absence. The First Apparition warns Macbeth to "Beware Macduff"; the Second Apparition *is* Macduff, and its prophecy deals with Macduff. The announcement of Macduff's departure for England leads to Macbeth's worst crime; this, in turn, leads to Macbeth's own death at the hands of the man he has so cruelly wronged.

In his interview with Lady Macduff, Ross describes her husband as "noble, wise, judicious", one who "best knows/The fits o' the season". Why, then, did Macduff leave his wife and family unprotected? Perhaps, there was a conflict of loyalties—love of country versus love of family—in his heart; realist though he was, Macduff may not have believed that Macbeth would stoop to such brutality and wickedness as the murder of women and children. Out of his great and terrible grief comes the vow of vengeance that is fulfilled at the end of the play.

The scene of the testing of Macduff, which follows the savage murder of his household, brings out many of his noble characteristics; his blunt honesty, his great patriotism, his true integrity, and the strength with which he masters his overwhelming grief make him a sympathetic and admirable character. He is throughout "a man faithful and honourable".

Malcolm

This is the sergeant
Who like a good and hardy soldier fought
'Gainst my captivity. Hail, brave friend!
Say to the king the knowledge of the broil,
As thou didst leave it.

Malcolm's first words in the play show that he remembers and appreciates service done. The fact that he greets the Sergeant as an equal indicates that he knows how to win the loyalty and support of men. It is Malcolm who reports the execution of the first Thane of Cawdor; this speech will be recalled when the death of a second treacherous Thane of Cawdor is later reported to him. The fact that he is named Prince of Cumberland in Act I, Scene 4 is one of the steps leading to the murder of Duncan. After his father's death, Malcolm shows in his plan to escape to England that he is both realistic and decisive. That he has won friends and influence there is indicated by the Lord's speech in Act III, Scene 6.

Malcolm's character is brought out most fully in Act IV, Scene 3, the scene of the testing of Macduff. We sense a cautious maturity and a cool, practical shrewdness, as he puts to the test Macduff's loyalty and his integrity of character; in this situation, he appears quite different from the gentle Duncan. Malcolm's analysis of himself shows his strength of character; he possesses the virtues of a good king as admired by James I; he is consistent, faithful, loyal, and truthful; a man of honour and a patriot. He may seem lacking in sympathy when he urges Macduff to sublimate his grief through action, but his own experience had taught him that this was the better, if harder, course.

As his army advances into Scotland, we see in him a natural

leader and commander. It is he who gives the orders to Siward and Macduff. He shows imagination and initiative in telling his soldiers to make use of camouflage, for he is indeed the "Child crowned, with a tree in his hand". The battle that follows is scarcely a test of his military skill, for, as he says, "We have met with foes/That strike beside us." It is to Malcolm, however, the newly hailed King of Scotland, that Shakespeare gives the last speech of the play, a speech in which the young monarch (contemptuously dismissed by Macbeth as "the boy Malcolm") shows touches of wise statesmanship. We feel that the Kingdom is in the hands of a ruler more capable, more practical, and more astute than Duncan, although he resembles his father in generosity and virtue:

> this, and what needful else
> That calls upon us, by the grace of Grace
> We will perform in measure, time, and place:
> So thanks to all at once, and to each one,
> Whom we invite to see us crown'd at Scone.

Duncan

"Thy royal father/Was a most sainted king." Macduff's summary of Duncan's character gives the picture of a ruler who was indeed a good man, but for those troublous times, not a good monarch. His nature was above reproach; even his murderer admitted it.

> Besides, this Duncan
> Hath borne his faculties so meek, hath been
> So clear in his great office, that his virtues
> Will plead like angels, trumpet-tongu'd against
> The deep damnation of his taking-off.

His generosity is evident in the rewards he gives to his victorious generals, and he is deeply grateful for their services. But Duncan lacks the shrewd realism necessary for the true welfare of his state. His misplaced idealism is brought out in his comment on the treacherous first Thane of Cawdor:

> There's no art
> To find the mind's construction in the face:
> He was a gentleman on whom I built
> An absolute trust.

Duncan's lack of judgement cost him his life, but our hearts are touched with pity for him. Even Lady Macbeth was moved to say: "Had he not resembled/My father as he slept, I had done 't."

Ross

Ross has been rather harshly described by Granville-Barker as "a politician, with a knack of remaining on the winning side". Macduff, though he may simply be using a polite form of address, greets him as "my ever gentle cousin".

In any case, his role is that of the bearer of news, both good and bad. It is he who brings Duncan the news of Macbeth's triumph over the Norwegians and who bears word that Macbeth is named Thane of Cawdor. Unlike Macduff, Ross is quite prepared to accept the new regime, and seems to typify all those who are following the line of least resistance.

He is among the first of the Scottish nobles to lose faith in Macbeth, although he is obviously somewhat afraid as he tells Lady Macduff of her husband's departure for England. His sympathy is well meant, but he is evidently unable or unwilling to take further action. To Ross also falls the unenviable task of breaking to Macduff the news of the murder of his wife and family, a duty that he performs reluctantly but conscientiously. Finally, Ross has to tell Siward that Young Siward has been killed in battle.

To judge by the part he plays, one would say that his friends must have considered him strong, sympathetic, and reliable, but despite his useful role, he lacks individuality; he seems more of an instrument than a distinctive personality.

Lennox and the Scottish Lords

Of the remaining Scottish nobles, only Lennox seems to stand out as an individual; Shakespeare may have had in mind a specific member of his acting company. Concerning the night of Duncan's death, Lennox says "My young remembrance cannot parallel/A fellow to it." There is an edge to his tongue as he comments on the supposed guilt of the grooms: "Those of his chamber, as it seem'd, had done 't." This sharp, sarcastic note is further emphasized in Act III, Scene 6, when he discusses ironically with an unnamed Lord the supposed guilt of Malcolm, Donalbain, and Fleance.

The remaining Scottish lords, Angus, Caithness, and Menteith, are not sharply distinguished or characterized in any way.

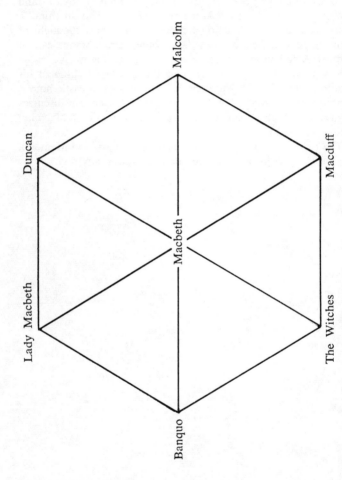

Malcolm

Duncan

Macduff

Macbeth

Lady Macbeth

The Witches

Banquo

Show how the diagram illustrates the various triangular relationships in the play.

The Main Events and Structural Pattern of Macbeth

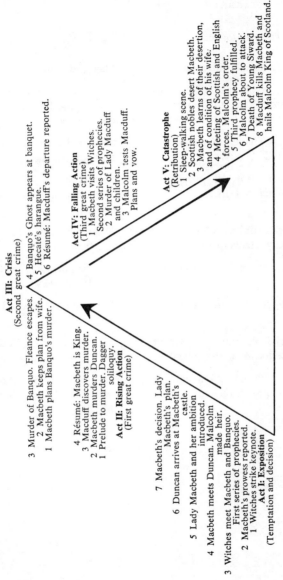

Act III: Crisis
(Second great crime)

4 Banquo's Ghost appears at banquet.
5 Hecate's harangue.
6 Résumé: Macduff's departure reported.
3 Murder of Banquo. Fleance escapes.
2 Macbeth keeps plan from wife.
1 Macbeth plans Banquo's murder.

Act IV: Falling Action
(Third great crime)
1 Macbeth visits Witches.
Second series of prophecies.
2 Murder of Lady Macduff
and children.
3 Malcolm tests Macduff.
Plans and vow.

Act V: Catastrophe
(Retribution)
1 Sleep-walking scene.
2 Scottish nobles desert Macbeth.
3 Macbeth learns of their desertion,
and of condition of his wife.
4 Meeting of Scottish and English
forces. Malcolm's order.
5 Third prophecy fulfilled.
6 Malcolm about to attack.
7 Death of Young Siward.
8 Macduff kills Macbeth and
hails Malcolm King of Scotland.

4 Résumé: Macbeth is King.
3 Macduff discovers murder.
2 Macbeth murders Duncan.
1 Prelude to murder. Dagger
soliloquy.

Act II: Rising Action
(First great crime)

7 Macbeth's decision. Lady
Macbeth's plan.
6 Duncan arrives at Macbeth's
castle.
5 Lady Macbeth and her ambition
introduced.
4 Macbeth meets Duncan. Malcolm
made heir.
3 Witches meet Macbeth and Banquo.
First series of prophecies.
2 Macbeth's prowess reported.
1 Witches strike keynote.

Act I: Exposition
(Temptation and decision)

Symmetry *in* Macbeth

1. Play begins with a battle.

2. Death of the rebel Macdonwald at the hands of Macbeth (I. i.).

3. First Thane of Cawdor executed (I. iv.).

4. First series of prophecies (Witches, I. iii.).

5. Dramatic introduction of Lady Macbeth (I. v.).

6. Murder of Duncan (II. i.).

7. Flight of King's sons (II. iii.).

---

1. Play ends with a battle.

2. Death of the usurper Macbeth at the hands of Macduff (V. viii.).

3. Second Thane of Cawdor slain (V. viii.).

4. Second series of prophecies (Witches and Apparitions, IV. i.).

5. Dramatic exit of Lady Macbeth (V. i.).

6. Murder of Lady Macduff and family (IV. ii.).

7. Departure of Macduff (III. vi.).

---

8. Crisis of play (murder of Banquo and escape of Fleance) occurs in mathematical centre of play (III. ii.).

9. Part played by Duncan and Banquo in opening acts.

9. Part played by Malcolm and Macduff in closing acts.

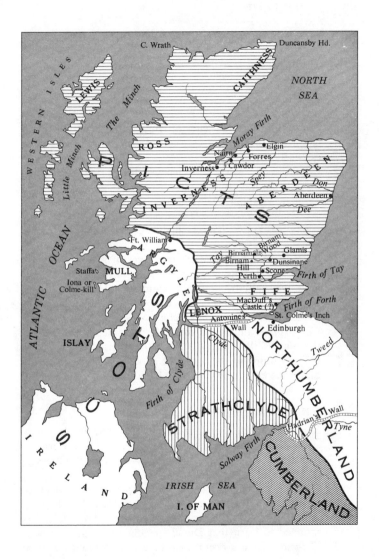

DRAMATIC DEVICES IN *MACBETH*

A STRUCTURAL DEVICES

1. *Exposition:* By the end of Act I, most of the main characters have been introduced and the plot has been established.
2. *Conflict:* the clash of opposing forces without which there is no drama:
   a) man vs. man i) Macbeth vs. Lady Macbeth—a clash of wills.
   ii) Macbeth vs. Macduff—a physical clash.
   b) man vs. himself: Macbeth's inner struggle.
3. *Crisis:* the turning point in the play. (In a Shakespearian play, it usually occurs in the third act.) Most critics consider that the murder of Banquo and the escape of Fleance mark the turning point in *Macbeth*.
4. *Catastrophe:* the dénouement, or outcome. The *climax* of the play is the death of Macbeth, whereas the outcome is the triumph of the forces of good as symbolized by the establishment of Malcolm as King of Scotland.

B DEVICES THAT ADD INTEREST

1. *Suspense:* a state of anxious uncertainty. In *Macbeth*, suspense is keen prior to each of the three great crimes; it is also marked in the last act, as we await the meeting of Macbeth and Macduff.
2. *Surprise:* the occurrence of the unexpected; *e.g.*, Macbeth is unpleasantly surprised to hear that Malcolm has been named Prince of Cumberland. Lady Macbeth is astounded to learn that Duncan is about to visit Inverness.
3. *Coincidence:* the occurrence of events without apparent

causal connection; *e.g.*, it is a grim coincidence that Duncan should arrive at Macbeth's castle at the very moment when Lady Macbeth has made up her mind that he must be murdered.

4. *Contrast:* the juxtaposition of opposites: a) within a character; *e.g.*, between the Lady Macbeth of I. v. and the Lady Macbeth of V. i., b) between characters; *e.g.*, Macduff and Banquo, c) in atmosphere; *e.g.*, between the scene following the murder of Duncan (II. ii.) and the episode of the drunken Porter (II. iii.).

5. *Parallelism:* here, the fact that characters and events in the earlier part of the play are balanced against those of the latter part; *e.g.*, Duncan against Malcolm, the first crime against the third, the first set of prophecies against the second.

6. *Principle of alternation:* a) a humorous scene following a tragic one; *e.g.*, the episode of the drunken Porter following the murder of Duncan, b) scenes alternating between rival factions, as in Act V; *e.g.*, the forces *opposed to* Macbeth, the forces *of* Macbeth.

7. *Nemesis:* the principle of retributive justice; *e.g.*, the fate that overtakes Macbeth and Lady Macbeth.

8. *Foreshadowing of events:* a premonitory warning of what may happen; *e.g.*, Banquo's statement:

> And oftentimes, to win us to our harm,
> The instruments of darkness tell us truths,
> Win us with honest trifles, to betray 's
> In deepest consequence.

9. *Irony:* the juxtaposition of incongruous elements; *e.g.*, that Macbeth should wish Duncan alive again after murdering him.

10. *Dramatic irony:* the effect produced when a speech or situation has one meaning for the actor and an inner or opposite one for the audience. *Macbeth* abounds in this device. Macbeth's entrance on the heels of Duncan's comment: "He was a gentleman, on whom I built/An

absolute trust", is full of dramatic irony because we know that already Macbeth has been toying with the idea of taking the crown. Banquo's promise to attend the feast is another illustration, since we know of Macbeth's plan to murder him. There is double dramatic irony here, since once we have read the play we know that Banquo fulfils his promise, but Macbeth is unaware that this will happen.

11. *Pathos:* that which excites pity; *e.g.*, the conversation between Lady Macduff and her son (IV. ii. 30-62).

12. *Supernatural:* an agency above or outside the forces of nature; *e.g.*, the Ghost of Banquo, the Apparitions.

13. *Humour:* a) word play; *e.g.*, Lady Macbeth's pun on the word "guilt" has a grim humour about it.

   b) satire: the use of irony or ridicule to expose or discourage vice or folly; *e.g.*, Young Macduff's comments on the depravity of man illustrate the use of irony to create satire.

   c) topical allusions: references to incidents contemporary with the period in which the play was written (here, 1606); *e.g.*, the allusion made by the drunken Porter to an equivocator would amuse an audience of the time.

CRITICS' COMMENTS

1. The Character of Macbeth: A Sympathetic Study

Throughout *Macbeth*, we watch the deterioration of a great man; but we never lose the sense of his greatness. As he becomes more desperate, Macbeth acquires something of the savagery of Euripides' Medea, though we cannot feel that he has been wronged. Yet if Macbeth is solely responsible, he himself pays the cost. Our repugnance for his savagery is qualified by the spectacle of his suffering; he himself suffers more than anybody else. In this universal pattern, we may recognize the common burden we share with Macbeth, those of us who pay some part of the price for our sins in this world. . . . Macbeth is constantly tormented by scruples—human scruples rather than religious; there is too much of the milk of human kindness in him to make him thoroughly successful. He is gradually transformed into a monster, after the murder of Duncan; and yet we can still catch glimpses of the different man he might have been—a man greatly loved, a courteous man, born to command:

> Now good digestion wait on appetite,
> And health on both,

he says to his guests, a most genial and characteristically profane grace. He is capable of greatness and generosity: there is a tender human love between him and his wife, though they are both abandoned to evil; we may recall the relation between Claudius and Gertrude, and Shakespeare's capacity for seeing some goodness even in wicked people. Above all, he is a poetic person, a man of great and imaginative sensitiveness, one of those rare persons we sometimes meet, if we are lucky, whose every word thrills us, who are incapable of dullness or the commoner kinds of stupidity, even though they may be guilty of greater crimes. All this, along with his wickedness, is part of the man we somehow value and feel for. . . . That such a man should sacrifice all the wealth of his human spirit—his kindness, his love, his very soul—to become a victim to continual fears, a tyrant ruthlessly murdering in the vain attempt to feel safe, finally to be killed like a foul beast of prey—this is terrible, and pitiful, too. . . . We see the necessity of Macbeth's destruction; we acquiesce in his punishment unreservedly; and yet we would find whatever excuses for him we can, because we admire the Promethean quality of his courage, because we recognize his conscience as like our own, and because we share his guilt.[1]

2. *Hubris*

Hubris is generally translated as 'insolence' or 'arrogance' or 'pride', but it means much more than any of these. It is a vice to which the successful, the powerful, and the strong are liable. Their success, their power, their strength carries them away, and they pay no regard to religion or justice or mercy; they rebel against the eternal laws which set bounds that men may not pass with impunity. Shakespeare described one form of *hubris* admirably when he spoke of "vaulting ambition, which o'erleaps itself". . . .

A perfect example of *hubris* is Hitler. There are many others. The Greeks saw in *hubris* one of the main forces working in history and the commonest cause of the downfall of men and of nations; and surely they were right. When Persia, confident in her great power, attacked their small country, it was *hubris*, and the *hubris* was punished. They would have seen it at work in Napoleon when, carried away by his success, he tried to dominate Europe, and they would have found in it the reason for his downfall. They would have seen it equally in the temper of Germany after her victory over France in 1870, leading gradually but inevitably to the disaster of the two world wars. Individuals of course are as liable to it as nations: the businessman who is carried on by success into speculations that ruin him is the victim of *hubris*. An excellent example of it in literature is Milton's Satan. Another is Macbeth: he begins as a successful general, and his success breeds *hubris* in him; his ambition grows and drives him on to murder his king and anyone else who stands in his way, and that finally leads to his ruin.[2]

[1]Harold S. Wilson, *On the Design of Shakespearean Tragedy* (Toronto, University of Toronto Press, 1957), pp. 77-78.
[2]R. W. Livingstone, *The Rainbow Bridge and Other Essays on Education* (Toronto, Clarke, Irwin & Company Limited, 1959), pp. 137-9.

3. The Conclusion of *Macbeth*: A Great Director's Interpretation

The Conclusion of *Macbeth* [the section comprising Act V, Scenes vii and viii] divides, dramatically, into three parts. The first runs to Macduff's discovery of Macbeth with

> Turn, hell-hound, turn.

This goes, as we say, ding-dong, and any possible half-pauses are filled up with 'alarums.' Macbeth is grim and deadly, a trapped beast; his comings and goings have no purpose in them. Moreover, as the battle goes forward he becomes conscious that his mind too has been trapped and tricked, though he cannot yet see how. He is invulnerable; again and again he returns to this. But, as certainly, with the battle against him, he is doomed. Is the answer to the riddle that he must kill himself? Must he 'play the Roman fool'? He fights, one would suppose, like an automaton and perhaps the more dangerously for that.

In clear contrast is the gallant, crusading figure of young Siward, flashing to his death.

There is none of the glow of battle upon Macduff. Methodically, determinedly, he pursues his single purpose. For a relief we have the interlude when the two generals, cool and confident still, enter the castle.

The second part concerns Macbeth and Macduff alone. Nice critics have found Macbeth's last fling of words—beloved of every schoolboy—too highly flavoured with bombast. They may be. But Shakespeare, having brought his play to the issue of sheer physical combat, might well think it appropriate to throw niceness behind him.[1] This is to be a mortal combat and a mighty combat. For Macduff to come easily by his vengeance would be unsatisfying. For Macbeth to go easily out would be incredible, and to give him a finely worded end might seem to redeem him, if ever so little. This Shakespeare will not do. He allows him one gleam of incorrigible pride, he leaves him his

[1] Not that he ever took much stock in it.

animal courage. For the rest, he sends him shouting to hell. And from the beginning the exchange of speeches between the two men should be like the exchange of blows.

The end of the play is contrived as a full and varied orchestra of voices with the trumpets of victory topping them. Malcolm and his soldiers enter processionally, and at once we are given the suggestion of order restored. The note of pity for the dead is struck, and upon it comes the practised soldier's stoic response. There is Ross's smooth sympathy. There is the defiant nobility with which Siward takes his own son's death; and for Malcolm there is a needed touch of impulsive generosity.

Macduff's entrance, lifting the severed head, changes the key almost violently. Here is an echo of the now ended tragedy. Vengeance is accomplished, but Macduff, widowed and childless, stands apart from all thoughtless rejoicing.

> I see thee compassed with thy kingdom's pearl.

But he is a man alone. His voice must have the music of a selfless and unforgettable sorrow in it.

Then, with the careful modulation of Malcolm's address to his people, Shakespeare brings us at his ease back to our work-a-day world.[1]

4. The Immediacy of *Macbeth*

The opening scene and the closing act of *Macbeth* are given to war; the rest of the first act and the second to murder; the third and fourth to tyranny—with further murder. The play leaves us with the feeling that offensive war, crime, and tyranny are merely different faces of the same monster. Tyranny is just war catching its breath. Under it the preponderance of power is so markedly on one side that open violence is no longer necessary. The Enemy is now the subjects. If the fragmentary passages describing Scotland under Macbeth are assembled, they read like a documented account of life in the countries subjugated by the "strong" men of the twentieth century. With its

[1]Granville-Barker, *op. cit.*, pp. lvi-lvii.

remote setting and ancient superstitions, *Macbeth* to a superficial mind may seem dated. On the contrary few of Shakespeare's plays speak more directly to our time.[1]

5. The Character of Macbeth, As Analysed by the Great Victorian Actor Sir Henry Irving: An Unsympathetic Study

[Macbeth] was a poet with his brain and a villain with his heart, and the mere appreciation and enjoyment of his own wickedness gave irony to his grim humour and zest to his crime. He loved throughout to paint himself and his deeds in the blackest pigments and to bring to the exercise of his wickedness the conscious deliberation of an intellectual voluptuary. All through the play his blackest deeds are heralded by high thoughts, told in the most glorious word-painting, so that after a little the reader or the hearer comes to understand that the excellence of the poetic thought is but a suggestion of the measure of the wickedness that is to follow. Of Macbeth's bravery there can be no doubt whatever, either historically or in the play. . . . Indeed, Shakespeare insists throughout on this great manly quality, and at the very outset of the tragedy puts into the mouths of other characters speeches couching their declaration in poetic form. It is to his moral qualities which I refer when I dub him villain.

Let it be sufficient that Macbeth—hypocrite, traitor, and regicide—threw over his crimes the glamour of his own poetic self-torturing thought. He was a Celt, and in every phase of his life his Celtic fervor was manifest. . . . A poetic mind on which the presages and suggestions of supernatural things could work; a nature sensitive to intellectual emotion, so that one can imagine him even in his contemplation of coming crimes to weep for the pain of the destined victim; self-torturing, self-examining, playing with conscience so that action and reaction of poetic thought might send emotional waves through the brain while

[1] H. C. Goddard, *The Meaning of Shakespeare*, Vol. 2 (Phoenix Books: Chicago, University of Chicago Press, 1962), p. 109.

the resolution was as firmly fixed as steel and the heart as cold as ice; a poet supreme in the power of words, with vivid imagination and quick sympathy of intellect; a villain cold-blooded, selfish, and remorseless, with a true villain's nerve and callousness when braced to evil work and the physical heroism of those who are born to kill: a moral nature with only sufficient weakness to quake momentarily before superstitious terrors— the man of sensibility and not the man of feeling. Such, I believe, was the mighty dramatic character which Shakespeare gave to the world in Macbeth.[1]

6. Lady Macbeth

When she (Charlotte Cushman) played Lady Macbeth, it was obviously the lady who wore the kilts in that castle. Booth's[2] own private idea of the character was of a red-haired little enchantress, very feminine in her ambitions. Cushman's Lady Macbeth was a raven-haired Amazon who bullied her husband, stalked him into a corner and then, as somebody who saw her put it, regularly "pitched into him" with lifted arm and large, meaty fist. It was a wonderful performance in its way, pitiless, macabre, and fascinating. Yet every time that Booth onstage felt the clamp of her muscular fingers on his shoulder and heard the cellolike tones rise out of her chest in her famous line

He that's coming must be provided for,

he was terribly tempted to snap back: "Well, why don't you kill him? You're a great deal bigger than I am."[3]

7. King James I on Witchcraft, 1597

Item, the saide *Agnis Sampson* confessed before the Kings Maiestie sundrye thinges which were so miraculous and strange, as that his Maiestie saide they were all extreame lyars, wherat she answered, she would not wishe his Maiestie to suppose her

---

[1] Furness, *op. cit.*, pp. 470-1.
[2] Edwin Booth (1833-1893) was the greatest Hamlet of his day.
[3] Eleanor Ruggles, *Prince of Players, Edwin Booth* (New York, W. W. Norton & Company, Inc., 1953), pp. 115-16.

woords to be false, but rather to beleeue them, in that she would discouer such matter vnto him as his maiestie should not any way doubt off.

And therupon taking his Maiestie a little aside, she declared vnto him the verye woordes which passed betweene the Kings Maiestie and his Queene at Vpslo in Norway the first night of their mariage, with their answere eache to other: whereat the Kinges Maiestie wondered greatlye, and swore by the liuing God, that he beleeued that all the Diuels in hell could not haue discouered the same: acknowledging her woords to be most true, and therefore gaue the more credit to the rest which is before declared.

Touching this *Agnis Tompson*, she is the onlye woman, who by the Diuels perswasion should haue entended and put in execution the Kings Maiesties death in this manner.

She confessed that she tooke a blacke Toade, and did hang the same vp by the heeles, three daies, and collected and gathered the venome as it dropped and fell from it in an Oister shell, and kept the same venome close couered, vntill she should obtaine any parte or peece of foule linnen cloth, that had appertained to the Kings Maiestie, as shirt, handkercher, napkin or any other thing which she practised to obtaine by meanes of one *Iohn Kers*, who being attendant in his Maiesties Chamber, desired him for olde acquaintance betweene them, to helpe her to one or a peece of such a cloth as is aforesaide, which thing the said *Iohn Kers* denyed to helpe her too, saying he could not help her too it.

And the said *Agnis Tompson* by her depositions since her apprehension saith, that if she had obtained any one peece of linnen cloth which the King had worne and fouled, she had bewitched him to death, and put him to such extraordinary paines, as if he had beene lying vpon sharp thornes and endes of Needles.[1]

---

[1]King James I, "Newes from Scotland, 1591", from *Daemonologie in Forme of a Dialogue, 1597* (London, The Bodley Head Ltd. and David Higham Associates, Ltd., 1924), pp. 15-16.

8. Witches and Witchcraft, 1584

And first *Ovid* affirmeth, that they can raise and suppresse lightening and thunder, raine and haile, clouds and winds, tempests and earthquakes. Others doo write, that they can pull downe the moone and the starres. Some write that with wishing they can send needles into the livers of their enimies. Some that they can transferre corne in the blade from one place to another. Some, that they can cure diseases supernaturallie, flie in the aire, and danse with divels. . . .

They can raise spirits (as others affirme) drie up springs, turne the course of running waters, inhibit the sunne, and staie both day and night, changing the one into the other. They can go in and out at awger holes, & saile in an egge shell, a cockle or muscle shell, through and under the tempestuous seas. . . .

And now to come to the definition of witchcraft, which hitherto I did deferre and put off purposelie: that you might perceive the true nature thereof, by the circumstances, and therefore the rather to allow of the same, seeing the varietie of other writers. Witchcraft is in truth a cousening art, wherin the name of God is abused, prophaned and blasphemed, and his power attributed to a vile creature. In estimation of the vulgar people, it is a supernaturall worke, contrived betweene a corporall old woman, and a spirituall divell. . . . The trade is though to be impious. The effect and end thereof to be some-times evill, as when thereby man or beast, grasse, trees, or corne, &c; is hurt: sometimes good, as whereby sicke folkes are healed, theeves bewraied, and true men come to their goods, &c. The matter and instruments, wherewith it is accomplished, are words, charmes, signes, images, characters, &c: the which words al-though any other creature doo pronounce, in maner and forme as they doo, leaving out no circumstance requisite or usuall for that action: yet none is said to have the grace or gift to performe the matter, except she be a witch, and so taken, either by hir owne consent, or by others imputation.[1]

[1]Reginald Scot, *The Discoverie of Witchcraft* (New York, Random House, Inc., 1930).

MACBETH

DRAMATIS PERSONAE

DUNCAN, *King of Scotland.*

MALCOLM,
DONALBAIN, } *his sons.*

MACBETH,
BANQUO, } *generals of the King's army.*

MACDUFF,
LENNOX,
ROSS,
MENTEITH,
ANGUS,
CAITHNESS, } *noblemen of Scotland.*

FLEANCE, *son to Banquo.*

SIWARD, *earl of Northumberland, general of the English forces.*

Young SIWARD, *his son.*

SEYTON, *an officer attending on Macbeth.*

BOY, *son to Macduff.*

An English Doctor.

A Scotch Doctor.

A Sergeant.

A Porter.

An Old Man.

Lady MACBETH.

Lady MACDUFF.

Gentlewoman attending on Lady Macbeth.

HECATE.

Three Witches.

Apparitions.

Lords, Gentlemen, Officers, Soldiers, Murderers, Attendants, and Messengers.

SCENE: *Scotland; England.*

S.D. **Thunder and lightning:** From time immemorial, thunder has been associated with the supernatural. Why? **Enter three Witches:** Note the prevalence of the number "three" in this play. In the text, Shakespeare refers to the Witches as "the Weird Sisters"; only in the S.D. are they "witches". (The word "weird" occurs six times in *Macbeth*.)

1 **When shall . . . again:** Note that many scenes (in Act I especially) begin with a question. Why?

3 **hurlyburly:** uproar, commotion, especially of battle.

4 **battle:** described in the following scene. (The whole play deals with the struggle between good and evil.)

5 **That will . . . sun:** The Third Witch exhibits supernatural knowledge.

7 **There to . . . Macbeth:** Note how Shakespeare prepares us for a future scene, and thereby creates suspense.

8 **I come, Graymalkin:** The line is in answer to her attendant demon, who cries with the voice of a cat; **Graymalkin:** a name for a grey cat. ("Malkin" is a diminutive of *Matilda*.)

9 **Paddock:** The Second Witch's familiar spirit summons her with the cry of a toad. 10 **anon:** in a moment.

11-12 **Fair is . . . fair:** The Witches stand for a reversal of the moral order. To them, right is wrong, and wrong, right. The rhyming couplet that closes the scene provides an air of finality. It is possible that the Witches disappeared through a trap-door in the stage, screened by smoke created by the burning of resin.

See also p. 155.

S.D. **Forres:** See map, p. xliii; **Alarum:** call to arms, sounded by a trumpet; **within:** the curtained recess at the rear of the Elizabethan stage; **Sergeant:** F reads *Captaine*. In the sixteenth century, a sergeant-major was a commissioned officer, often a member of the King's bodyguard.

1 **bloody:** It is significant that the human action of the play should begin with a reference to blood, an image that prevails throughout *Macbeth*. It is mentioned more than one-hundred times.

2 **revolt:** the battle referred to by the Witches; a rebellion led by the chieftain Macdonwald. 3 **the newest state:** the latest news.

5 **my captivity:** It is unlikely that Malcolm was at the battle referred to. His statement serves here to give the impression that he is grateful for services done him.

6 **the king:** This is Shakespeare's way of indicating Duncan's identity; **the:** thy; **broil:** tumult, quarrel, perhaps from the Italian *broglio*, hurly-burly.

ACT I
Scene 1

A DESERT PLACE.

Thunder and lightning. Enter three Witches.

First Witch.   When shall we three meet again?
  In thunder, lightning, or in rain?
Second Witch.   When the hurlyburly's done,
  When the battle's lost, and won.
Third Witch.   That will be ere the set of sun.   5
First Witch.   Where the place?
Second Witch.   Upon the heath.
Third Witch.   There to meet with Macbeth.
First Witch.   I come, Graymalkin.
Second Witch.   Paddock calls.
Third Witch.   Anon!   10
All.   Fair is foul, and foul is fair.
  Hover through the fog and filthy air.   *Exeunt.*

Scene 2

A CAMP NEAR FORRES.

*Alarum within. Enter Duncan, Malcolm, Donalbain,
Lennox, with Attendants, meeting a bleeding Sergeant.*

Duncan.   What bloody man is that? He can report,
  As seemeth by his plight, of the revolt
  The newest state.
Malcolm.   This is the sergeant
  Who like a good and hardy soldier fought
  'Gainst my captivity. Hail, brave friend!   5
  Say to the king the knowledge of the broil,
  As thou didst leave it.

3

7-9 **Doubtful it . . . art:** The simile used to suggest deadlock reminds us of the desperate clutch of two drowning men.

10 **to that:** for that purpose.

11-12 **The multiplying . . . him:** The metaphor suggests lice; **the western isles:** the Hebrides. See map, p. xliii.

13 **kerns and gallowglasses:** light-armed and heavy-armed foot soldiers from Ireland.

14-15 **damned quarrel:** detestable cause; **fortune, on . . . whore:** Fortune, a fickle strumpet, deceived Macdonwald by granting him her favour to begin with, only to withdraw her support.

16 **brave Macbeth:** Note the first adjective applied to Macbeth.

17 **brandish'd steel:** This suggests the strength and skill with which Macbeth flourished his great two-handed sword.

18 **smok'd:** The sword reeked of hot blood.

19 **minion:** darling (Macbeth is not fortune's, but "valour's", favourite); **carv'd:** Note the power of this imitative verb.

20 **the slave:** Macdonwald (a term of contempt).

21 **which ne'er . . . him:** who did not part from him politely. The antecedent of "which" is usually taken to be "Macbeth".

22 **unseam'd him . . . chops:** ripped him open from stomach to jaws.

17-23 This picture of a doughty warrior is both vivid and violent. Note the words that suggest action and the heat of battle.

24 **cousin:** kinsman. Holinshed states that Macbeth and Duncan were first cousins. Duncan's praise is sincere and genuine.

25-28 **As whence . . . swells:** The sun rises in the east, but storms also come from the east; even so, the victory over Macdonwald was followed by the attack of Sweno, King of Norway; **reflection:** shining.

30 The line seems to suggest in its sound the scorn felt by the speaker for those who fled in such undignified haste.

31 **surveying vantage:** seeing an opportunity.

32 **furbish'd:** burnished, renovated.

34-35 **Yes, as . . . lion:** not at all (ironic).

36 **say sooth:** tell the truth.

37 **cannons overcharg'd . . . cracks:** doubly charged. The reference to "cannons" is an anachronism in respect to eleventh-century Scotland. Cannon were first used in European warfare in the fourteenth century (perhaps at the Battle of Crecy, 1346).

40 **memorize another Golgotha:** make the place as memorable as "Golgotha", the place of the skull, where the Crucifixion took place.

Sergeant.   Doubtful it stood,
  As two spent swimmers, that do cling together
  And choke their art. The merciless Macdonwald
  (Worthy to be a rebel, for to that   10
  The multiplying villainies of nature
  Do swarm upon him) from the western isles
  Of kerns and gallowglasses is supplied;
  And fortune, on his damned quarrel smiling,
  Show'd like a rebel's whore: but all's too weak: 15
  For brave Macbeth (well he deserves that name)
  Disdaining fortune, with his brandish'd steel,
  Which smok'd with bloody execution,
  Like valour's minion, carv'd out his passage,
  Till he fac'd the slave;   20
  Which ne'er shook hands, nor bade farewell to him,
  Till he unseam'd him from the nave to the chops,
  And fix'd his head upon our battlements.
Duncan. O valiant cousin, worthy gentleman!
Sergeant. As whence the sun 'gins his reflection   25
  Shipwrecking storms and direful thunders break,
  So from that spring, whence comfort seem'd to come,
  Discomfort swells. Mark, king of Scotland, mark,
  No sooner justice had, with valour arm'd,
  Compell'd these skipping kerns to trust their heels,   30
  But the Norweyan lord, surveying vantage,
  With furbish'd arms, and new supplies of men,
  Began a fresh assault.
Duncan.   Dismay'd not this
  Our captains, Macbeth and Banquo?
Sergeant.   Yes,
  As sparrows eagles; or the hare the lion.   35
  If I say sooth, I must report they were
  As cannons overcharg'd with double cracks;
  So they doubly redoubled strokes upon the foe:
  Except they meant to bathe in reeking wounds,
  Or memorize another Golgotha,   40

6 • MACBETH

41 To create suspense, Shakespeare causes the Sergeant to break off at this critical point.
44 **smack of honour both:** Your words and your wounds have a flavour of honour.
45 **thane:** the Scottish equivalent of the English *earl*.
47 **strange:** "The word, like the witches, is always somewhere doing its work" (Mark Van Doren). It hints at the abnormality of Macbeth's behaviour; **God save the king:** The prayer is ironic in view of Duncan's fate.
48 **Fife:** See map, p. xliii. Three military campaigns have been telescoped here: Macdonwald's rebellion, the defeat of Sweno, King of Norway, and the defeat of Canute (Sweno's brother).
49 **flout:** mock. The line suggests the snapping of the flags in a stiff breeze and implies that the banners themselves are scornful.
50 **fan our people cold:** fill our people with cold terror at the impact of an invasion. It is not the banners that cause fear, but what they stand for.
53 **the thane of Cawdor:** Dover Wilson believes that the Thane of Cawdor was secretly in league with both the King of Norway and the rebel Macdonwald. For "Cawdor", see map, p. xliii.
54 **Bellona's bridegroom:** husband of the goddess of war; hence, Mars; a tribute to Macbeth's martial prowess; **lapp'd in proof:** encased in tested, hence impenetrable, armour.
55 **confronted him with self-comparisons:** If we accept the fact that Macbeth was genuinely surprised to learn of Cawdor's treachery, the pronoun "him" refers to "Norway". The expression means: "faced him with courage that matched his own".
56 **point, rebellious:** F has the comma as indicated. Some editors prefer it after "rebellious". "Rebellious" is thought by some to refer to Cawdor rather than Sweno. What are the difficulties in such an interpretation?
57 **lavish:** insolent.
60 **craves composition:** longs for terms of peace.
61 **deign:** grant.
62 **Saint Colme's inch:** See map, p. xliii. St. Columba's island, or "inch" (Erse), in the Firth of Forth. Here, the remains of St. Columba's monastery can be found.
63 **dollars:** an anachronism. The coin was originally minted from silver found in Joachims*thal* (dale) in Bohemia about 1518.
64-65 **deceive our bosom interest:** betray our intimate confidence; **present:** immediate.
68 **noble Macbeth:** No one can speak too highly of Macbeth.
67-68 The rhyming couplet locks the scene up and leaves us with a picture of a heroic Macbeth.
See also p. 157.

I cannot tell—
But I am faint, my gashes cry for help.

Duncan. So well thy words become thee as thy wounds;
They <u>smack of honour both</u>. Go get him surgeons.

                    Exit Sergeant, attended.

Who comes here?

          Enter Ross and Angus.

Malcolm.   The worthy <u>thane</u> of Ross.   45

Lennox. What a haste looks through his eyes! So should he
   look
That seems to speak things <u>strange</u>.

Ross.   God save the king!

Duncan. Whence cam'st thou, worthy thane?

Ross.   From <u>Fife</u>, great king,
Where the Norweyan banners <u>flout</u> the sky
And <u>fan our people cold.</u>   50
Norway himself, with terrible numbers,
Assisted by that most disloyal traitor,
The <u>thane of Cawdor</u>, began a dismal conflict,
Till that <u>Bellona's bridegroom</u>, lapp'd in proof,
<u>Confronted him</u> with self-comparisons,   55
Point against <u>point, rebellious</u> arm 'gainst arm,
Curbing his <u>lavish</u> spirit: and, to conclude,
The victory fell on us.

Duncan.   Great happiness!

Ross. That now
Sweno, the Norways' king, <u>craves composition</u>:   60
Nor would we <u>deign</u> him burial of his men,
Till he disbursed, at <u>Saint Colme's inch</u>
Ten thousand <u>dollars,</u> to our general use.

Duncan. No more that thane of Cawdor shall <u>deceive</u>
<u>Our bosom interest</u>: go pronounce his <u>present</u> death,   65
And with his former title greet Macbeth.

Ross. I'll see it done.

Duncan. What he hath lost, <u>noble Macbeth</u> hath won.

                    Exeunt.

2 **Killing swine:** The destructive nature of the Witches is brought out in this reference to one of their recognized activities.

5 **munch'd:** a very imitative word, especially when repeated.

6 **Aroint thee:** Begone; away with you; **rump-fed:** Of the various possible meanings, *fat-bottomed* (pampered, fed on the best joints) seems the most appropriate; **ronyon:** scabby, mangy creature.

7 **Aleppo:** In medieval times, this city, in what was then North Syria, was the centre of a great import and export trade; **the Tiger:** This was a popular Elizabethan name for a ship.

4-7 Note the realistic details of the picture. They suggest a fat, lazy, complacent woman.

8 **in a sieve:** evidence of supernatural powers.

9 **rat without a tail:** A witch could take the shape of any animal she pleased, but the tail would be missing.

10 **I'll do:** The use of the verb without an object allows the imagination to conjure up horrid pictures; its repetition brings out the vindictive nature of the speaker. The verb "do" appears frequently in the play.

11 **a wind:** Witches were reported to be able to sell winds, which were then to be tied in the corner of a handkerchief until needed. See also IV. i. 52-53.

15 **blow:** Add *upon*. The Witches could keep a ship from reaching port if they so desired.

17 **shipman's card:** the compass-card used by the steersman.

18 **I will:** F reads *Ile*, which Pope emended to *I will*; **drain:** a vivid picture of dehydration and excessive thirst.

19-20 **Sleep shall . . . lid:** Sleeplessness is one of the recurring themes in the play; **pent-house lid:** eye-lid. A "pent-house" was the sloping roof over a door or window. It sometimes referred to the overhanging roof of a shed; on occasion, the shed itself was referred to as a pent-house. Note the modern meaning and account for it.

21 **forbid:** under a curse.

22 **se'nnights:** weeks; cf. *fortnights*; **nine times nine:** "Nine" was a magic number.

23 **dwindle, peak, and pine:** These imitative verbs suggest a growing thinness and emaciation as the body wastes away under a spell (perhaps that of a waxen image stuck with pins and melting in a fire).

28 **a pilot's thumb:** To make their charms, the Witches opened graves and took from the bodies small bones such as fingers, toes, and knees. Today, a rabbit's foot is carried by some people "for luck".

Scene 3

THE HEATH.

Thunder. Enter the three Witches.

First Witch.   Where hast thou been, sister?
Second Witch.   Killing swine.
Third Witch.   Sister, where thou?
First Witch.   A sailor's wife had chestnuts in her lap,
And munch'd, and munch'd, and munch'd. "Give me," quoth I: 5
"Aroint thee, witch!" the rump-fed ronyon cries.
Her husband's to Aleppo gone, master o' the Tiger;
But in a sieve I'll thither sail,
And, like a rat without a tail,
I'll do, I'll do, and I'll do.   10
Second Witch.   I'll give thee a wind.
First Witch.   Thou'rt kind.
Third Witch.   And I another.
First Witch.   I myself have all the other,
And the very ports they blow,   15
All the quarters that they know
I' the shipman's card.
I will drain him dry as hay:
Sleep shall neither night nor day
Hang upon his pent-house lid;   20
He shall live a man forbid:
Weary se'nnights, nine times nine,
Shall he dwindle, peak, and pine:
Though his bark cannot be lost,
Yet it shall be tempest-tost.   25
Look what I have.
Second Witch.   Show me, show me.
First Witch.   Here I have a pilot's thumb,
Wreck'd as homeward he did come.   *Drum within.*

[handwritten marginal note: witches unreal — treatment by women real. *]*

30 **A drum:** Since Macbeth and Banquo are unaccompanied, the sound may be of supernatural origin.

32 **weird:** F reads *weyward*, but Holinshed writes "weird". The Anglo Saxon noun *wyrd* meant fate, but Shakespeare's Witches are not synonymous with the Greek Fates, though they are connected with Macbeth's destiny. (The old Highland saying runs "He maun dree his wyrd": He must endure his fate.)

33 **posters:** swift travellers.

32-37 The Witches do a grotesque dance, moving widdershins. They stand like withered tree-stumps.

37 S.D. Macbeth makes his first entrance, which has been carefully prepared for by Shakespeare.

38 **So foul . . . seen:** Dramatic irony is created by this echo of the Witches' couplet. "Fair" is usually taken to refer to Macbeth's victories, "foul", to the weather.

39 **Forres:** See map, p. xliii. Duncan's camp was at Forres. A mound, now known as Macbeth's Hillock, rises between Forres and Nairn on the Moray Firth; **What are these:** Holinshed says: "There met them three women in strange and wild attire, resembling creatures of elder world."

44 **choppy:** chapped.

46 **beards:** These were a recognized characteristic of witches. "The sort of such as are said to be witches are women which be commonly old, lame, blear-eied, pale, fowle, and full of wrinkles" (Scot).

47 **Speak, if you can:** Note the difference between the reactions of the two men. Why do the Witches answer Macbeth?

48 **Glamis:** See map, p. xliii. In Scotland, this word is a monosyllable; Shakespeare frequently scans it as two syllables.

48-50 The triple salutation is found in Holinshed. Of what significance is the order? What evidence is there of dramatic irony?

51 **why do you start:** Why are you startled? "To start" is to make a sudden movement as a result of surprise or another emotion. In Shakespeare, it implies guilt. The implication is that Macbeth has previously contemplated the kingship and therefore is not an innocent man when the Witches accost him.

53 **fantastical:** illusory, imaginary, creatures of fancy.

54 **show:** appear to be.

55-56 **with present . . . hope:** Banquo refers to each of the three salutations; **having:** fortune.

57 **rapt:** transported, in a daze.

58-59 **if you . . . not:** a singularly appropriate metaphor to suggest supernatural powers of foretelling the future.

60-61 Banquo's conscience is clear. He neither begs their favours nor fears their hate.

Third Witch.   A drum, a drum!   30
   Macbeth doth come.
All.   The weird sisters, hand in hand,
   Posters of the sea and land,
   Thus do go, about, about,
   Thrice to thine, and thrice to mine,   35
   And thrice again, to make up nine.
   Peace, the charm's wound up.
        Enter Macbeth and Banquo.
Macbeth.   So foul and fair a day I have not seen.
Banquo.   How far is 't call'd to Forres? What are these
   So wither'd, and so wild in their attire,   40
   That look not like the inhabitants o' the earth,
   And yet are on 't? Live you? or are you aught
   That man may question? You seem to understand me,
   By each at once her choppy finger laying
   Upon her skinny lips: you should be women,   45
   And yet your beards forbid me to interpret
   That you are so.
Macbeth.   Speak, if you can: what are you?
First Witch.   All hail, Macbeth! hail to thee, thane of Glamis!
Second Witch.   All hail, Macbeth! hail to thee, thane of Cawdor!
Third Witch.   All hail, Macbeth! that shalt be king hereafter!   50
Banquo.   Good sir, why do you start, and seem to fear
   Things that do sound so fair? I' the name of truth,
   Are ye fantastical, or that indeed
   Which outwardly ye show? My noble partner
   You greet with present grace, and great prediction   55
   Of noble having, and of royal hope,
   That he seems rapt withal: to me you speak not:
   If you can look into the seeds of time,
   And say which grain will grow, and which will not,
   Speak then to me, who neither beg nor fear   60
   Your favours, nor your hate.
First Witch.   Hail!
Second Witch.   Hail!

62-64 The Witches seem to speak grudgingly, and to spit out their pronouncements unwillingly.

65-66 Note the paradoxes.

67 **get:** beget, be the father of.

70 **Stay:** The Witches prepare to leave; Dover Wilson suggests that a mist rises and begins to shroud them; **imperfect:** saying only part of what you mean.

71 **Sinel:** Macbeth's father, the name being a corruption of the modern *Finlay*.

74 **stands not . . . belief:** is not believable.

76 **owe:** possess. Note also the word "strange" again.

77 **blasted:** blighted, withered.

79 The fact that the Witches have vanished like bubbles suggests their sudden, supernatural disappearance.

81-82 **corporal:** corporeal, having a physical body; **melted as . . . wind:** The simile reminds one of seeing his breath on a frosty morning and watching it disappear; **Would they had stay'd:** Macbeth speaks with great longing.

83 Banquo expresses incredulity.

84 **insane root:** henbane, a narcotic, poisonous plant, productive of insanity. (Note the transferred epithet.) Shakespeare may have been reading Plutarch's *Life of Antony*, which contains a similar reference.

86 **Your children . . . kings:** Already the prophecy rankles, although some editors state that Macbeth merely wanted to hear Banquo repeat the prophecy regarding the kingship. According to Holinshed, Macbeth and Banquo jested about the prophecies.

88 **S.D. Ross:** Once more, this Thane is the bearer of tidings.

91 **personal venture:** actual part played.

92-93 **His wonders . . . his:** Duncan is bewildered; his own amazement vies with his admiration. (Hence, he can find no words.)

95 **stout:** bold.

96 **nothing afeard:** not a bit afraid.

Third Witch.   Hail!

First Witch.   Lesser than Macbeth, and greater.   65

Second Witch.   Not so happy, yet much happier.

Third Witch.   Thou shalt get kings, though thou be none:

  So all hail, Macbeth and Banquo!

First Witch.   Banquo and Macbeth, all hail!

Macbeth.   Stay, you imperfect speakers, tell me more: 70

  By Sinel's death I know I am thane of Glamis,

  But how of Cawdor? the thane of Cawdor lives,

  A prosperous gentleman; and to be king

  Stands not within the prospect of belief,

  No more than to be Cawdor. Say from whence   75

  You owe this strange intelligence, or why

  Upon this blasted heath you stop our way

  With such prophetic greeting? Speak, I charge you.

                            Witches vanish.

Banquo.   The earth hath bubbles, as the water has,

  And these are of them: whither are they vanish'd?   80

Macbeth.   Into the air: and what seem'd corporal melted

  As breath into the wind. Would they had stay'd!

Banquo.   Were such things here, as we do speak about?

  Or have we eaten on the insane root,

  That takes the reason prisoner?   85

Macbeth.   Your children shall be kings.

Banquo.   You shall be king.

Macbeth.   And thane of Cawdor too: went it not so?

Banquo.   To the selfsame tune and words. Who's here?

      Enter Ross and Angus.

Ross.   The king hath happily receiv'd, Macbeth,

  The news of thy success: and when he reads   90

  Thy personal venture in the rebels' fight,

  His wonders and his praises do contend,

  Which should be thine, or his: silenc'd with that,

  In viewing o'er the rest o' the selfsame day,

  He finds thee in the stout Norweyan ranks,   95

  Nothing afeard of what thyself didst make,

97   **strange images of death:** Macbeth is likened to a sculptor. Cf. "carv'd out his passage" (I. ii. 19).

98   **post:** swift-riding courier.

99   **thy praises:** praises of thee.

104   **earnest:** pledge; **of a greater honour:** Such a promise might give Macbeth reason to hope that he would be named the King's heir.

106   **addition:** title.

107   **the devil:** Banquo has no doubt that the Witches are evil.

108-9   **dress me . . . robes:** The image of clothing is a recurring one. Throughout the play, Macbeth, the usurper-King, is dressed in "borrow'd robes", which seem to symbolize hypocrisy.

111-12   **combined with . . . Norway:** in league with the Norwegians; **line the rebel:** support or reinforce Macdonwald.

113   **vantage:** favourable opportunity.

111-14   Angus is somewhat vague, as Shakespeare deliberately intended to imply.

115   **capital:** punishable by death.

117   **behind:** yet to come; **Thanks for your pains:** Macbeth's courtesy at the outset is one of his positive characteristics.

118   **do you not hope:** Why does Macbeth appeal to Banquo?

120   **that:** the prophecy; **home:** fully.

124   **instruments of darkness:** the Witches, who are agents of evil.

126   **in deepest consequence:** in matters of the highest importance.

123-6   Banquo's prophecy is a warning that ultimately proves true.

Strange images of death. As thick as hail
Came post with post, and every one did bear
Thy praises in his kingdom's great defence,
And pour'd them down before him.
Angus.   We are sent   100
   To give thee from our royal master thanks,
   Only to herald thee into his sight,
   Not pay thee.
Ross.   And for an earnest of a greater honour,
   He bade me, from him, call thee thane of Cawdor: 105
   In which addition, hail, most worthy thane,
   For it is thine.
Banquo.   What, can the devil speak true?
Macbeth.   The thane of Cawdor lives: why do you dress me
   In borrow'd robes?
Angus.   Who was the thane, lives yet,
   But under heavy judgement bears that life,   110
   Which he deserves to lose. Whether he was com-
      bin'd
   With those of Norway, or did line the rebel
   With hidden help and vantage, or that with both
   He labour'd in his country's wreck, I know not;
   But treasons capital, confess'd, and prov'd,   115
   Have overthrown him.
Macbeth (aside).   Glamis, and thane of Cawdor:
   The greatest is behind.—Thanks for your pains.—
   Do you not hope your children shall be kings,
   When those that gave the thane of Cawdor to me
   Promis'd no less to them?
Banquo.   That, trusted home,   120
   Might yet enkindle you unto the crown,
   Besides the thane of Cawdor. But 'tis strange:
   And oftentimes, to win us to our harm,
   The instruments of darkness tell us truths,
   Win us with honest trifles, to betray's   125
   In deepest consequence.

127 **Cousins, a word:** He deliberately turns away.
128-9 **happy prologues . . . theme:** The metaphor here, one of Shakespeare's favourites, is drawn from the world of the theatre. Just as a prologue precedes a play, so the first two salutations are a prelude to the glorious drama of my becoming King; **swelling:** increasing in splendour.
130 **soliciting:** incitement, temptation. 134 **suggestion:** temptation.
135-8 **horrid image:** his own murder of Duncan; **doth unfix . . . nature:** The idea of the murder is at this stage hideously repugnant; **doth unfix my hair:** makes my hair stand on end; **seated:** firm-set; **use:** custom; **Present fears . . . imaginings:** This speech is a key to an understanding of Macbeth's character.
139-42 The thought of the murder, which is as yet only in my imagination, so perturbs the kingdom of my being (single state of man) that the power to act (function) is swallowed up in speculation (smother'd in surmise), and only the unreal seems real. (The whole passage suggests a chaos of bewilderment.)
142 **Look how . . . rapt:** an indirect stage direction, indicating that Macbeth looks as if he is in a trance.
127-42 Macbeth's first soliloquy shows his vivid imagination and his fear of wrong-doing. It brings out the conflict that will continue to rage within him until he has made his decision. His ambition is clearly indicated, along with the fact that the fear of an enemy in the flesh is as nothing compared with the terrors his imagination conjures up. "This is the moment of the birth of evil in Macbeth" (Wilson Knight).
143-4 **If chance . . . stir:** Macbeth seems to put aside the thought of taking direct action.
144-6 New clothes may seem stiff and awkward until they become comfortable after being worn. Note the clothing image.
147 **Time and . . . day:** The future will bring what it will bring.
148 **we stay . . . leisure:** a courteous reminder that they are waiting for him.
149-50 **Give me your favour:** I beg your pardon; **my dull . . . forgotten:** an obvious bit of hypocrisy; **wrought:** concerned, busy.
150-2 **your pains . . . them:** Macbeth's memory is a book in which their kindnesses are recorded for him to recall daily. Macbeth again shows winning courtesy; **pains:** the trouble you take; **Let us . . . king:** thought by some to have an ominous meaning.
153-5 **and at . . . other:** This remark to Banquo reveals that Macbeth has not really forgotten the third prophecy; **at more time:** when we have more of an opportunity; **the interim . . . it:** when time has permitted us to consider it.
See also p. 159.

In this scene we see how prophecies affect macbeth.

Cousins, a word, I pray you.
Macbeth (aside).   Two truths are told,
  As happy prologues to the swelling act
  Of the imperial theme.—I thank you, gentlemen.—
  (aside) This supernatural soliciting   130
  Cannot be ill; cannot be good: if ill,
  Why hath it given me earnest of success,
  Commencing in a truth? I am thane of Cawdor:
  If good, why do I yield to that suggestion,
  Whose horrid image doth unfix my hair,   135
  And make my seated heart knock at my ribs,
  Against the use of nature? Present fears
  Are less than horrible imaginings:
  My thought, whose murder yet is but fantastical,
  Shakes so my single state of man that function   140
  Is smother'd in surmise, and nothing is,
  But what is not.

appears & real.
good or evil.
paradox

Banquo.   Look how our partner's rapt.
Macbeth (aside). If chance will have me king, why,
  chance may crown me,
  Without my stir.
Banquo.   New honours come upon him,
  Like our strange garments, cleave not to their mould,   145
  But with the aid of use.
Macbeth (aside).   Come what come may,
  Time and the hour runs through the roughest day.
Banquo. Worthy Macbeth, we stay upon your leisure.
Macbeth. Give me your favour: my dull brain was wrought
  With things forgotten. Kind gentlemen, your pains   150
  Are register'd where every day I turn
  The leaf to read them. Let us toward the king;
  Think upon what hath chanc'd; and at more time,
  The interim having weigh'd it, let us speak
  Our free hearts each to other.
Banquo.   Very gladly.   155
Macbeth. Till then, enough. Come, friends.   *Exeunt.*

1-2   Why is Duncan impatient? **those in commission:** men in charge of the execution. Some editors think this refers to Ross and Angus in view of I. ii. 67.

9   **as one . . . studied:** like an actor who had rehearsed the part and memorized his lines, so well he did it.

10   **ow'd:** possessed.

11   **as 'twere:** as if it were; **careless:** worthless, unvalued.

2-11   This speech is sometimes entitled "The Repentant Traitor". It has been suggested that Shakespeare was thinking of the execution of the ill-fated Earl of Essex.

11-14   **There's no . . . trust:** Macbeth's entrance on the heels of this remark is a startling instance of dramatic irony. It also indicates that Duncan, the idealist, is not realistic in his judgement of character; **There's no . . . face:** It is impossible to deduce a man's true character from his facial appearance. One cannot judge a book by its cover.

16-20   **thou art . . . thee:** My eagerness to reward you cannot catch up with your merits. The image is that of a falcon overtaking its prey. Shakespeare seems to have observed with accuracy the grace and power of birds in flight; **proportion:** adjustment; **Would thou . . . mine:** If only you had deserved less, I might have been able to repay and reward you more fittingly.

21   **More is . . . pay:** I cannot possibly pay you what you deserve.

14-21   Some critics are of the opinion that Duncan is too lavish in his praise. How valid is this criticism?

22-23   **The service . . . itself:** Virtue is its own reward.

24-27   **out duties . . . honour:** Just as children and servants owe love and obedience to parents and masters respectively, so I, a subject, am but doing my duty to you as King in trying to protect and preserve you.

22-27   Some find in these lines a contrived and stilted expression of allegiance.

Scene 4

FORRES. THE PALACE.

Flourish. Enter Duncan, Malcolm, Donalbain,
Lennox, and Attendants.

Duncan.   Is execution done on Cawdor? Are not
  Those in commission yet return'd?
Malcolm.   My liege,
  They are not yet come back. But I have spoke
  With one that saw him die; who did report
  That very frankly he confess'd his treasons,   5
  Implor'd your highness' pardon, and set forth
  A deep repentance: nothing in his life
  Became him like the leaving it; he died
  As one that had been studied in his death,
  To throw away the dearest thing he ow'd   10
  As 'twere a careless trifle.
Duncan.   There's no art
  To find the mind's construction in the face:
  He was a gentleman on whom I built
  An absolute trust.
          Enter Macbeth, Banquo, Ross, and Angus.
                O worthiest cousin!
  The sin of my ingratitude even now   15
  Was heavy on me: thou art so far before,
  That swiftest wing of recompense is slow
  To overtake thee. Would thou hadst less deserv'd,
  That the proportion both of thanks, and payment,
  Might have been mine! only I have left to say,   20
  More is thy due than more than all can pay.
Macbeth.   The service and the loyalty I owe,
  In doing it, pays itself. Your highness' part
  Is to receive our duties: and our duties
  Are to your throne, and state, children, and servants;   25
  Which do but what they should, by doing everything

28-29 **plant, growing:** The image of growth appears frequently in the play. Cf. "seeds of time" (I. iii. 58).

29-32 **Noble Banquo . . . heart:** The King's praise of Banquo seems more spontaneous and sincere than his praise of Macbeth.

32-33 **There if . . . own:** My increasing importance will only increase my devotion to you. Banquo's brief speech is evidence of his sincerity and loyalty; **grow:** a) cling to, as the vine does to the tree, b) advance in dignity.

34 **wanton in fulness:** overflowing. Duncan's joy expresses itself in tears.

36 **whose places . . . nearest:** whose rank is closest to our own.

37 **establish our estate:** settle the succession to the throne. Since it was the custom in Scotland during the eleventh century for the crown to pass to the strongest person in the family group, Macbeth might have expected that he would be named heir-apparent instead of Malcolm.

39 **Prince of Cumberland:** next in line to the throne; cf. Prince of Wales; **Cumberland:** See map, p. xliii. The present county was held by Scotland as a fief of the crown of England.

41 **signs of nobleness:** insignia of nobility; **like stars:** The insignia would take the form of a jewel, on a chain or in a brooch.

42 **Inverness:** One of the chief towns in the Scottish Highlands. See map, p. xliii.

43 **bind us . . . you:** increase our indebtedness to you.

44 **The rest . . . you:** Leisure is weariness to me when it is not devoted to serving you.

45 **harbinger:** forerunner, one whose duty it was to make provision for the King's lodging; **make joyful:** but not in the sense that Duncan would interpret it; hence, dramatic irony.

47 **My worthy Cawdor:** It is ominous that Macbeth has been honoured with a traitor's title.

48 **step:** obstacle. To get the crown, Macbeth must take action.

50-51 **Stars hide . . . desires:** Macbeth feels that his evil deed must be accomplished in utter darkness, not only because it is wicked, but lest it be discovered. Many critics have pointed out that darkness, symbolic of evil, broods over the whole play.

52 **The eye wink at the hand:** Let the eye not see the deeds of the hand; **that:** the murder; **be:** come to pass.

55-56 **And in . . . me:** It is meat and drink to me to hear him praised. Duncan's unsuspicious generosity creates dramatic irony.

57 **whose care:** who in his concern (for my well-being).

See also p. 160.

Safe toward your love and honour.
Duncan.   Welcome hither: ~honie~
   I have begun to plant thee, and will labour
   To make thee full of growing. Noble Banquo,
   That hast no less deserv'd, nor must be known   30
   No less to have done so: let me enfold thee,
   And hold thee to my heart.
Banquo.   There if I grow,
   The harvest is your own.
Duncan.   My plenteous joys,
   Wanton in fulness, seek to hide themselves
   In drops of sorrow. Sons, kinsmen, thanes,   35
   And you whose places are the nearest, know,   ~will eventually be king (phrophesy)~
   We will establish our estate upon
   Our eldest, Malcolm, whom we name hereafter
   The Prince of Cumberland: which honour must
   Not unaccompanied invest him only,   40
   But signs of nobleness, like stars, shall shine
   On all deservers. From hence to Inverness,
   And bind us further to you.
Macbeth.   The rest is labour, which is not us'd for you:
   I'll be myself the harbinger, and make joyful   45
   The hearing of my wife with your approach;
   So humbly take my leave.
Duncan.   My worthy Cawdor!
Macbeth (aside).   The Prince of Cumberland! that is a step,
   On which I must fall down, or else o'erleap,
   For in my way it lies. Stars, hide your fires!   50
   Let not light see my black and deep desires: ~(kill duncan)~
   The eye wink at the hand; yet let that be,
   Which the eye fears, when it is done, to see.   *Exit.*
Duncan.   True, worthy Banquo; he is full so valiant,
   And in his commendations I am fed;   55
   It is a banquet to me. Let's after him,
   Whose care is gone before, to bid us welcome:
   It is a peerless kinsman.   *Flourish.   Exeunt.*

S.D. Lady Macbeth: Lady Macbeth makes her first appearance in one production wearing a "Long gown of pale blue silk gathered at waist by a belt of cloth of gold web" (French's Acting Edition). Many readers picture her as small, dark, and intense. In some productions, she makes her entrance descending the stairs as she reads her letter. She is the first person in the play to appear alone on the stage.

2 **the perfect'st report:** Macbeth may be referring to the proof that he had experienced, or to information gained by inquiry about the Witches.

3-4 **mortal:** human; **burn'd in desire:** Note his intense longing.

6 **missives:** messengers.   7 **all-hail'd:** greeted.

8-9 **referr'd me . . . time:** reminded me of the future.

10-11 **deliver:** communicate to; **my dearest . . . greatness:** Macbeth's love for his wife is shown by this phrase and also by the fact that he hastened to write her a letter about his strange encounter.

12 **dues of rejoicing:** right to share my joy.

15 **shalt be:** Note the tense—the future of determination. Lady Macbeth's first words in the play illustrate the iron quality of her will.

17 **the milk . . . kindness:** Most critics interpret this metaphor to mean *mildness* or *gentleness*. (Lady Macbeth views this as a weakness.) Others maintain that *humankindness* (one word) refers to the qualities that Macbeth shares with other human beings.

18 **the nearest way:** *i.e.*, the way of murder.

19 **not without ambition:** You have a certain amount of ambition; an understatement surely! In *Julius Caesar* and *Henry VIII*, Shakespeare shows the effect of inordinate ambition.

20-22 **illness:** wickedness. Ambition often requires that a man be unscrupulous; **What thou . . . holily:** The things on which you set a high value, you would prefer to achieve by lawful means; **wouldst not . . . win:** You do not like cheating, but you would rather win by cheating than lose.

23 **that which cries:** the crown.

24 **that which . . . do:** the murder.

25 **undone:** not done; **Hie thee:** Hasten.

26 **may pour . . . ear:** may express to you my determination. The metaphor reminds us of the poison poured in the ear of Hamlet's father.

27-28 **chastise with . . . round:** drive away (whip) with my courageous words all the scruples that stand between you and the crown.

Scene 5

INVERNESS. MACBETH'S CASTLE.

Enter Lady Macbeth, reading a letter.

Lady Macbeth. "They met me in the day of success; and I have learn'd by the perfect'st report, they have more in them than mortal knowledge. When I burn'd in desire to question them further, they made themselves air, into which they vanish'd. Whiles I stood   5 rapt in the wonder of it, came missives from the king, who all-hail'd me thane of Cawdor, by which title, before, these weird sisters saluted me, and referr'd me to the coming on of time, with 'Hail, king that shalt be!' This have I thought good to deliver thee, my   10 dearest partner of greatness, that thou mightst not lose the dues of rejoicing by being ignorant of what greatness is promis'd thee. Lay it to thy heart, and farewell."

Glamis thou art, and Cawdor, and shalt be   15
What thou art promis'd: yet do I fear thy nature,
It is too full o' the milk of human kindness
To catch the nearest way. Thou wouldst be great,
Art not without ambition, but without
The illness should attend it. What thou wouldst
    highly,   20
That wouldst thou holily; wouldst not play false,
And yet wouldst wrongly win. Thou 'ldst have,
    great Glamis,
That which cries "Thus thou must do if thou have it;"
And that which rather thou dost fear to do,
Than wishest should be undone. Hie thee hither,   25
That I may pour my spirits in thine ear,
And chastise with the valour of my tongue
All that impedes thee from the golden round,

29   **metaphysical:** supernatural.

15-30   Lady Macbeth's great soliloquy gives not only an analysis of her husband's character but an insight into her own.

31-33   **Thou'rt mad . . . preparation:** Lady Macbeth is caught off guard. It seems incredible to her that such an opportunity would be presented at such a moment.

35-37   **One of . . . message:** A breathless servant who preceded Macbeth could scarcely give the news.

38-40   **great news:** Little does the servant realize what his mistress means; **raven:** a bird of ill omen. Such a dreadful deed is planned that even the raven croaks more hoarsely than usual. The reference is symbolic; **The raven . . . battlements:** Note the onomatopoeia.

41   **mortal thoughts:** murderous schemes; **unsex:** Remove all womanly feelings.

42   **crown to the toe:** head to foot, completely; **top-full:** brimful.

43   **make thick my blood:** This would make her insensitive.

44   **Stop up . . . remorse:** Let no compassion gain entrance or proceed to my heart.

45-47   **that no . . . purpose:** that no natural feelings of pity interfere with my cruel design; **nor keep . . . it:** nor prevent the deed from being carried out, as a peacemaker would intervene between two disputants.

48   **take my . . . gall:** change "the milk of human kindness" to "gall"; *i.e.*, bitterness. Since it was believed that demons were suckled by witches, the expression may mean: "Take my milk now turned to gall as your nourishment, agents of murder."

49   **sightless substances:** invisible forms.

50   **wait on:** are ready to carry out; **nature's mischief:** the evil in human nature; **thick:** dark.

51   **pall:** hide, as in a shroud; **dunnest:** darkest.

52   **that my . . . makes:** Lady Macbeth apparently intended to commit the deed herself.

53   **blanket:** The earth is asleep under the covering of night; a homely image. Perhaps, heaven (the stars) peeps through this blanket (the darkness). Her speech has risen to an awesome climax.

54-55   **Great Glamis . . . hereafter:** The threefold salutation reminds us that Lady Macbeth may be considered the Fourth Witch; **hereafter:** in the future.

38-54   Lady Macbeth's invocation to the spirits of evil and to darkness shows inhuman determination. Yet, if she were not womanly and kindly, she would not need to steel herself.

56-57   **transported me . . . present:** enabled me to see into the future, beyond the unknowing "now".

Which fate and metaphysical aid doth seem
To have thee crown'd withal.
    Enter a Messenger.

                      What is your tidings?   30
Messenger.   The king comes here to-night.
Lady Macbeth.   Thou 'rt mad to say it:
  Is not thy master with him? who, were't so,
  Would have inform'd for preparation.
Messenger.   So please you, it is true: our thane is coming:
  One of my fellows had the speed of him,   35
  Who, almost dead for breath, had scarcely more
  Than would make up his message.
Lady Macbeth.   Give him tending,
  He brings great news.   *Exit Messenger.*
          The raven himself is hoarse
That croaks the fatal entrance of Duncan
Under my battlements. Come, you spirits   40
That tend on mortal thoughts, unsex me here,
And fill me, from the crown to the toe, top-full
Of direst cruelty: make thick my blood,
Stop up the access and passage to remorse,
That no compunctious visitings of nature   45
Shake my fell purpose, nor keep peace between
The effect and it! Come to my woman's breasts,
And take my milk for gall, you murdering ministers,
Wherever in your sightless substances
You wait on nature's mischief! Come, thick night,   50
And pall thee in the dunnest smoke of hell,
That my keen knife see not the wound it makes,
Nor heaven peep through the blanket of the dark,
To cry "Hold, hold!"
    Enter Macbeth.

                Great Glamis! worthy Cawdor!
Greater than both, by the all-hail hereafter!   55
Thy letters have transported me beyond
This ignorant present, and I feel now

57-58 I feel . . . instant: I can already see you as King.

58-59 My dearest . . . to-night: Macbeth's passionate greeting is combined with a statement that is more than an announcement.

60 To-morrow, as he purposes: A pause after "to-morrow" indicates that Macbeth may have other plans for him, as Lady Macbeth is quick to see. So close are husband and wife that they seem able to read each other's thoughts.

62-63 Your face . . . matters: Macbeth must learn to play the hypocrite more skilfully. The days of a frank and open countenance are behind him; **to beguile the time:** to deceive the world.

65-66 look like . . . under't: Again comes the Machiavellian advice to play the hypocrite. "The medal commemorating the Gunpowder Plot depicts a serpent lurking among flowers" (Muir).

67-70 provided for: a grisly euphemism; **and you . . . masterdom:** Note the dominant "s" sound that hisses through these lines; **great business:** The thought of the murder does not seem to be in any sense wicked or evil to Lady Macbeth. She has become more of a monster than a woman; **dispatch:** management; **solely sovereign sway:** royal power to us alone.

71 We will speak further: Macbeth finds his wife's tidal energy overpowering. An obstacle in his path rouses his determination, but being thrust forward too eagerly makes him balky.

72 To alter . . . fear: To change countenance makes others suspicious.

73 How confident she is!

See also p. 161.

S.D. hautboys: oboes; **torches:** The need for torches has been questioned by some editors, but doubtless the castle would be growing dark.

1-3 a pleasant seat: an attractive situation; **the air . . . senses:** If the castle were located strategically on an eminence, it would be fanned by cooling breezes in warm weather. Such an atmosphere would be soothing to the senses; **gentle:** made gentle, soothed. Duncan's speech provides a sharp contrast with the tension of the preceding scene. His appreciation of his hosts' castle is grimly ironic.

4 temple-haunting: flying about churches; **martlet:** a kind of swallow; **does approve:** proves.

5 loved mansionry: nest to which the bird fondly returns. F reads *mansonry*, which was emended to *masonry* by Pope. "Mansionry" is Theobald's conjecture.

The future in the instant.
Macbeth.   My dearest love,
   Duncan comes here to-night.
Lady Macbeth.   And when goes hence?
Macbeth.   To-morrow, as he purposes.
Lady Macbeth.   O, never   60
   Shall sun that morrow see! *irony – duncan says can read face.*
   Your face, my thane, is as a book, where men
   May read strange matters. To beguile the time,
   Look like the time; bear welcome in your eye,
   Your hand, your tongue: look like the innocent flower,   65
   But be the serpent under't. He that's coming
   Must be provided for: and you shall put
   This night's great business into my dispatch,
   Which shall to all our nights and days to come
   Give solely sovereign sway and masterdom.   70
Macbeth.   We will speak further.
Lady Macbeth.   Only look up clear;
   To alter favour ever is to fear: *real + unreal.*
   Leave all the rest to me.   *Exeunt.*

Scene 6

BEFORE MACBETH'S CASTLE.

Hautboys and torches. Enter Duncan, Malcolm,
Donalbain, Banquo, Lennox, Macduff, Ross,
Angus, and Attendants.   *irony – audience*

Dramatic

Duncan.   This castle hath a pleasant seat; the air *now going be*
   Nimbly and sweetly recommends itself   *dead.*
   Unto our gentle senses.
Banquo.   This guest of summer,
   The temple-haunting martlet, does approve,
   By his loved mansionry, that the heaven's breath   5

6 **jutty:** projecting part; **frieze:** an ornamental band of sculpture on a wall.

7 **buttress:** perhaps a flying buttress, used as an arch support to a high wall; **coign of vantage:** convenient corner for nesting.

8 **pendent bed:** hanging nest; **procreant cradle:** place for begetting young.

10 **delicate:** pleasant.

3-10 Banquo's knowledge of birds shows that he is observant and that he appreciates nature. The play contains a number of references to birds.

11-14 **The love . . . love:** The love of my subjects sometimes causes me trouble, but I am thankful none the less for this evidence of their affection; **Herein I . . . trouble:** My visit causes you trouble, but it is evidence of my love for you. Hence, you should pray God to reward me (God 'ild us) and be thankful for my visit.

14-18 **All our . . . house:** Lady Macbeth's hypocrisy does not hide the fact that she has the social sense of a good hostess and knows how to welcome a guest gracefully; **single business . . . against:** unworthy in comparison with.

19 **late dignities:** recent honours.

20 **We rest your hermits:** We remain bound to pray for you. Duncan's question again reminds us of treachery. Why does Macbeth not appear to welcome the King?

21 **We cours'd . . . heels:** We followed him closely.

22 **purveyor:** forerunner; an officer sent in advance to provide food for the King and his company.

23 **great love:** for his wife or for Duncan? The latter would be more ironic, the former a more gracious compliment; **holp:** helped.

24-25 **Fair and . . . guest:** This phrase throws into sharp relief the horror of the deed contemplated, a violation of the ancient laws of hospitality.

25-28 **Your servants . . . own:** The Macbeths are merely stewards, holding all they possess in trust for Duncan; **in compt:** under obligation to render an account; **audit:** report; **still:** always; **Give me your hand:** This mark of the King's trust and affection may have moved Lady Macbeth more than she let on. The phrase reappears, in another context, in the sleep-walking scene (V. i. 66).

31 **By your leave:** According to Granville-Barker, the King with courtly politeness kissed Lady Macbeth's cheek, as was the custom of the time.

See also p. 162.

Smells wooingly here: no jutty, frieze,
Buttress, nor coign of vantage, but this bird
Hath made his pendent bed and procreant cradle:
Where they most breed and haunt, I have observ'd
The air is delicate.
   Enter Lady Macbeth.

Duncan.   See, see, our honour'd hostess!   10
 The love that follows us sometime is our trouble,
 Which still we thank as love. Herein I teach you
 How you shall bid God 'ild us for your pains,
 And thank us for your trouble.
Lady Macbeth.   All our service,
 In every point twice done, and then done double,   15
 Were poor and single business, to contend
 Against those honours deep and broad wherewith
 Your majesty loads our house: for those of old,
 And the late dignities heap'd up to them,
 We rest your hermits.
Duncan.   Where's the thane of Cawdor?   20
 We cours'd him at the heels, and had a purpose
 To be his purveyor: but he rides well,
 And his great love, sharp as his spur, hath holp him
 To his home before us. Fair and noble hostess,
 We are your guest to-night.
Lady Macbeth.   Your servants ever   25
 Have theirs, themselves, and what is theirs, in compt,
 To make their audit at your highness' pleasure,
 Still to return your own.
Duncan.   Give me your hand;
 Conduct me to mine host: we love him highly,
 And shall continue our graces towards him.   30
 By your leave, hostess.   *Exeunt.*

S.D. Sewer: an official who looked after the arrangements for a banquet; **divers:** various; **service:** the various receptacles in which food and drink were served.

1-2 **If it . . . quickly:** If the murder were finished with once it had been completed, then it would be a good thing to do it soon. The idea has been going round in Macbeth's mind.

3 **trammel up:** entangle in a net from which escape is impossible.

4 **his surcease:** Duncan's death; some editors interpret *its end*, the end of the assassination; **that but:** if only.

6 **here:** in this life; **bank and . . . time** (Theobald): Life is pictured as a sand-bar in the great sea of eternity. F reads *banke and schoole*.

7 **jump:** risk, chance; **the life to come:** This may imply that Macbeth is not sure whether there is an after-life. It could mean, however, that he is prepared to take a chance on not being punished in the next world.

8-16 **still:** always; **that we . . . inventor:** Evil is a kind of boomerang; **This even-handed . . . lips:** Justice is depicted as impartial; **commends:** offers; **ingredience:** so F; **He's here . . . myself:** Macbeth gives three valid reasons for not committing the murder. He is mercilessly clear-sighted.

17 **hath borne . . . meek:** has exercised his powers with such moderation.

18-20 **clear:** blameless, honest; **that his . . . taking-off:** Duncan's good qualities, angels with voices like ringing trumpets, will cry out against the terrible evil of his murder (onomatopoeia).

21-23 **and pity . . . blast:** a vivid image of helplessness and tenderness; **the blast:** the wind; **cherubin:** plural, *angels*; **hors'd upon . . . air:** riding upon the winds, their invisible steeds.

24-25 **shall blow . . . wind:** Shakespeare was aware that rain (tears) often followed a high wind (rage) and seemed to cause the latter to abate.

16-25 **Besides, this . . . wind:** Macbeth shows his poetic imagination and his realization of the horror of the murder.

25-28 **I have . . . other:** I have no motive for the deed except overweening ambition, which like a horseman trying to leap into the saddle jumps too far and falls on the other side. Thus, in over-reaching myself, I may destroy myself.

1-28 This powerful soliloquy is justly well known, presenting as it does a clear insight into Macbeth's character. His doubts and fears, his scruples, his imagination, all make him seem very human; he does express fear of the consequences, but according to Bradley, what really holds him back is the hideous vileness of the deed.

Scene 7

MACBETH'S CASTLE.

Hautboys and torches. Enter a Sewer, and divers Servants with dishes and service, and pass over the stage. Then enter Macbeth.

Macbeth. If it were done, when 'tis done, then 'twere well
It were done quickly: if the assassination
Could trammel up the consequence, and catch,
With his surcease, success; that but this blow
Might be the be-all and the end-all, here,   5
But here, upon this bank and shoal of time,
We'ld jump the life to come. But in these cases
We still have judgement here; that we but teach
Bloody instructions, which being taught, return
To plague the inventor. This even-handed justice   10
Commends the ingredience of our poison'd chalice
To our own lips. He's here in double trust;
First, as I am his kinsman, and his subject,
Strong both against the deed; then, as his host,
Who should against his murderer shut the door,   15
Not bear the knife myself. Besides, this Duncan
Hath borne his faculties so meek, hath been
So clear in his great office, that his virtues
Will plead like angels, trumpet-tongu'd against
The deep damnation of his taking-off;   20
And pity, like a naked new-born babe,
Striding the blast, or heaven's cherubin, hors'd
Upon the sightless couriers of the air,
Shall blow the horrid deed in every eye,
That tears shall drown the wind. I have no spur   25
To prick the sides of my intent, but only
Vaulting ambition, which o'erleaps itself,
And falls on the other.

28   S.D. Lady Macbeth's arrival creates dramatic irony when we think of the statement: "I have no spur. . . ." Her appearance is well-timed.

28-30   Note the effect of tension created by the short, sharp questions.

31-35   Macbeth's better self comes to the fore, and it is evident that he values the esteem of his fellows. Once more, his new honours are compared to new garments; **bought:** won.

35-38   **Was the . . . freely:** Lady Macbeth draws herself up to her full height and lashes Macbeth with all the scorn at her command. Hope is first personified (drunk) and then regarded as a garment (dress'd). Lady Macbeth's emotion makes her incoherent, but her contempt for Macbeth's cowardice is easily understood; **and wakes . . . pale:** Hope is compared to a man recovering from a drunken orgy.

39-41   **Such I . . . love:** In view of the strong feelings between them, this threat would cut deep; **Art thou . . . desire:** Are you afraid to match ambition with deeds?

42   **the ornament of life:** the crown.

45   **the adage:** The proverb: "The cat would eat fish but would not wet her feet." Similarly, Macbeth would like the crown, but is unwilling to take the necessary, unpleasant steps.

46-47   **I dare . . . none:** This has been referred to as "the last rally of Macbeth's better self"; **none:** Such a one is less than a man.

47-48   **What beast . . . me:** This question and the lines that follow seem to refer to a lost scene in which plans were definitely discussed by Macbeth. "Beast" is used in contrast to a "man".

50-51   **And, to . . . man:** When he had the courage to do it, he was superhuman.

52   **did then adhere:** were then favourable; **you would make both:** You were ready to create an opportunity.

53-54   **They have . . . you:** Now that the opportunity offers itself, you shrink back.

54-59   **I have . . . this:** The lines suggest that Macbeth had definitely promised to seize the crown. Lady Macbeth taunts him with faithlessness. To show the enormity of his crime, she says that rather than break such an oath, she would destroy her suckling infant (perhaps a child by a previous marriage, or perhaps hypothetical only); this indicates some tender feelings.

Enter Lady Macbeth.

Lady Macbeth. How now? what news?
He has almost supp'd: why have you left the
    chamber?

Macbeth. Hath he ask'd for me?

Lady Macbeth. Know you not he has? 30

Macbeth. We will proceed no further in this business:
He hath honour'd me of late, and I have bought
Golden opinions from all sorts of people,
Which would be worn now in their newest gloss,
Not cast aside so soon.

Lady Macbeth. Was the hope drunk, 35
Wherein you dress'd yourself? hath it slept since?
And wakes it now to look so green, and pale,
At what it did so freely? From this time,
Such I account thy love. Art thou afeard
To be the same in thine own act and valour 40
As thou art in desire? Wouldst thou have that
Which thou esteem'st the ornament of life,
And live a coward in thine own esteem?
Letting "I dare not" wait upon "I would,"
Like the poor cat i' the adage?

Macbeth. Prithee peace: 45
I dare do all that may become a man,
Who dares do more, is none.

Lady Macbeth. What beast was't then
That made you break this enterprise to me?
When you durst do it, then you were a man;
And, to be more than what you were, you would 50
Be so much more the man. Nor time, nor place,
Did then adhere, and yet you would make both:
They have made themselves, and that their fitness
    now
Does unmake you. I have given suck, and know
How tender 'tis to love the babe that milks me: 55
I would, while it was smiling in my face,

59 **If we should fail:** Macbeth, under the charges of cowardice, fickleness, and faithlessness, is beginning to weaken.

60 **We fail?:** So F. The question mark implies incredulous contempt. What emotions would be suggested by a period? an exclamation mark?

61 **screw your . . . sticking-place:** The metaphor is drawn from the tuning of a musical instrument, such as a viol. It may refer to the tightening of the cord of a cross-bow.

65 **wassail:** carousing; **convince:** overcome.

66-68 **that memory . . . only:** Imagine the brain as a kind of silex, a coffee-maker. The lower receptacle is the memory (keeper of the brain). When it is heated with alcohol, its "liquid" rises into the second receptacle (reason), leaving only fumes behind. Eventually, if the heat (alcohol) is still applied, the upper receptacle will be full of vapours. The image is that of a man stupefied; **limbec:** "alembic, distilling vessel full of alcoholic fumes" (Dover Wilson); **swinish sleep:** Lady Macbeth speaks contemptuously of such intoxication, though it will serve her purpose well.

69 **drenched:** sodden.

70 **you and I:** She sees it as a joint matter.

72 **spongy:** drunken, a term of contempt.

73 **great quell:** the murder. Lady Macbeth consistently regards the crime as a high and noble achievement, in contrast to Macbeth.

71-73 **What not . . . quell:** This feature of the crime is particularly revolting.

62-73 Lady Macbeth's dastardly plan shows her to be without conscience. The scheme is found in Holinshed.

73-75 **Bring forth . . . males:** To Macbeth, his wife's strength of spirit is admirable. She is fitted to be the mother of sons.

75-78 **Will it . . . done't:** It is tragic to realize that the cowardly plan appeals to Macbeth because it will enable them to escape the consequences.

78 **other:** otherwise.

79-80 **As we . . . death:** The thought of such hollow grief is repulsive; **bend up:** as one would string a bow.

81 **corporal agent:** physical faculty.

82 **mock the time:** delude the world.

83 In yielding to temptation, Macbeth must now dress himself symbolically in the garment of hypocrisy. Should the act end with a faint burst of mocking laughter, a moaning wind, distant thunder, or a slamming door?

See also p. 162.

Have pluck'd my nipple from his boneless gums,
And dash'd the brains out, had I so sworn
As you have done to this.
Macbeth.   If we should fail?
Lady Macbeth.   We fail?   60
But screw your courage to the sticking-place,
And we'll not fail: when Duncan is asleep,
(Whereto the rather shall his day's hard journey
Soundly invite him) his two chamberlains
Will I with wine and wassail so convince,   65
That memory, the warder of the brain,
Shall be a fume, and the receipt of reason
A limbec only: when in swinish sleep
Their drenched natures lie as in a death,
What cannot you and I perform upon   70
The unguarded Duncan? what not put upon
His spongy officers, who shall bear the guilt
Of our great quell?
Macbeth.   Bring forth men-children only!
For thy undaunted mettle should compose
Nothing but males. Will it not be receiv'd,   75
When we have mark'd with blood those sleepy
    two
Of his own chamber, and us'd their very daggers,
That they have done't?
Lady Macbeth.   Who dares receive it other,
As we shall make our griefs and clamour roar
Upon his death?
Macbeth.   I am settled, and bend up   80
Each corporal agent to this terrible feat.
Away, and mock the time with fairest show:
False face must hide what the false heart doth know.
                                        Exeunt.

1 **How goes . . . boy:** What purposes are served by this opening question?

2 **The moon is down:** the title of a novel by John Steinbeck. What other book titles are derived from the works of Shakespeare? What is Shakespeare trying to establish by the fact that the moon has set?

3 Evidently a young moon.

4 **husbandry:** thrift. The angels are good housekeepers.

5 **candles:** a favourite Shakespearian metaphor. In what ways are stars like candles? **take thee that too:** an indirect stage direction. Shakespeare frequently saw in his mind's eye what was happening onstage; **that:** probably, his sword belt. Other pieces of equipment have been suggested.

6 **A heavy . . . me:** I have an overwhelming urge to sleep. Note the imitative effect of the line, which is both smooth and weighty.

7-9 **would not:** refuse, am unwilling to; **Merciful powers . . . repose:** What has Banquo been dreaming of? See line 20. What is indicated by his refusal to sleep?

9-10 **Give me . . . there:** Why does he make his request before asking the question?

11 **A friend:** dramatic irony.

14 **largess:** presents; **offices:** the servants' quarters.

15 **diamond:** In Holinshed, the diamond was given to the husband, not the wife. Why does Shakespeare make this change? **withal:** with.

16 **shut up:** retired to rest.

17-18 **Being unprepar'd . . . defect:** Since we had no time to make suitable preparations, what we wished to do was limited by what we were able to do. Macbeth's apology is awkward, as is the unrelated participle.

20 **I dreamt . . . sisters:** Why should Banquo mention this?

ACT II

Scene 1

INVERNESS. MACBETH'S CASTLE.

Enter Banquo, and Fleance bearing a torch before him.

Banquo.   How goes the night, boy?
Fleance.   The moon is down; I have not heard the clock.
Banquo.   And she goes down at twelve.
Fleance.   I take't, 'tis later, sir.
Banquo.   Hold, take my sword: there's husbandry in heaven,
   Their candles are all out: take thee that too.   5
   A heavy summons lies like lead upon me,
   And yet I would not sleep. Merciful powers,
   Restrain in me the cursed thoughts that nature
   Gives way to in repose!
         Enter Macbeth, and a Servant with a torch.
                  Give me my sword:
   Who's there?   10
Macbeth.   A friend.
Banquo.   What, sir, not yet at rest? The king's a-bed:
   He hath been in unusual pleasure, and
   Sent forth great largess to your offices:
   This diamond he greets your wife withal,   15
   By the name of most kind hostess, and shut up
   In measureless content.
Macbeth.   Being unprepar'd,
   Our will became the servant to defect,
   Which else should free have wrought.
Banquo.   All's well.
   I dreamt last night of the three weird sisters: 20
   To you they have show'd some truth.
Macbeth.   I think not of them:

37

21-24 I think . . . time: Macbeth's speech is not only contradictory but also hypocritical.

25 cleave to . . . 'tis: support me when the time comes. This may mean when Duncan dies, but it is open to another interpretation.

26-27 so I . . . it: provided I do not forfeit any honour in trying to increase it.

28 my bosom franchis'd: my conscience free. This may be interpreted as a warning to Macbeth of Banquo's suspicions. Some editors maintain that Banquo suspected nothing.

30 the like to you: dramatic irony. Macbeth will have no time for sleep. Macbeth looks at Fleance as he and his father depart; Banquo puts his arm protectively around his son's shoulder. Comment on this as a possible piece of stage business.

32 She strike . . . bell: a signal that all is in readiness.

33 Is this a dagger: To begin with, Macbeth is incredulous and horrified.

34 The handle . . . hand: Of what significance is this? Why is "clutch" a better word than *seize* or *snatch*? Note also the indirect stage direction.

36-37 fatal: ominous; **sensible to:** perceptible by, capable of being perceived by.

39 heat-oppressed: raised to a feverish pitch (close to delirium).

40 palpable: substantial.

41 which now I draw: indirect stage direction.

42 thou marshall'st me: The dagger, air-borne, moves towards the King's room as though manifesting Macbeth's thoughts.

44-45 Mine eyes . . . rest: Either my eyes are being tricked by the other senses (which tell me that the dagger is not there), or else my sense of sight is more reliable (and the other senses are faulty).

46 dudgeon: handle; **gouts:** drops.

47 There's no such thing: Passing his hand over his eyes, Macbeth exerts his will to banish the phenomenon.

48-49 bloody business: murder (Macbeth shrinks from using the word "murder"); **informs thus:** creates this vision; **one half-world:** our hemisphere.

50 abuse: deceive.

51 curtain'd: Curtains were drawn around a four-poster bed when the occupant retired; **sleep:** sleeper.

Yet when we can entreat an hour to serve,
We would spend it in some words upon that business,
If you would grant the time.
Banquo.   At your kind'st leisure.
Macbeth.   If you shall cleave to my consent, when 'tis,   25
It shall make honour for you.
Banquo.   So I lose none,
In seeking to augment it, but still keep
My bosom franchis'd, and allegiance clear,
I shall be counsell'd.
Macbeth.   Good repose the while!
Banquo.   Thanks, sir: the like to you!   30
                    Exeunt Banquo and Fleance.
Macbeth.   Go bid thy mistress, when my drink is ready,
She strike upon the bell. Get thee to bed.
                              Exit Servant.
Is this a dagger, which I see before me,
The handle toward my hand? Come, let me clutch
    thee.
I have thee not, and yet I see thee still.   35
Art thou not, fatal vision, sensible
To feeling, as to sight? or art thou but
A dagger of the mind, a false creation,
Proceeding from the heat-oppressed brain?
I see thee yet, in form as palpable   40
As this which now I draw.
Thou marshall'st me the way that I was going,
And such an instrument I was to use.
Mine eyes are made the fools o' the other senses,
Or else worth all the rest: I see thee still;   45
And on thy blade and dudgeon, gouts of blood,
Which was not so before. There's no such thing:
It is the bloody business which informs
Thus to mine eyes. Now o'er the one half-world
Nature seems dead, and wicked dreams abuse   50
The curtain'd sleep; witchcraft celebrates

52 **pale Hecate's offerings:** the rites of the goddess of witchcraft, who presided over the dark of the moon, black magic, and the underworld; **wither'd:** spectre-like. 53 **alarum'd:** roused.

54 **whose howl's his watch:** The howl of the wolf indicates to murder (personified) the progress or passage of the dark hours; **thus:** Macbeth suits the action to the word.

55 **with Tarquin's ravishing strides:** Tarquinius Sextus, son of Tarquinius Superbus, the last of the legendary kings of Rome, was guilty of ravishing Lucretia, a virtuous Roman matron.

58 **thy very stones prate:** a Biblical reference (Luke 19:40).

59-60 **and take . . . it:** and cause me to postpone this horrid deed to some less suitable time.

61 Talk paralyses action.

62-64 **I go . . . hell:** The lines have the ominous sound and rhythm of a tolling bell. The couplet adds emphasis and finality to Macbeth's departure; we see him crouched over, ascending the steps; his dagger flashes; his shadow looms on the wall.

33-64 The great Dagger Soliloquy shows that Macbeth's imagination is overwrought. It has been pointed out that when Macbeth's conscience is troubled he is likely to be the victim of hallucinations, visual or aural. Some editors have stated that the dagger is "a manifestation of his subconscious desire to kill Duncan". On the modern stage, it is possible to present the image of a floating dagger. Give the case for and against. See also p. 166.

This scene is "one of the finest examples of atmosphere in all drama" (Harrison).

2 **quench'd:** stupefied; **hath given me fire:** has kindled my courage.

1-2 Her nervous behaviour belies her words.

3-4 **owl:** a bird of ill-omen. Lady Macbeth is startled by its weird cry; **fatal:** ominous; **bellman:** watchman, who by night called out the hour and the weather. He also visited condemned persons the night before their execution; **He is about it:** Why is the brief statement with its pronouns more dramatic than: "Macbeth is now committing the murder"?

6 **mock their . . . snores:** Their snores make their responsibility of guarding the King seem utterly ridiculous; **drugg'd:** to make assurance doubly sure; **possets:** "night caps" made of hot milk, wine, sugar, eggs, and grated biscuit, heated till thick.

7-8 **that death . . . die:** They actually seem dead, so deeply unconscious are they.

5-8 Why does Lady Macbeth rehearse all these details?

8 S.D. **within:** offstage. Macbeth's cry adds to the suspense.

10-11 **the attempt . . . us:** An unsuccessful attempt will ruin us.

Pale Hecate's offerings; and wither'd murder,
Alarum'd by his sentinel, the wolf,
Whose howl's his watch, thus with his stealthy pace,
With Tarquin's ravishing strides, towards his design   55
Moves like a ghost. Thou sure and firm-set earth,
Hear not my steps, which way they walk, for fear
Thy very stones prate of my whereabout,
And take the present horror from the time,
Which now suits with it. Whiles I threat, he lives: 60
Words to the heat of deeds too cold breath gives.

                        A bell rings.

I go, and it is done: the bell invites me.
Hear it not, Duncan, for it is a knell
That summons thee to heaven, or to hell.   *Exit.*

Scene 2

Enter Lady Macbeth.

Lady Macbeth.   That which hath made them drunk hath
    made me bold;
  What hath quench'd them hath given me fire. Hark!
    Peace!
  It was the owl that shriek'd, the fatal bellman,
  Which gives the stern'st good-night. He is about it;
  The doors are open: and the surfeited grooms   5
  Do mock their charge with snores: I have drugg'd
    their possets,
  That death and nature do contend about them,
  Whether they live or die.
Macbeth (within).   Who's there? what ho!
Lady Macbeth.   Alack, I am afraid they have awak'd,
  And 'tis not done: the attempt, and not the deed,   10
  Confounds us. Hark! I laid their daggers ready,
  He could not miss 'em. Had he not resembled

12-13 **Had he . . . done't:** an unmistakably Shakespearian touch. Lady Macbeth's humanity is illustrated in contrast to all her cold-blooded planning. The statement also helps to establish Duncan's age; **My husband:** This is the only occasion in the play on which Lady Macbeth so refers to Macbeth. With what emotion does she speak?

14 **I have . . . deed:** The terse statement, spoken dully, suggests in the "d" sounds the ideas of death and doom; **a noise:** See line 22.

16-19 **descended:** Explain why this verb is used; **second chamber:** Presumably, the King slept in the first, the Princes in the second, bedroom; **Did not . . . Donalbain:** The quick brief speeches add to the tension.

20 **sorry:** wretched; **S.D. Looking on his hands:** Dover Wilson points out that Garrick and others carried a dagger in each hand, but it would be more logical if one blood-covered hand were free, since Lady Macbeth does not notice the daggers, behind Macbeth's back to begin with, until line 48. Wilson also refers to a manuscript note in Sir Henry Irving's copy of the play: "Don't look at each other."

21 **A foolish . . . sight:** Lady Macbeth speaks sternly.

22 **one did . . . "Murder!":** The references are to Malcolm and Donalbain. How grimly ironic it is that one should have cried "Murder" just as the deed was done! Macbeth's feelings as he stood there can readily be imagined.

24 **address'd them:** composed themselves.

25 **There are . . . together:** Lady Macbeth tries to speak matter-of-factly.

26 **"Amen":** So be it.

27 **as:** as if; **hangman's hands:** The hangman in Elizabethan times was obliged to draw and quarter his victim; hence, the blood-stained hands.

28 **listening:** Supply *to*.

32-33 **"Amen" stuck . . . throat:** Macbeth has cut himself off from all the good in the universe and cannot say "So be it" or the prayer "God bless us." His tormented and tortured conscience makes him at this point a profoundly tragic figure.

33-34 **These deeds . . . mad:** Lady Macbeth begins to speak a little desperately, unaware that she speaks truly.

35 **a voice:** an aural hallucination, perhaps his conscience; **Sleep no more:** Dover Wilson calls this "one of the leading motifs of *Macbeth*". "Sleep in Shakespeare is ever the privilege of the good and the reward of the innocent" (Mark Van Doren).

37 **knits up . . . care:** smooths out the frayed and tangled skein of worry; the restorative aspect of sleep is stressed.

My father as he slept, I had done't.
    Enter Macbeth.

                        My husband!
Macbeth.   I have done the deed. Didst thou not hear a noise?
Lady Macbeth.   I heard the owl scream and the crickets cry. 15
    Did not you speak?
Macbeth.   When?
Lady Macbeth.   Now.
Macbeth.   As I descended?
Lady Macbeth.   Ay.
Macbeth.   Hark!
    Who lies i' the second chamber?
Lady Macbeth.   Donalbain.
Macbeth.   This is a sorry sight.   *Looking on his hands.*   20
Lady Macbeth.   A foolish thought, to say a sorry sight.
Macbeth.   There's one did laugh in's sleep, and one cried
    "Murder!"
    That they did wake each other: I stood and heard
    them:
    But they did say their prayers, and address'd them
    Again to sleep.
Lady Macbeth.   There are two lodg'd together.   25
Macbeth.   One cried, "God bless us!", and "Amen" the
    other,
    As they had seen me with these hangman's hands:
    Listening their fear, I could not say "Amen,"
    When they did say "God bless us!"
Lady Macbeth.   Consider it not so deeply.   30
Macbeth.   But wherefore could not I pronounce "Amen"?
    I had most need of blessing, and "Amen"
    Stuck in my throat.
Lady Macbeth.   These deeds must not be thought
    After these ways; so, it will make us mad.
Macbeth.   Methought I heard a voice cry "Sleep no more!   35
    Macbeth does murder sleep"—the innocent sleep,
    Sleep that knits up the ravell'd sleeve of care,

38 **the death . . . life:** Sleep ends the daily round of activity as death ends life; **sore labour's bath:** The soothing quality of a warm bath after hard physical work is well known.

39 **balm:** a healing ointment. The mind is bruised by the problems of the day, which are like physical blows. Sleep also heals; **great nature's second course:** Sleep is like food in the banquet of life. The second course is thought to have been the meat course.

40 **What do you mean:** Lady Macbeth, lacking Macbeth's poetic imagination, tries wildly to bring him back to reality.

36-40 Shakespeare apparently set a very high value on sleep.

41 **still it cried:** Macbeth is oblivious of his wife's pleas.

42-43 **Glamis hath . . . more:** The voice gives him all his titles and dooms him forever to sleeplessness.

45 **unbend:** slacken.   46 **brainsickly:** madly.

47 **witness:** evidence. Seeing the blood-stained daggers, Lady Macbeth gasps.

49-50 **smear the . . . blood:** Her presence of mind is admirable; **I'll go no more:** Lady Macbeth's influence is at an end.

54-55 **as pictures:** They have no reality and are not terrifying; **'tis the . . . devil:** Only a child fears the devil's picture.

56-57 **gild the . . . guilt:** This grisly pun is used by Lady Macbeth for its shock value. "To gild" is to cover with gold, which is sometimes described as *red. Gilt* is gold paint; *guilt,* a sense of being at fault.

55-57 Lady Macbeth nerves herself to do what must be done.

57 S.D. **Knocking within:** Already, nemesis is shadowing Macbeth. The timing of this stage business is superb. See De Quincey's famous essay on the subject.

59 **What hands are here:** He holds them away from himself in horror; **ha:** a shudder of hideous repulsion.

60-63 **great Neptune's . . . hand:** Note the contrast; **Neptune:** Roman god of the sea; **No; this . . . red:** This startling image shows us the sea turning to blood in accusation of Macbeth. The blood-stained hand is one of the persistent images in the play; it becomes the symbol of guilt. Note the contrast between the powerful polysyllables and the simple monosyllables. Line 62 is imitative of the undulations of the sea and its vast extent; **incarnadine:** dye blood-red. Shakespeare invented this verb; **making the . . . red:** The green sea will become completely and utterly red. ("One" is not a pronoun in this interpretation. F reads: *making the green one, red.*) S.D. **Re-enter Lady Macbeth:** Despite her brave words, she has been through an ordeal from which she will never completely recover.

The death of each day's life, sore labour's bath,
Balm of hurt minds, great nature's second course, *going crasy*
Chief nourisher in life's feast,—
Lady Macbeth.   What do you mean?   40
Macbeth.   Still it cried "Sleep no more!" to all the house:
   "Glamis hath murder'd sleep, and therefore Cawdor
   Shall sleep no more: Macbeth shall sleep no more."
Lady Macbeth.   Who was it that thus cried. Why, worthy thane, *manic*
   You do unbend your noble strength, to think   45
   So brainsickly of things. Go get some water,
   And wash this filthy witness from your hand.
   Why did you bring these daggers from the place?
   They must lie there: go carry them, and smear
   The sleepy grooms with blood.
Macbeth.   I'll go no more: 50
   I am afraid to think what I have done;
   Look on't again I dare not.
Lady Macbeth.   Infirm of purpose!
   Give me the daggers: the sleeping and the dead
   Are but as pictures: 'tis the eye of childhood,
   That fears a painted devil. If he do bleed,   55
   I'll gild the faces of the grooms withal,
   For it must seem their guilt.
                    Exit. Knocking within.
Macbeth.   Whence is that knocking?
   How is't with me, when every noise appals me?
   What hands are here? ha! they pluck out mine eyes!
   Will all great Neptune's ocean wash this blood   60
   Clean from my hand? No; this my hand will rather
   The multitudinous seas incarnadine,
   Making the green one red.
            Re-enter Lady Macbeth.
Lady Macbeth.   My hands are of your colour: but I shame
   To wear a heart so white. *(Knocking within.)* I hear
      a knocking   65
   At the south entry: retire we to our chamber:

64-67 **I hear . . . deed:** Her resourcefulness saves them from certain discovery. To Macbeth, the knocking "brings the final realization of what he has done; to Lady Macbeth, it means that the business of removing the traces must be done quickly" (Harrison); **a little . . . deed:** dramatic irony, in view of V. i.

68-69 **Your constancy . . . unattended:** Your courage has deserted you.

70-72 **nightgown:** dressing-gown; **lest occasion . . . watchers:** lest we should be summoned and shown to be still up; **be not . . . thoughts:** Does she scream, hiss, or plead?

73 I would rather be lost in my thoughts than realize what I have done.

74 The irony is supreme. Now that Macbeth has committed the murder, he wishes the victim alive again. The speech makes a poignant and powerful conclusion to the scene.

See also p. 167.

S.D. **Enter a Porter:** Various pieces of stage business have been used to illustrate the befuddled intoxication of the Porter. In some productions, he speaks in dialect. Why might this device be introduced?

2 **old:** an emphatic colloquial expression meaning *plenty of*, or, *a high old time*.

4-6 **Beelzebub:** "Lord of the flies"; in the Old Testament, the chief god of the pagan peoples; in the New Testament, the prince of evil spirits; **a farmer . . . plenty:** one of three topical allusions that help to fix the date of the play. The farmer bought up corn, thinking it would be scarce. He paid a good price for it, expecting to sell it for still more, but when the harvest was good, the price went down, and he was ruined. See The Date, p. xxv; **come in time:** "Come in, time-server" (Dover Wilson); **napkins enow:** handkerchiefs enough.

8 **th' other devil's name:** This he has forgotten; **equivocator:** This is generally believed to be a reference to the trial of the Jesuit Henry Garnet on March 28, 1606, for complicity in the Gunpowder Plot. So great was the interest in this trial that James I himself was present incognito. Garnet confessed that he had been guilty of equivocation, was convicted of treason, and hanged on May 3. Equivocation is the use of ambiguous expressions, with attempt to deceive the listener and conceal the truth. See also V. v. 43-44, and The Date, p. xxv.

See p. 48 for notes on lines 9-19.

A little water clears us of this deed: ? *novine*.
How easy is it then! Your constancy
Hath left you unattended. *(Knocking within.)* Hark!
  more knocking:
Get on your nightgown, lest occasion call us   70
And show us to be watchers: be not lost
So poorly in your thoughts.
Macbeth.   To know my deed, 'twere best not know myself.
                                    Knocking within.
Wake Duncan with thy knocking! I would thou
  could'st!   *Exeunt.*

Scene 3

Enter a Porter. Knocking within.

Porter.   Here's a knocking indeed! If a man were porter
of hell-gate, he should have old turning the key.
(Knocking within.) Knock, knock, knock! Who's there,
i' the name of Beelzebub? Here's a farmer, that
hang'd himself on th' expectation of plenty: come in   5
time; have napkins enow about you; here you'll sweat
for't. *(Knocking within.)* Knock, knock! Who's there,
in th'other devil's name? Faith, here's an equivocator,
that could swear in both the scales against either
scale, who committed treason enough for God's sake,   10
yet could not equivocate to heaven: O, come in,
equivocator. *(Knocking within.)* Knock, knock, knock!
Who's there? Faith, here's an English tailor come
hither, for stealing out of a French hose: come in
tailor, here you may roast your goose. *(Knocking   15
within.)* Knock, knock; never at quiet! What are you?
But this place is too cold for hell. I'll devil-porter it
no further: I had thought to have let in some of all
professions, that go the primrose way to the everlasting

9-10 **could swear . . . scale:** could commit perjury; **scale:** of justice; **who committed . . . sake:** Garnet's motives in taking part in the Plot were religious ones. (The Jesuits were thought to teach that the end justified the means.)

11 **could not . . . heaven:** The Porter notes the irony.

13-14 **English tailor . . . hose:** One explanation is that the tailor stole part of his customer's material. The Englishman of the time aped French fashions; Shakespeare satirizes this habit; **roast your goose:** heat your iron for pressing clothes.

4-15 What have all three arrivals in common? (Note the use of the number "three".)

17 **too cold for hell:** Dramatic irony is illustrated in that unconsciously the Porter *is* gate-keeper of hell, the Macbeths' castle.

19 **the primrose way:** Shakespeare associated primroses with the gay and thoughtless pleasures of life. Ophelia refers to "the primrose path of dalliance" (*Hamlet*, I. iii. 50).

19-20 **the everlasting bonfire:** seemingly a euphemism until we recall that a bonfire was originally a *bonefire*; **Anon:** Coming.

21 **remember the porter:** with a tip.

24-25 **second cock:** three a.m.

28 **nose-painting:** Drinking makes for red noses.

31 **be an equivocator with:** play fast and loose with (Dover Wilson), and thus deceive.

35-36 **equivocates him . . . sleep:** tricks him into falling asleep; **giving him the lie:** deceiving him.

37 **gave thee the lie:** got the better of thee.

40 **took up my legs:** a play on the effect of drinking (made him unsteady) and the action of wrestling.

41 **made a . . . him:** managed to get the better of him (throw him down). Other coarse interpretations have been suggested.

43 **Our knocking . . . him:** more dramatic irony.

44-47 Note the terseness of Macbeth's tight-lipped replies.

48 **joyful trouble:** an example of oxymoron, the juxtaposition of antithetical terms. Cf. Tennyson's description of Sir Lancelot:

> His honour rooted in dishonour stood
> And faith unfaithful kept him falsely true.

Why is it supposedly a joyful trouble?

bonfire. *(Knocking within.)* Anon, anon! I pray you, 20
remember the porter. *Opens the gate.*
     Enter Macduff and Lennox.
Macduff. Was it so late, friend, ere you went to bed,
That you do lie so late?
Porter. Faith, sir, we were carousing till the second
    cock: and drink, sir, is a great provoker of three 25
    things.
Macduff. What three things does drink especially
    provoke?
Porter. Marry, sir, nose-painting, sleep, and urine.
    Lechery, sir, it provokes and unprovokes; it provokes
    the desire, but it takes away the performance: there- 30
    fore much drink may be said to be an equivocator with
    lechery: it makes him and it mars him; it sets him
    on and it takes him off; it persuades him and dis-
    heartens him; makes him stand to, and not stand to;
    in conclusion, equivocates him in a sleep, and giving 35
    him the lie, leaves him.
Macduff. I believe drink gave thee the lie last night.
Porter. That it did, sir, i' the very throat on me: but
    I requited him for his lie, and, I think, being too
    strong for him, though he took up my legs sometime, 40
    yet I made a shift to cast him.
Macduff. Is thy master stirring?
     Enter Macbeth.
  Our knocking has awak'd him; here he comes.
Lennox. Good morrow, noble sir.
Macbeth.   Good morrow, both.
Macduff. Is the king stirring, worthy thane?
Macbeth.   Not yet. 45
Macduff. He did command me to call timely on him;
  I have almost slipp'd the hour.
Macbeth.   I'll bring you to him.
Macduff. I know this is a joyful trouble to you;
  But yet 'tis one.

50 **physics:** relieves, is a remedy for.

51 **This is the door:** We wonder what Macbeth's feelings are.

52 **limited service:** appointed duty.

53 **He does . . . so:** Knowing what he knows, Macbeth alters his statement.

54 **lay:** lodged.

58 **dire combustion:** dread confusion.

59 **new hatch'd . . . time:** a new brood of horrors, in keeping with this unhappy age; **the obscure bird:** the owl. See also II. ii. 3 and 15; **obscure:** living in the dark.

60-61 **clamour'd:** wailed; **livelong night:** all night long; **the earth . . . shake:** Note the personification. The earth, suffering from fever and ague, shook violently and thereby caused an earthquake. Hotspur gives a different explanation in *Henry IV, Part 1*, III. i. 26-33.

54-61 Lennox's speech illustrates pathetic fallacy (a mistaken belief that nature sympathizes with man).

61 **'Twas a rough night:** Surely a masterpiece of understatement!

62 **young remembrance:** Lennox must be cast in keeping with this remark. Shakespeare may have had a specific actor of the company in mind.

64 **O horror, horror, horror:** A shout or a whisper?

66 **Confusion now . . . masterpiece:** Destruction has completed its greatest work.

67 **sacrilegious:** profane.

68-69 **the Lord's anointed temple:** the temple of the Lord's anointed, a double Biblical reference to the *King* who is anointed with holy oil at his coronation and to the *man*: "ye are the temple of the living God" (II Cor., 6:16). The phrase suggests also the Divine Right of Kings, which was firmly upheld by James I. Hence, regicide is the most heinous of crimes; **and stole . . . building:** There is a further crime of theft involved in the taking of the life from the body or building; **What is't . . . life:** Macbeth feigns incredulity and bewilderment; **destroy your . . . Gorgon:** Anyone who looked at the face (head) of Medusa, one of the Gorgons, was turned to stone. The sight of Duncan's murdered body would blind one who looked upon it.

74 **alarum-bell:** The great bell of the castle was rung in time of emergency. There is such a bell in the Shakespearian theatre at Stratford, Ontario; one also hung in the Globe Theatre.

76 **downy:** soft; **counterfeit:** image.

Macbeth.   The labour we delight in physics pain: 50
   This is the door.
Macduff.   I'll make so bold to call,
   For 'tis my limited service.   *Exit.*
Lennox.   Goes the king hence to-day?
Macbeth.   He does: he did appoint so.
Lennox.   The night has been unruly: where we lay,
   Our chimneys were blown down, and, as they say,   55
   Lamentings heard i' the air, strange screams of death,
   And prophesying, with accents terrible,
   Of dire combustion, and confus'd events,
   New hatch'd to the woful time: the obscure bird
   Clamour'd the livelong night: some say, the earth   60
   Was feverous, and did shake.
Macbeth.   'Twas a rough night.
Lennox.   My young remembrance cannot parallel
   A fellow to it.
        Re-enter Macduff.
Macduff.   O horror, horror, horror! Tongue nor heart
   Cannot conceive nor name thee.
Macbeth. ⎰   What's the matter?   65
Lennox. ⎱
Macduff.   Confusion now hath made his masterpiece.
   Most sacrilegious murder hath broke ope
   The Lord's anointed temple, and stole thence
   The life o' the building.
Macbeth.   What is't you say? the life?
Lennox.   Mean you his majesty?   70
Macduff.   Approach the chamber, and destroy your sight
   With a new Gorgon: do not bid me speak;
   See, and then speak yourselves.
                Exeunt Macbeth and Lennox.
                   Awake, awake!
   Ring the alarum-bell. Murder and treason!
   Banquo and Donalbain! Malcolm, awake!   75
   Shake off this downy sleep, death's counterfeit,

78 **the great doom's image:** a picture of the Day of Judgement. Why does Macduff use this metaphor?

73-78 **Awake, awake . . . Banquo:** The exclamations create a mood of excitement. Note the names of those summoned by Macduff.

79 **As from . . . sprites:** At the Day of Judgement, the dead, it was believed, would rise from their graves; the comparison from the preceding lines is continued; **sprites:** spirits.

80 **countenance:** be in keeping with or look upon; **Ring the bell:** It was suggested by Theobald that this command was really a stage direction that had crept into the text.

81-83 **What's the . . . speak:** Lady Macbeth has elected to play the outraged hostess whose guests have been disturbed. She compares the sound of the bell and the shouting to the summons to discussion that often preceded a battle; **O gentle lady:** further dramatic irony.

85 **repetition:** recital. Such a dreadful announcement would be a death blow to a woman of sensitivity.

86 Macduff greets Banquo as a friend and, like him, a loyal subject. Note Banquo's rejoinder: "Dear Duff."

87-88 **Woe, alas . . . house:** Lady Macbeth has perhaps calculated that the selfish remark would seem more natural. Most readers, however, think that a comment about the fate of Duncan would show some human feeling, instead of this concern for her reputation; **Too cruel, anywhere:** Banquo's rebuke is curt.

91 **chance:** event.

92 **a blessed time:** under the reign of Duncan.

93 **serious in mortality:** worth living for in human existence.

94 **toys:** trifles; **is:** Shakespeare sometimes uses a singular verb where modern usage would require a plural.

95-96 **wine, drawn, lees, vault:** Macbeth compares life to a wine-cellar or to a vault. The best wine (Duncan's life) has been drained away, and only the dregs (inferior men) are left for us to boast about. "Vault" may also have the meaning *the over-arching sky*, and thus, *our world*.

91-96 In spite of Macbeth's feigned grief, it is possible to detect here a peculiar kind of honesty in his lament.

97 **What is amiss:** What is wrong, or in the sense in which Macbeth answers, What is lacking? (Donalbain is lacking a father.)

97-99 Note the roundabout speech of Macbeth as contrasted with Macduff's blunt statement. Which is more desirable? Why?

100 **O:** a gasp of horror; **by whom:** To what extent is this a logical question? 101 **as it seem'd:** How does Lennox say these words?

And look on death itself! up, up, and see
The great doom's image! Malcolm! Banquo!
As from your graves rise up, and walk like sprites,
To countenance this horror. Ring the bell.   80

Bell rings.

      Enter Lady Macbeth.
Lady Macbeth.   What's the business,
That such a hideous trumpet calls to parley
The sleepers of the house? speak, speak!
Macduff.   O gentle lady,
'Tis not for you to hear what I can speak:
The repetition, in a woman's ear,   85
Would murder as it fell.

      Enter Banquo.

                        O Banquo, Banquo!
Our royal master's murder'd.
Lady Macbeth.   Woe, alas!
What, in our house?
Banquo.   Too cruel, any where.
Dear Duff, I prithee, contradict thyself,
And say it is not so.   90

      Re-enter Macbeth and Lennox, with Ross.
Macbeth.   Had I but died an hour before this chance,
I had lived a blessed time; for from this instant
There's nothing serious in mortality:
All is but toys: renown and grace is dead;
The wine of life is drawn, and the mere lees   95
Is left this vault to brag of.

      Enter Malcolm and Donalbain.
Donalbain.   What is amiss?
Macbeth.   You are, and do not know't:
The spring, the head, the fountain of your blood
Is stopp'd; the very source of it is stopp'd.
Macduff.   Your royal father's murder'd.
Malcolm.   O, by whom?   100
Lennox.   Those of his chamber, as it seem'd, had done't:

102 **badg'd:** plainly marked as with a badge.

105 **star'd, and were distracted:** We can imagine their wretched plight.

107-8 **O, yet . . . them:** When had Macbeth done this? Why? To what extent was it wise? **fury:** frenzy; **Wherefore did you so:** A pregnant pause precedes Macduff's question. He is suspicious.

109-10 **Who can . . . moment:** He attempts to explain his chaotic feelings and thus to justify his unjustifiable deed; **amaz'd:** confused; **loyal:** as a subject; **neutral:** as a judge.

111 **expedition:** haste. The picture is of one runner outdistancing another; just so, love (emotion) acts more quickly than reason (thought).

112-19 **Here lay . . . known:** "It is not improbable that Shakespeare put these forced and unnatural metaphors into the mouth of Macbeth as a mark of artifice and dissimulation, to show the difference between the studied language of hypocrisy and the natural outcries of real passion" (Dr. Johnson); **silver skin . . . blood:** The comparison, though poetic, is exaggerated; **lac'd:** streaked; **his gash'd . . . entrance:** The image is that of the storming of a castle. His gaping wounds allowed death, the conqueror, to enter; **steep'd:** soaked and sodden; **colours of their trade:** blood; **unmannerly breech'd:** rudely clothed, with blood instead of their sheaths; possibly, another clothing image; **who could . . . known:** We wonder how Macbeth can speak of love and courage at such a moment.

119 **Help me hence, ho:** Why might Lady Macbeth wish to create a diversion at this point? Why, on the other hand, might she be truly overcome?

120 **Look to the lady:** Macduff's thoughtful consideration is brought out; Macbeth says nothing. How can his silence be explained?

120-1 **Why do . . . ours:** Malcolm considers that their silence may cause them to be suspected.

123 **auger-hole:** An "auger" is a carpenter's tool used to bore small holes; here, a minute spot.

125-6 **Our tears . . . brew'd:** The shock of sorrow is as yet too great for the show of tears; **Nor our . . . motion:** Our deep grief cannot yet be expressed in action.

120-6 It seems strange that no one says a word to the King's sons, even though Malcolm had been named his father's heir.

127 **naked frailties:** scantily clothed bodies. They have rushed to the scene in dressing-gowns.

128 **suffer in exposure:** The night is cold; **let us meet:** Banquo takes the lead in the investigation but makes no accusations.

130 **scruples:** doubts.

Their hands and faces were all badg'd with blood,
So were their daggers, which unwip'd we found
Upon their pillows:
They star'd, and were distracted; no man's life   105
Was to be trusted with them.
Macbeth.   O, yet I do repent me of my fury,
That I did kill them.
Macduff.   Wherefore did you so?
Macbeth. Who can be wise, amaz'd, temperate and furious,
Loyal and neutral, in a moment? No man: 110
The expedition of my violent love
Outran the pauser, reason. Here lay Duncan,
His silver skin lac'd with his golden blood,
And his gash'd stabs look'd like a breach in nature
For ruin's wasteful entrance: there the murderers,   115
Steep'd in the colours of their trade; their daggers
Unmannerly breech'd with gore: who could refrain,
That had a heart to love, and in that heart
Courage to make's love known?
Lady Macbeth.   Help me hence, ho!
Macduff.   Look to the lady.
Malcolm (aside to Donalbain). Why do we hold our tongues,   120
That most may claim this argument for ours?
Donalbain (aside to Malcolm).   What should be spoken
here, where our fate,
Hid in an auger-hole, may rush and seize us?
Let's away;
Our tears are not yet brew'd.
Malcolm (aside to Donalbain).   Nor our strong sorrow   125
Upon the foot of motion.
Banquo.   Look to the lady:
          Lady Macbeth is carried out.
And when we have our naked frailties hid,
That suffer in exposure, let us meet,
And question this most bloody piece of work,
To know it further. Fears and scruples shake us: 130

131-3 **In the . . . malice:** Banquo asserts his innocence, and though he says nothing about it, must surely suspect Macbeth; **undivulg'd pretence:** secret design.

134 **briefly put . . . readiness:** quickly don clothes and armour.

137-9 **To show . . . easy:** They see through Macbeth's protestations; **easy:** easily; **to England. to Ireland:** Holinshed mentions their separate destinations, although to begin with they both fled to Cumberland. In some stage productions, Macduff listens from behind a pillar to the boys' conversation. Why? How convincing would such a move be? Some think that Macbeth is more likely to eavesdrop. Comment.

141 **There's daggers . . . smiles:** Cf. *Hamlet* "That one may smile, and smile, and be a villain" (I. v. 108); **near:** the comparative of *nigh*; hence, the meaning is: "the nearer in blood". The reference may be to Macbeth, who was their father's first cousin.

142-4 **the nearer bloody:** the more likely to be bloodthirsty and to murder us; **shaft, shot, lighted, aim:** Malcolm sees the first murder as an arrow that has not yet reached its target. Whoever murdered Duncan to get his throne will want to get rid of them too.

145 **dainty:** particular.

146-7 **shift away:** escape; **warrant:** authority for, justification for; **that theft . . . itself:** In stealing away, they have stolen themselves. Such a "crime" is justified in that remaining would be certain death.

See also p. 168.

1 **Threescore and . . . well:** The Old Man must be well over seventy. Why does Shakespeare emphasize his age? Why is he not named? It has been suggested that he is blind.

2 **volume:** Life is a book.

3 **sore:** dreadful.

4 **hath trifled former knowings:** has made previous events seem trivial or insignificant; **father:** a common form of address to older people.

5-6 **as:** as if; **act, stage:** The theatrical metaphor recurs; **threatens:** so F. Many editors read *threaten*.

In the great hand of God I stand, and thence
Against the undivulg'd pretence I fight
Of treasonous malice.
Macduff.   And so do I.
All.   So all.
Macbeth.   Let's briefly put on manly readiness,
  And meet i' the hall together.
All.   Well contented.   135
            Exeunt all but Malcolm and Donalbain.
Malcolm.   What will you do? Let's not consort with them:
  To show an unfelt sorrow is an office
  Which the false man does easy. I'll to England.
Donalbain.   To Ireland, I; our separated fortune
  Shall keep us both the safer: where we are,   140
  There's daggers in men's smiles: the near in blood,
  The nearer bloody.
Malcolm.   This murderous shaft that's shot
  Hath not yet lighted, and our safest way
  Is to avoid the aim. Therefore to horse;
  And let us not be dainty of leave-taking,   145
  But shift away: there's warrant in that theft
  Which steals itself, when there's no mercy left.
                                Exeunt.

Scene 4

Enter Ross with an Old Man.

Old Man.   Threescore and ten I can remember well,
  Within the volume of which time I have seen
  Hours dreadful and things strange: but this sore
    night
  Hath trifled former knowings.
Ross.   Ah, good father,
  Thou seest the heavens, as troubled with man's act,   5
  Threatens his bloody stage: by the clock 'tis day,

7 **strangles the travelling lamp:** blots out the sun, as on July 20, 1963.

8 **Is't night's . . . shame:** Is night's evil influence prevalent or is the light of day ashamed to look upon what has been done? "For the space of six moneths together, after this heinous murther thus committed, there appeered no sunne by day, nor moone by night in anie part of the realme, but still was the skie covered with continual clouds . . ." (Holinshed); **predominance:** influence, a term borrowed from astrology.

11 **the deed that's done:** an echo of Macbeth's words, II. ii. 14; **Tuesday last:** Shakespeare has a way of referring to a specific day of the week in order to give an impression of verisimilitude.

12-13 **towering:** circling higher and higher; **place:** the highest point of flight before the downward swoop; **A falcon . . . kill'd:** a most unnatural incident. It has been interpreted symbolically to refer to Duncan (the royal falcon) and Macbeth seeking for the crown (an owl in search of mice). The falcon is found in the Shakespeare coat of arms as the family crest; **hawk'd at:** attacked on the wing.

15 **minions:** darlings, the pride and flower.

17 **as:** as if.

14-18 Shakespeare's picture of the disturbed horses is found in Holinshed: "Horses in Louthian [see map, p. xliii], being of singular beautie and swiftnesse, did eate their owne flesh, and would in no wise taste anie other meate."

18 **eat:** pronounced *et*, a past tense of *eat*.

20 **good:** a significant adjective.

23 **Those that . . . slain:** Macduff speaks ironically.

24 **pretend:** intend, aspire to; **suborn'd:** incited to it, bribed.

25-27 Fortunately for Macbeth!

27 **'gainst nature still:** further unnatural behaviour.

28 **ravin up:** utterly devour, swallow greedily.

29 **thine own life's means:** the source of its existence (Duncan).

31 **nam'd:** chosen; **Scone:** See map, p. xliii. It is locally pronounced *Scoon*. The abbey is two-and-a-half miles from Perth. Here, the early Scottish Kings were crowned on the famous Stone of Destiny, which was thought to have been Jacob's pillow. The stone was taken to Westminster Abbey in 1296 by Edward I and was recently purloined by Scottish nationalists. It is now in safe-keeping, and a replica is kept beneath the Chair of St. Edward.

32 **invested:** endued with the insignia of kingship.

And yet dark night strangles the travelling lamp:
Is't night's predominance, or the day's shame,
That darkness does the face of earth entomb
When living light should kiss it?

Old Man. 'Tis unnatural, 10
Even like the deed that's done. On Tuesday last,
A falcon towering in her pride of place
Was by a mousing owl hawk'd at, and kill'd.

Ross. And Duncan's horses (a thing most strange and certain)
Beauteous, and swift, the minions of their race, 15
Turn'd wild in nature, broke their stalls, flung out,
Contending 'gainst obedience, as they would
Make war with mankind.

Old Man. 'Tis said they eat each other.

Ross. They did so; to the amazement of mine eyes,
That look'd upon't.

Enter Macduff.

Here comes the good Macduff. 20
How goes the world, sir, now?

Macduff. Why, see you not?

Ross. Is't known who did this more than bloody deed?

Macduff. Those that Macbeth hath slain. *worit*

Ross. Alas, the day!
What good could they pretend?

Macduff. They were suborn'd:
Malcolm and Donalbain, the king's two sons, 25
Are stol'n away and fled, which puts upon them
Suspicion of the deed.

Ross. 'Gainst nature still:
Thriftless ambition, that wilt ravin up
Thine own life's means! Then 'tis most like
The sovereignty will fall upon Macbeth. 30

Macduff. He is already nam'd, and gone to Scone
To be invested.

Ross. Where is Duncan's body?

33 **Colme-kill:** See map, p. xliii. Iona, an island of the Inner Hebrides, where St. Columba landed in 563 to preach Christianity. It was the burial place of ancient Scottish kings, among them Duncan and Macbeth. Holinshed writes: "The bodie of Duncan was first conveied unto Elgine, and there buried in kingly wise; but afterwards it was removed and conveied unto Colmekill, and there laid in a sepulture amongst his predecessors, in the year after the birth of our Saviour, 1046."

36 **I'll to Fife:** In this terse, blunt statement, Macduff indicates his lack of sympathy with the new regime; **Well, I will thither:** Ross has been accused of being a time-server; he seems to represent the quiescent nobility.

38 **Lest our . . . new:** Macduff utters a cryptic warning in terms of the familiar clothing image.

40-41 Some have criticized this rather jingling couplet, but it does express the contrast between good and evil that is at the heart of the play.

See also p. 170.

3 **play'dst most foully:** This line seems to indicate that Banquo suspects Macbeth. It echoes Lady Macbeth's "wouldst not play false" (I. v. 21).

4 **stand:** remain.

7 **shine:** are bright with truth.

8 **verities on . . . good:** actualities proved true for you.

9 **oracles:** prophets.

1-10 In Holinshed's edition, Banquo was an accomplice. ("At length therefore communicating his purposed intent with his trustie friends, amongst whome Banquho was the chiefest, upon confidence of their promised aid, he slue the king at Enverns [Inverness] . . . in the sixt yeare of his reigne.") It has been suggested that Shakespeare made the change in view of the fact that James I regarded Banquo as one of his ancestors. This soliloquy "reminds us of the prophecies and thus sets the new episode in the same atmosphere of fate and destiny; and it brings out Macbeth's real danger, for Banquo, though he has hitherto been discreetly silent, quite clearly knows who murdered Duncan and seeing how, and by what means, Macbeth has taken a hand in fulfilling Destiny, is himself more encouraged to do the like" (Harrison).

10 S.D. **sennet:** a set of notes on a trumpet. The King and Queen enter richly costumed; yet, their faces are not happy.

Macduff.   Carried to Colme-kill,
The sacred storehouse of his predecessors,
And guardian of their bones.
Ross.   Will you to Scone?   35
Macduff.   No, cousin, I'll to Fife.   ~~not loyal to Macbeth.~~
Ross.   Well, I will thither.
Macduff.   Well, may you see things well done there: adieu—
  |Lest our old robes sit easier than our new!| *clothing image.*
Ross.   Farewell, father.
Old Man.   God's benison go with you, and with those   40
That would make good of bad and friends of foes!
                                        Exeunt.

ACT III

Scene 1

FORRES. THE PALACE.

Enter Banquo.

Banquo.   Thou hast it now, king, Cawdor, Glamis, all,
As the weird women promis'd, and I fear
Thou play'dst most foully for't: yet it was said
It should not stand in thy posterity,
But that myself should be the root and father   5
Of many kings. If there come truth from them,
As upon thee, Macbeth, their speeches shine,
Why, by the verities on thee made good,
May they not be my oracles as well
And set me up in hope? But hush, no more.   10
            Sennet sounded. Enter Macbeth, as king, Lady
            Macbeth, as queen, Lennox, Ross, Lords, Ladies,
            and Attendants.
Macbeth.   Here's our chief guest.

13 **all-thing:** altogether.

14 **we:** the royal plural, now that Macbeth is king; **solemn supper:** formal banquet.

17 **indissoluble:** that cannot be dissolved.

19, 24, 36 Note the diabolically casual way in which Macbeth tucks in his questions.

22 **still:** always; **grave and prosperous:** weighty and profitable.

21-23 Banquo has been a loyal and helpful supporter of Macbeth.

23 **we'll take tomorrow:** Tomorrow will serve.

26 **go not . . . better:** if my horse does not go faster than usual.

28 **a dark hour:** The phrase has a deeper significance than that implied by Banquo.

29 **My lord . . . not:** perhaps the most striking example of dramatic irony in the play.

30-31 **We hear . . . Ireland:** This speech indicates the passage of time; **bloody cousins are bestow'd:** murderous kinsmen are settled.

32 **parricide:** the murder of one's father.

33-35 Note the subject of the next day's council-meeting; **strange invention:** Ironically, these tales are the truth; **hie you:** go quickly.

37 **our time . . . upon's:** It is time for us to be away.

39 **commend you . . . backs:** Dover Wilson refers to this as a friendly jest in which Macbeth recommends them to the hospitality of the horses' saddles.

42-44 **seven at night:** when it will obviously be dark; **to make . . . alone:** If Macbeth does not mingle too much with his subjects, his presence will be the more appreciated. He banishes even Lady Macbeth. This is also a manoeuvre to enable him to consult the murderers in privacy; **while:** until.

Lady Macbeth.   If he had been forgotten,
  It had been as a gap in our great feast,
  And all-thing unbecoming.
Macbeth.   To-night we hold a solemn supper, sir,
  And I'll request your presence.
Banquo.   Let your highness   15
  Command upon me, to the which my duties
  Are with a most indissoluble tie
  For ever knit.
Macbeth.   Ride you this afternoon?
Banquo.   Ay, my good lord.   20
Macbeth.   We should have else desir'd your good advice,
  (Which still hath been both grave and prosperous)
  In this day's council; but we'll take to-morrow.
  Is't far you ride?
Banquo.   As far, my lord, as will fill up the time   25
  'Twixt this and supper: go not my horse the better,
  I must become a borrower of the night,
  For a dark hour or twain.
Macbeth.   Fail not our feast. *ironic* *killed*
Banquo.   My lord, I will not.
Macbeth.   We hear our bloody cousins are bestow'd   30
  In England, and in Ireland, not confessing *dramatic irony*
  Their cruel parricide, filling their hearers
  With strange invention. But of that to-morrow,
  When therewithal we shall have cause of state
  Craving us jointly. Hie you to horse: adieu,   35
  Till you return at night. Goes Fleance with you?
Banquo.   Ay, my good lord: our time does call upon's.
Macbeth.   I wish your horses swift, and sure of foot, *irony*
  And so I do commend you to their backs.
  Farewell.   *Exit Banquo.*   40
  Let every man be master of his time *dramatic irony*
  Till seven at night; to make society
  The sweeter welcome, we will keep ourself
  'Till supper-time alone: while then, God be with you!

45   **Sirrah:** a form of *sir*, used to address inferiors.
49   **But to . . . thus:** Add *would be everything*. He speaks with deep-seated anguish. His suffering is part of the penalty he pays; **in:** with regard to.
50-51   **stick deep:** go deep, like a dagger; **in his . . . fear'd:** As the ancestor of James I, Banquo possesses an innate nobility that inspires Macbeth's fear and jealousy. Compare this to I. vii. 16-20.
51-54   Banquo is both soldier and statesman, bold as well as prudent. Macbeth may fear that Banquo is plotting against him.
55   **being:** existence.
56-57   **Genius:** guardian spirit; **as it . . . Caesar:** It is as if Banquo gives Macbeth an inferiority complex, in the same way as Mark Antony was affected by Octavius, Caesar's heir. The reference is found in North's translation of Plutarch, which Shakespeare knew well; **chid:** rebuked.
61   **fruitless:** without issue.   62   **gripe:** grasp.
63   **with an unlineal hand:** by one who is not of my line.
65   **fil'd:** defiled.
67   **put rancours . . . peace:** as if his peace of mind were contained in a receptacle into which poisoning hatred had been dropped; **rancours:** malice.
68   **mine eternal jewel:** my immortal soul, a pearl of great price. How conscience-stricken is Macbeth?
69   **given to . . . man:** surrendered to the devil. In his soliloquy, I. vii. 7, he was ready to take a chance on the afterworld.
71-72   **Rather than . . . utterance:** Macbeth pictures two knights in combat, Fate and himself; **list:** the space enclosed by movable barriers, in which the tournament took place; **champion:** fight against; **to the utterance:** to the death.
48-72   This soliloquy reveals that although he has secured the crown, Macbeth has achieved neither true happiness nor peace of mind. Compare this with I. vii. 1-28. His speech ends on a note of defiance. Why does Macbeth want Banquo out of the way?
72   S.D. **two Murderers:** Of these, Masefield writes: "He had looked about for his murderers, and made enquiries, had chosen them shrewdly and tempted them with cunning, knowing one to be a possible killer, from outraged vanity [2nd M.], the other a likely killer from desperation." Comment. Another suggestion is that they were soldiers, possibly disgraced and dismissed for some offence.
74   **Was it . . . together:** The audience is thus spared the introductory discussion.

       Exeunt all but Macbeth and an Attendant.
Sirrah, a word with you: attend those men   45
Our pleasure?
Attendant.   They are, my lord, without the palace-gate.
Macbeth.   Bring them before us.   *Exit Attendant.*
              To be thus is nothing;
But to be safely thus: our fears in Banquo
Stick deep, and in his royalty of nature   50
Reigns that which would be fear'd: 'tis much he dares,
And, to that dauntless temper of his mind,
He hath a wisdom that doth guide his valour
To act in safety. There is none but he
Whose being I do fear: and under him   55
My Genius is rebuk'd, as it is said
Mark Antony's was by Caesar. He chid the sisters,
When first they put the name of king upon me,
And bade them speak to him. Then prophet-like
They hail'd him father to a line of kings.   60
Upon my head they plac'd a fruitless crown,
And put a barren sceptre in my gripe,
Thence to be wrench'd with an unlineal hand,
No son of mine succeeding. If't be so,
For Banquo's issue have I fil'd my mind,   65
For them the gracious Duncan have I murder'd,
Put rancours in the vessel of my peace
Only for them, and mine eternal jewel
Given to the common enemy of man,
To make them kings, the seed of Banquo kings!   70
Rather than so, come fate into the list,
And champion me to the utterance! Who's there?
       Re-enter Attendant, with two Murderers.
Now go to the door, and stay there till we call.
                    Exit Attendant.
Was it not yesterday we spoke together?
First Murderer.   It was, so please your highness.
Macbeth.   Well then, now   75

77-79 **it was . . . self:** Banquo is blamed for an action that Macbeth had taken; **made good:** plainly showed.

80 **pass'd in . . . you:** proved point by point.

81 **borne in hand:** deceived; **cross'd:** thwarted; **the instruments:** the means.

83 **to a notion craz'd:** even to an insane mind.

88 **so gospell'd:** such Christian fellows.

91 **We are men:** and therefore can endure only so much by way of insult.

86-91 The questions, appealing to their pride, are asked scornfully.

92 Macbeth looks at them contemptuously, hating himself because he must make use of such creatures; **catalogue:** general list.

94 **shoughs:** shaggy dogs; **water-rugs:** rough-haired water-dogs; **demi-wolves:** crosses between dogs and wolves. To maintain the strength and endurance of sled dogs in the North, they are sometimes crossed with wolves; **clept:** called.

95 **the valued file:** the list that showed dogs graded according to their value.

97 **housekeeper:** watchdog.

99 **clos'd:** enclosed.

100 **particular addition:** special title; **bill:** general list. All dogs are dogs, just as all men are men, but each has its own particular characteristics.

92-101 The Dog Speech gives Shakespeare's feeling that social harmony results when everything remains in its rightful place. It also points up Shakespeare's knowledge of dogs.

102 **station:** position.

103 **rank:** grade, level.

104 **I will . . . bosoms:** I will confide to you a scheme.

105 **takes your enemy off:** Macbeth's euphemism for *murder*.

106 **grapples:** The picture is of one ship being brought close to another by means of grappling irons.

107 **who wear . . . life:** whose health is impaired while he lives. Banquo is like a virus, sapping Macbeth's strength.

Have you consider'd of my speeches? Know
That it was he in the times past which held you
So under fortune, which you thought had been
Our innocent self: this I made good to you
In our last conference, pass'd in probation with you;   80
How you were borne in hand, how cross'd; the
    instruments;
Who wrought with them; and all things else that
    might
To half a soul, and to a notion craz'd,
Say "Thus did Banquo."
First Murderer.   You made it known to us.
Macbeth.   I did so; and went further, which is now   85
    Our point of second meeting. Do you find
    Your patience so predominant in your nature,
    That you can let this go? Are you so gospell'd,
    To pray for this good man, and for his issue,
    Whose heavy hand hath bow'd you to the grave,   90
    And beggar'd yours for ever?
First Murderer.   We are men, my liege.
Macbeth.   Ay, in the catalogue ye go for men,
    As hounds and greyhounds, mongrels, spaniels, curs,
    Shoughs, water-rugs, and demi-wolves, are clept
    All by the name of dogs: the valued file   95
    Distinguishes the swift, the slow, the subtle,
    The housekeeper, the hunter, every one
    According to the gift which bounteous nature
    Hath in him clos'd, whereby he does receive
    Particular addition, from the bill   100
    That writes them all alike: and so of men.
    Now if you have a station in the file,
    Not i' the worst rank of manhood, say it,
    And I will put that business in your bosoms,
    Whose execution takes your enemy off,   105
    Grapples you to the heart and love of us,
    Who wear our health but sickly in his life,

110 **hath:** So F; most editors read *have*.

112 **tugg'd with fortune:** pulled hither and thither by ill-luck.

114-15 **Both of . . . enemy:** At least, this is what you are supposed to think. They are quite prepared to accept Macbeth's interpretation.

108-15 How are the two Murderers alike and different?

116 **bloody distance:** deadly enmity.

117-18 **thrusts against . . . life:** is an attack on my vitals.

120 **bid my . . . it:** take the responsibility for a deed I wished done; play the dictator whose acts are not to be questioned.

121 **for:** because of.

122 **wail:** I must bewail.

123 **who:** *Whom* would be required today.

124 **make love:** appeal.

128 Impatiently, Macbeth cuts them short; **spirits:** courage. Some interpret the meaning as *spirits of hatred and revenge*; **Your spirits . . . you:** The line is probably ironic, if the first meaning is accepted.

130 **acquaint you . . . time:** let you know the ideal moment as determined by close observation; **perfect spy:** the result of perfect spying. Macbeth appears to have had an elaborate network of agents (III. iv. 131-2).

131 **to-night:** for fear of what Banquo might say at the next day's council meeting.

132 **something:** some distance; **always thought:** It must always be remembered.

133 **I require a clearness:** I must not be implicated.

134 **rubs:** hitches. The metaphor is drawn from bowling, where a "rub" is an unevenness in the green; **botches:** flaws, bungling errors.

136 **absence is . . . material:** removal is just as important.

Which in his death were perfect.
Second Murderer.   I am one, my liege,
  Whom the vile blows and buffets of the world
  Hath so incens'd that I am reckless what   110
  I do to spite the world.
First Murderer.   And I another,
  So weary with disasters, tugg'd with fortune,
  That I would set my life on any chance,
  To mend it, or be rid on't.
Macbeth.   Both of you
  Know Banquo was your enemy.
Both Murderers.   True, my lord.   115
Macbeth. So is he mine; and in such bloody distance,
  That every minute of his being thrusts
  Against my near'st of life: and though I could
  With barefac'd power sweep him from my sight,
  And bid my will avouch it, yet I must not,   120
  For certain friends that are both his, and mine,
  Whose loves I may not drop, but wail his fall
  Who I myself struck down: and thence it is
  That I to your assistance do make love,
  Masking the business from the common eye,   125
  For sundry weighty reasons.
Second Murderer.   We shall, my lord,
  Perform what you command us.
First Murderer.   Though our lives—
Macbeth. Your spirits shine through you. Within this hour,
    at most,
  I will advise you where to plant yourselves,
  Acquaint you with the perfect spy o' the time,   130
  The moment on't, for't must be done to-night,
  And something from the palace; always thought,
  That I require a clearness; and with him,
  To leave no rubs nor botches in the work,
  Fleance, his son, that keeps him company,   135
  Whose absence is no less material to me

138 **that dark hour:** dark in a double sense. See also III. i. 28; **apart:** offstage. In some productions, the First Murderer demurs at the thought of the second murder, but is easily overborne by the Second Murderer.

139 **anon:** in a moment; **We are resolv'd:** Our minds are made up. Some editors give this speech to the Second Murderer. Which is more logical?

141-2 Macbeth appears confident and exultant.
See also p. 172.

1 Why does Lady Macbeth ask about Banquo?

3 It is ironic that Lady Macbeth must now ask for an audience with the King.

4 **Nought's had, all's spent:** Nothing is gained; everything is wasted.

5 **content:** peace of mind.

6-7 **'Tis safer . . . joy:** Macbeth also expresses envy of their victim; **doubtful joy:** happiness nullified by suspicion and anxiety.

4-7 Lady Macbeth is bitterly disillusioned. We sense a great weariness of spirit.

8 **Why do . . . alone:** This is Lady Macbeth's great tragedy. She has sacrificed all for her husband, only to find that they are being driven farther and farther apart. Macbeth deliberately isolates himself from her in his misery.

9 **sorriest:** most wretched.

10 **using:** harbouring.

11 **them they think on:** him (Duncan) on whom his thoughts concentrate.

12 **without regard:** ignored; **what's done, is done:** It's no use crying over spilt milk. Note the use of the verb "do".

13-15 The snake represents all the obstacles that stand between them and the security of the crown. By killing Duncan, they have merely removed one obstacle (scotch'd the snake). Danger will reappear (as the wound heals and the snake becomes powerful again). The snake image is found several times; **scotch'd:** cut, gashed; **poor:** feeble.

16 **let the . . . disjoint:** let the whole universe fall to pieces; **both the worlds suffer:** heaven and earth perish.

17-19 **ere we . . . fear:** Why should he fear to eat? **and sleep . . . nightly:** Macbeth's conscience is torturing him as he relives the murder of Duncan. It has been suggested that he dreams of being murdered by Banquo.

Than is his father's, must embrace the fate
Of that dark hour: resolve yourselves apart,
I'll come to you anon.
Both Murderers.   We are resolv'd, my lord.
Macbeth.   I'll call upon you straight: abide within.   140
                                    Exeunt Murderers.

It is concluded: Banquo, thy soul's flight,
If it find heaven, must find it out to-night.   *Exit.*

Scene 2

Enter Lady Macbeth and a Servant.

Lady Macbeth.   Is Banquo gone from court?
Servant.   Ay, madam, but returns again to-night.
Lady Macbeth.   Say to the king, I would attend his leisure
For a few words.
Servant.   Madam, I will.   *Exit.*
Lady Macbeth.   Nought's had, all's spent,
Where our desire is got without content:
'Tis safer to be that which we destroy
Than by destruction dwell in doubtful joy.
    Enter Macbeth.
How now, my lord, why do you keep alone,
Of sorriest fancies your companions making,
Using those thoughts which should indeed have died   10
With them they think on? Things without all remedy
Should be without regard: what's done, is done.
Macbeth.   We have scotch'd the snake, not kill'd it:
She'll close, and be herself, whilst our poor malice
Remains in danger of her former tooth.   15
But let the frame of things disjoint, both the worlds
    suffer,
Ere we will eat our meal in fear, and sleep
In the affliction of these terrible dreams,

21-22 Than on . . . ecstasy: The metaphor (an anachronism) is drawn from the practice of stretching prisoners on the rack; **ecstasy:** here, frenzy, extreme mental torture.

22-23 Duncan is . . . well: said to be the finest lines in Shakespeare. Note the metaphor, the emotional intensity, and the onomatopoeia. Why is life like a fever? **fitful:** spasmodic.

24-25 his: its, unless "treason" is personified. Note the evils that can beset a king; **malice domestic:** civil war.

13-26 This passage is one of the great poetic speeches of the play. It is full of irony, music, and imaginative phrasing.

27 sleek o'er . . . looks: smooth your rough appearance, as one would brush shaggy hair.

29-30 So shall . . . Banquo: Macbeth seems to make a supreme effort to be himself; **remembrance:** remember your responsibility as hostess to Banquo.

31 Present him eminence: Treat him with the distinction befitting an honoured guest.

32 unsafe the while: since we are unsafe for the time being.

33 lave our honours: Our honour can only be kept clean (laved) by flattering Banquo.

34 vizards: masks. Macbeth is now the hypocrite.

35 leave this: dismiss such thoughts.

36 full of scorpions: a hideous image to suggest the tormented suspicions that throng his brain.

38 copy's: tenure (a legal term) or pattern. Neither Banquo nor Fleance is immortal (eterne); hence, they are not to be feared.

39 assailable: open to attack.

40-41 jocund: joyful. The reason he gives her for being gay is macabre; **ere the . . . flight:** at dusk; **cloister'd:** among the covered walks of college or cathedral buildings.

42 shard-borne: carried on scaly wings, though "shard" suggests rather the horny wing-cases. Shard-born could mean *dung-bred.*

41-43 ere to . . . peal: The imitative harmony brought out by the humming, droning sounds is very expressive; **hath rung . . . peal:** has sounded a sleepy curfew. **44** The sound of "d" is dominant.

46 seeling: eye-closing. "Seel", a term drawn from falconry, means *to draw a thread through the bird's eyelids.*

47 scarf up: blindfold; **tender eye . . . day:** Day is compared to a falcon, and is also associated with good rather than evil.

49 bond: The lives of Banquo and Fleance are compared to a legal document between them and nature that is to be destroyed by the hand of darkness (evil): possibly, the Witches' prophecies.

45-50 Compare Macbeth's invocation to night and Lady Macbeth's speech, I. v. 50-51.

That shake us nightly: better be with the dead,
Whom we, to gain our peace, have sent to peace,   20
Than on the torture of the mind to lie
In restless ecstasy. Duncan is in his grave:
After life's fitful fever, he sleeps well;
Treason has done his worst: nor steel, nor poison,
Malice domestic, foreign levy, nothing,   25
Can touch him further.
Lady Macbeth.   Come on;
  Gentle my lord, sleek o'er your rugged looks,
  Be bright and jovial among your guests to-night.
Macbeth.   So shall I, love, and so, I pray, be you:
  Let your remembrance apply to Banquo,   30
  Present him eminence, both with eye and tongue:
  Unsafe the while, that we
  Must lave our honours in these flattering streams,
  And make our faces vizards to our hearts,
  Disguising what they are.
Lady Macbeth.   You must leave this.   35
Macbeth.   O, full of scorpions is my mind, dear wife!
  Thou know'st that Banquo and his Fleance, lives.
Lady Macbeth.   But in them nature's copy's not eterne.
Macbeth.   There's comfort yet, they are assailable;
  Then be thou jocund: ere the bat hath flown   40
  His cloister'd flight, ere to black Hecate's summons
  The shard-borne beetle, with his drowsy hums,
  Hath rung night's yawning peal, there shall be done
  A deed of dreadful note.
Lady Macbeth   What's to be done?   *not going to till her.*
Macbeth.   Be innocent of the knowledge, dearest chuck,   45
  Till thou applaud the deed. Come, seeling night,
  Scarf up the tender eye of pitiful day,
  And with thy bloody and invisible hand
  Cancel and tear to pieces that great bond
  Which keeps me pale! Light thickens, and the crow   50
  Makes wing to the rooky wood:

52 **Good things . . . drowse:** Goodness grows weak and sleepy as night falls. Why?

55 **Things bad . . . ill:** Wickedness requires more wickedness to conceal itself. Lines 52 and 55 have both been called "the motto of the tragedy". Which one more accurately expresses the central idea?

See also p. 173.

S.D. Enter three Murderers: It is interesting to speculate on the identity of the Third Murderer. Some maintain that in view of Macbeth's comments in III. iv. 21 and 50, he could not have been present. Why might he have sent the Third Murderer?

1 The First Murderer is rightly suspicious. If the Third Murderer were Macbeth, would the others recognize him?

2-4 **He needs . . . just:** We need not be suspicious; he reports our duties exactly as Macbeth outlined them.

5 **The west . . . day:** This poetic line seems out of place on the lips of a murderer. Comment.

6 **lated:** belated.

7 **timely:** welcome.

9 **Give us . . . ho:** This is said to his attendants who, not hearing the scuffle, go off with the horses.

10 **within the . . . expectation:** on the list of invited guests.

11 **go about:** take the longer route to the stables.

15 **Stand to 't:** Be bold.

11-15 Note how Shakespeare makes a virtue of necessity in explaining the dismissal of the horses.

16 **It will . . . to-night:** Banquo's powers of observation have been illustrated in I. vi. 3-10 and II. i. 4-5.

Good things of day begin to droop and drowse,
Whiles night's black agents to their preys do rouse.
Thou marvell'st at my words: but hold thee still;
Things bad begun make strong themselves by ill: 55
So, prithee go with me.   *Exeunt.*

Scene 3

A PARK NEAR THE PALACE.

Enter three Murderers.

First Murderer.   But who did bid thee join with us?
Third Murderer.   Macbeth.
Second Murderer.   He needs not our mistrust, since he delivers
   Our offices and what we have to do,
   To the direction just.
First Murderer.   Then stand with us:
   The west yet glimmers with some streaks of day: 5
   Now spurs the lated traveller apace
   To gain the timely inn, and near approaches
   The subject of our watch.
Third Murderer.   Hark! I hear horses.
Banquo (within).   Give us a light there, ho!
Second Murderer.   Then 'tis he: the rest
   That are within the note of expectation   10
   Already are i' the court.
First Murderer.   His horses go about.
Third Murderer.   Almost a mile: but he does usually—
   So all men do—from hence to the palace gate
   Make it their walk.
Second Murderer.   A light, a light!
         Enter Banquo, and Fleance with a torch.
Third Murderer.   'Tis he.
First Murderer.   Stand to 't.   15
Banquo.   It will be rain to-night.

16 **Let it come down:** Note the grisly pun.
17 Note the urgency with which Banquo speaks to Fleance. How can this be explained? Why does the boy not stay to aid his father?
18 **Thou mayst revenge:** Banquo mentions no name. Why not? **slave:** villain; S.D. **Fleance escapes:** Muir states that this is "the turning point of the play". According to tradition, Fleance escaped into Wales and married a Welsh princess. Their son Walter became Lord High Steward of Scotland, took "Steward" (Stuart) as his surname, and was the ancestor of James I.
19 Why did the Third Murderer put out the light? What was the result?

See also p. 174.

S.D. **A banquet prepared:** There have been many famous banquets in literature and in history; *e.g.*, Belshazzar's Feast, the Wedding Feast of Peleus and Thetis, the Last Supper. Harrison regards this as "the second masterly scene of the play".
1-2 **degrees:** rank, precedence; **at first and last:** from the beginning to the end of the banquet, or as some editors suggest, once and for all.
4 **play the humble host:** a metaphor from the theatre.
5 **keeps her state:** remains in her canopied chair of state. The implication is that Lady Macbeth cannot endure the strain of mingling with the guests; **in best time:** at the proper time.
6 **require her welcome:** request her to bid you welcome.
9 **encounter:** respond to; an indirect stage direction, probably suggesting that they are drinking to the lady's health.
10 **Both sides are even:** a reference to the seating of the guests on either side of the table; **i' the midst:** evidence of his desire to "play the humble host".
11 **large:** free. He notices the Murderer, and with this remark he covers his withdrawal.
12 **There's blood . . . face:** With what emotion does he speak— alarm, fascination, hope, or warning?
13 **'Tis Banquo's then:** He speaks grimly.

irony / rain

First Murderer   Let it come down.
        They set upon Banquo.

macbeth
witch
servant

Banquo.   O, treachery! Fly, good Fleance, fly, fly, fly!
    Thou mayst revenge. O slave!
            Dies. Fleance escapes.
Third Murderer.   Who did strike out the light?
First Murderer.   Was't not the way?
Third Murderer.   There's but one down; the son is fled.
Second Murderer.   We have lost   20
    Best half of our affair.
First Murderer.   Well, let's away, and say how much is done.
                                Exeunt.

Scene 4

HALL IN THE PALACE.

A banquet prepared. Enter Macbeth, Lady Macbeth,
Ross, Lennox, Lords, and Attendants.

Macbeth.   You know your own degrees, sit down: at first
    And last the hearty welcome.
Lords.   Thanks to your majesty.
Macbeth.   Ourself will mingle with society,
    And play the humble host.
    Our hostess keeps her state, but in best time   5
    We will require her welcome.
Lady Macbeth.   Pronounce it for me, sir, to all our friends,
    For my heart speaks they are welcome.
            Enter First Murderer to the door.
Macbeth.   See, they encounter thee with their hearts' thanks.
    Both sides are even: here I'll sit i' the midst.   10
    Be large in mirth, anon we'll drink a measure
    The table round. (*Approaching the door.*) There's
        blood upon thy face.
First Murderer.   'Tis Banquo's then.

14 **'Tis better . . . within:** a callous comment. It is better that his blood be on your face than in his veins. "He" should then be *him*. Another interpretation is: "It is better that you should be outside the hall than that he should be inside."

15 **dispatch'd:** put to death.

16 **My lord . . . him:** In some productions, the Murderer shows Banquo's ring, which Macbeth immediately takes from him.

19 **the nonpareil:** one who has no equal; model of excellence.

20 An embarrassed confession. Why is he embarrassed?

21 **my fit:** Possibly, Macbeth is referring to the spasms of insecurity and fear that shake him periodically.

22 **whole:** solid; **founded:** firm.

23 **broad and . . . air:** free and unfettered as the surrounding air.

22-23 The three similes suggest stability and freedom.

24 **cabin'd, cribb'd, confin'd:** Macbeth speaks like one choking for air; **cabin'd:** enclosed in a small space; **cribb'd:** cramped, imprisoned, as in a hovel or hut.

25 **saucy:** insolent; **But Banquo's safe:** He clutches at this straw.

26-28 **Ay, my . . . nature:** Why does he emphasize the details? **safe:** Dover Wilson calls this a callous euphemism; **trenched:** deep-cut; **the least . . . nature:** each a death stroke; **Thanks for that:** a terse expression of gratitude.   29 **worm:** snake.

29-31 **There the . . . present:** Macbeth consoles himself with thinking that Fleance does not present an immediate danger.

33-37 **give the cheer:** welcome the guests; **the feast . . . welcome:** If Macbeth does not assure the guests that they are welcome, it will seem as if they are dining at an inn where they would have to pay for their meal, rather than being guests at a pleasant entertainment; **to feed . . . it:** If one is mainly interested in the food and wants a good meal, he would be better to eat at home. When one is at a banquet or social gathering, the toasts and speeches add zest and the spice of formality; **sauce:** medieval cooks specialized in highly spiced sauces, which were sometimes used to conceal the taste of unpalatable food.

32-37 Lady Macbeth, herself an experienced hostess, reminds her husband of his social duties.

37 **S.D. The Ghost . . . place:** The explicit stage direction indicates that an actual figure appeared on the Elizabethan stage, probably out of the trap-door. Macbeth is the only one who sees it, but a contemporary allusion supports the idea of a "real ghost". 37 **remembrancer:** one appointed to remind another.

40-41 **Here the . . . present:** If only Banquo were present, all the flower of Scottish nobility would be gathered under one roof; **grac'd:** gracious.

Macbeth.   'Tis better thee without than he within.
    Is he dispatch'd?   15
First Murderer.   My lord, his throat is cut, that I did for him.
Macbeth.   Thou are the best o' the cut-throats; yet he's good
    That did the like for Fleance: if thou didst it,
    Thou art the nonpareil.
First Murderer.   Most royal sir,
    Fleance is 'scap'd.   20
Macbeth (aside).   Then comes my fit again: I had else been
        perfect,
    Whole as the marble, founded as the rock,
    As broad and general as the casing air:
    But now I am cabin'd, cribb'd, confin'd, bound in
    To saucy doubts and fears.—But Banquo's safe?   25
First Murderer.   Ay, my good lord: safe in a ditch he bides,
    With twenty trenched gashes on his head;
    The least a death to nature.
Macbeth.   Thanks for that.
    (aside) There the grown serpent lies, the worm that's fled
    Hath nature that in time will venom breed,   30
    No teeth for the present. Get thee gone; to-morrow
    We'll hear ourselves again.   *Exit Murderer.*
Lady Macbeth.   My royal lord,
    You do not give the cheer, the feast is sold
    That is not often vouch'd, while 'tis a making
    'Tis given with welcome: to feed were best at home;   35
    From thence, the sauce to meat is ceremony,
    Meeting were bare without it.
            *The Ghost of Banquo enters, and sits in
            Macbeth's place.*
Macbeth.   Sweet remembrancer!
    Now good digestion wait on appetite,
    And health on both!
Lennox.   May't please your highness sit?
Macbeth.   Here had we now our country's honour roof'd,   40
    Were the grac'd person of our Banquo present;

42-43 **who may . . . mischance:** whom I hope I may accuse of unkindness rather than pity on account of some accident.

46-48 **The table's . . . highness:** At first, Macbeth sees only that there is no empty place. On seeing the hideous apparition, he draws back in horror. It is this that prompts Lennox's remark.

49 **Which of . . . this:** He thinks it is a practical joke played on him by one of his lords.

50-51 **Thou canst . . . it:** This indicates that the Ghost is not that of Duncan; **never shake . . . me:** an indirect stage direction; the Ghost nods its head up and down as if in accusation.

55 **upon a thought:** in a moment.

57 **extend his passion:** prolong his agitation.

53-58 Lady Macbeth shows presence of mind as she seeks to protect her husband.

60 **O proper stuff:** ridiculous nonsense.

61 **This is . . . fear:** This is merely a picture created (painted) by your fear.

62 **air-drawn:** visionary, unreal. Macbeth had apparently told his wife about the dagger. Why would he do this?

63 **flaws:** outbursts, like gusts of wind.

64 **impostors to:** pretenders in comparison with.

66 **authoriz'd by her grandam:** vouched for by her grandmother. His behaviour would be appropriate in an old wives' tale full of superstitious nonsense.

67 **Why do . . . faces:** Macbeth's countenance works convulsively. Lady Macbeth lashes him with her taunts and scorn as she did when urging him to commit the murder of Duncan. She is less successful now in her contemptuous appeals to his pride.

69-70 Macbeth is almost incoherent.

71 **charnel-houses:** vaults in which dead bodies or bones are piled. It has been suggested that Shakespeare's aversion from such a place led to his putting a curse (in his epitaph) on any one who should move his bones.

Who may I rather challenge for unkindness,
Than pity for mischance!
Ross.   His absence, sir,
Lays blame upon his promise. Please 't your highness
To grace us with your royal company?   45
Macbeth.   The table's full.
Lennox.   Here is a place reserv'd, sir.
Macbeth.   Where?
Lennox.   Here, my good lord. What is't that moves your
highness?
Macbeth.   Which of you have done this?
Lords.   What, my good lord?
Macbeth.   Thou canst not say I did it: never shake   50
Thy gory locks at me.
Ross.   Gentlemen, rise, his highness is not well.
Lady Macbeth.   Sit, worthy friends: my lord is often thus,
And hath been from his youth: pray you, keep seat;
The fit is momentary, upon a thought   55
He will again be well. If much you note him,
You shall offend him, and extend his passion;
Feed, and regard him not. Are you a man?
Macbeth.   Ay, and a bold one, that dare look on that
Which might appal the devil.
Lady Macbeth.   O proper stuff!   60
This is the very painting of your fear:
This is the air-drawn dagger which you said
Led you to Duncan. O, these flaws and starts,
(Impostors to true fear) would well become
A woman's story at a winter's fire,   65
Authoriz'd by her grandam. Shame itself,
Why do you make such faces? When all's done,
You look but on a stool.
Macbeth.   Prithee see there! behold! look! lo! how say you?
Why, what care I? If thou canst nod, speak too.   70
If charnel-houses and our graves must send
Those that we bury back, our monuments

73 **maws of kites:** the stomachs of vultures. Only when devoured by birds of prey can the dead be prevented from returning to haunt the living; **unmann'd:** To accuse Macbeth of lacking manhood had always been one of Lady Macbeth's most effective taunts.

76 **ere humane . . . weal:** before civilized law cleansed society and made it peaceful as opposed to violent; **humane:** so F. The Elizabethans did not distinguish in meaning or spelling between *human* and "humane"; **purg'd:** a medical metaphor.

81 **twenty:** an echo of the Murderer's statement (III. iv. 27); **mortal murders . . . crowns:** deadly wounds on their heads.

82 **more strange:** The two monosyllables add emphasis.

58-83 These lines would be spoken as an aside.   84 **lack:** miss.

83-84 Lady Macbeth, unable to establish contact with Macbeth, makes her final appeal as a hostess.

85 **muse:** wonder.

86 **strange infirmity:** There have been various references to Macbeth's "health" of mind. Here, he pretends that his tendency towards hallucinations (brought on by an over-active conscience) is his own peculiar ailment. This explanation suggests that although we see the Ghost, Shakespeare may have intended it to be a figment of Macbeth's imagination.

88 **Give me . . . full:** The hand that takes the goblet trembles and the wine spills over.

91 **S.D. Re-enter Ghost:** Although F prints the stage direction after line 88, it has been dropped down by many editors to the middle of line 91 so that the Ghost enters obediently in response to Macbeth's express wish. (Its entrance after line 88 would, of course, prolong the dramatic irony.) **thirst:** desire to drink.

92 **all to all:** all good wishes to all.

93 **Avaunt:** Begone. Macbeth dashes down his cup, a piece of stage business used by David Garrick.

94 **marrowless:** hence, lifeless.

95 **speculation:** intelligence or power of sight.

96 **glare:** stare glassily, since the eyes are without expression.

98 **time:** occasion.

96-98 Lady Macbeth makes a heroic, if futile, effort.

100 **rugged:** rough, shaggy; **Russian bear:** Found in Russia, the animal is still used as a symbol of that country.

101 **arm'd:** with its horn; some say, with its tough hide; **Hyrcan:** Hyrcania was a province of the ancient Empire of Persia. Tigers abounded there. It is significant that Macbeth mentions three of the fiercest animals known. Of these, he is not afraid.

Shall be the maws of kites.　　　　　　*Exit Ghost*.
Lady Macbeth.　　　　　What, quite unmann'd in folly?
Macbeth.　If I stand here, I saw him.
Lady Macbeth.　　　　　　Fie, for shame!
Macbeth.　Blood hath been shed ere now, i' the olden time,　75
　Ere humane statute purg'd the gentle weal;
　Ay, and since too, murders have been perform'd
　Too terrible for the ear: the time has been,
　That, when the brains were out, the man would die,
　And there an end; but now they rise again,　　　80
　With twenty mortal murders on their crowns,
　And push us from our stools: this is more strange
　Than such a murder is.
Lady Macbeth.　　　　My worthy lord,
　Your noble friends do lack you.
Macbeth.　　　　　　　I do forget.
　Do not muse at me, my most worthy friends;　　85
　I have a strange infirmity, which is nothing
　To those that know me. Come, love and health to all;
　Then I'll sit down. Give me some wine; fill full.
　I drink to the general joy o' the whole table,
　And to our dear friend Banquo, whom we miss;　90
Would he were here! (*Re-enter Ghost*.) To all and him we thirst,
　And all to all.
Lords.　　　　Our duties, and the pledge.
Macbeth.　Avaunt! and quit my sight! let the earth hide thee!
　Thy bones are marrowless, thy blood is cold;
　Thou hast no speculation in those eyes　　　95
　Which thou dost glare with.
Lady Macbeth.　　　　Think of this, good peers,
　But as a thing of custom: 'tis no other,
　Only it spoils the pleasure of the time.
Macbeth.　What man dare, I dare:
　Approach thou like the rugged Russian bear,　　100
　The arm'd rhinoceros, or the Hyrcan tiger,

102 **nerves:** sinews.

104 **desert:** a deserted place, where they could not be interrupted.

105 **if trembling . . . then:** a line "much discussed and emended". "If I then harbour a single tremour" (Dover Wilson).

106 **the baby of a girl:** girl's doll. Other interpretations are "a baby girl", "the baby of an immature mother". In any case, it is contemptuously symbolic of weakness.

106-8 **Hence, horrible . . . hence:** As Macbeth exerts his will power, the apparition vanishes; **Why so . . . still:** He looks about him like a man emerging from a trance, and notices the disorder.

109 **displac'd:** dispelled. 110 **admir'd disorder:** amazing confusion.

111 **overcome:** pass over. Are such things no more to be wondered at than the casual passage of a summer cloud over our heads?

112-16 **You make . . . fear:** You make me wonder whether I am a coward or not, since you are so obviously unafraid; **disposition that I owe:** my own nature; **blanch'd:** white and pinched.

119-20 **Stand not . . . once:** Ceremonial leave-taking in order of rank is to be dispensed with in the interest of speed.

117-20 With admirable presence of mind, Lady Macbeth makes a superhuman effort to prevent Macbeth from betraying himself irrevocably.

120-1 **Good night . . . majesty:** Lennox's remark is heavily sarcastic. Lady Macbeth ignores it. Of their departure, Harrison says: "the Scottish lords withdraw [from the banquet] with full knowledge of the murder of Banquo." Comment.

122 **it:** the murder of Banquo; possibly the Ghost.

123 **stones:** under which the corpse has been concealed by the murderer; **trees to speak:** This was said to be a reference to the *Aeneid*, in which the ghost of a murdered man speaks from a tree (Steevens).

124 **augures:** auguries; *i.e.*, predictions; **understood relations:** incidents thought to relate to the question. Another meaning is: "properly interpreted phenomena".

125-6 **by maggot-pies . . . blood:** Magpies, jackdaws, and rooks have thus been the agents through which the most secret murderer has been discovered.

127 **at odds with:** having an argument with. It is hard to tell whether it is day or night. She utters no recriminations.

128-9 **How say'st thou, that:** what do you think of the fact that; **Macduff denies . . . bidding:** Macbeth's restless, tormented mind turns towards another source of trouble, but he will never find peace of mind; **Did you . . . sir:** Lady Macbeth speaks in a voice drained of all emotion after her efforts.

Take any shape but that, and my firm nerves
Shall never tremble. Or be alive again,
And dare me to the desert with thy sword;
If trembling I inhabit then, protest me   105
The baby of a girl. Hence, horrible shadow!
Unreal mockery, hence!   *Exit Ghost.*
                        Why so, being gone,
I am a man again: pray you, sit still.
Lady Macbeth.   You have displac'd the mirth, broke the
     good meeting,
With most admir'd disorder.
Macbeth.   Can such things be,   110
And overcome us like a summer's cloud,
Without our special wonder? You make me strange
Even to the disposition that I owe,
When now I think you can behold such sights,
And keep the natural ruby of your cheeks,   115
When mine is blanch'd with fear.
Ross.   What sights, my lord? nick of time
Lady Macbeth.   I pray you, speak not; he grows worse and worse;
Question enrages him: at once, good night.
Stand not upon the order of your going,
But go at once.
Lennox.   Good night, and better health   120
Attend his majesty!
Lady Macbeth.   A kind good night to all!
          Exeunt all but Macbeth and Lady Macbeth.
Macbeth.   It will have blood; they say, blood will have blood:
Stones have been known to move, and trees to speak;
Augures and understood relations have
By maggot-pies, and choughs, and rooks brought forth   125
The secret'st man of blood. What is the night?
Lady Macbeth.   Almost at odds with morning, which is which.
Macbeth.   How say'st thou, that Macduff denies his person
At our great bidding?
Lady Macbeth.   Did you send to him, sir?

130 **by the way:** casually. Macduff did not apparently send a deliberate refusal to attend the banquet.

131-2 **There's not . . . fee'd:** Macbeth trusts nobody. Holinshed states: "For Makbeth had, in everie noble mans house, one slie fellow or other in fee with him, to reveale all that was said or doone within the same. . . ."

133 **betimes:** early. It is evidence of the deterioration of Macbeth's character that now he should seek out "the instruments of darkness".

134 **bent:** The word suggests determination and desperation.

135-8 **the worst:** Supply *news*; **for mine . . . way:** Everything must take second place to what I want. The speech reveals a supreme, almost savage, selfishness; **I am . . . o'er:** The image of a man wading through a river of blood is a powerful one. He says, in effect: "There is no turning back now that I am half-way over."

139-40 **Strange things . . . scann'd:** This ominous speech implies that from now on Macbeth plans to carry out his deeds on the impulse of the moment without thought or reason. The implication is that the deeds will be too unnatural to contemplate. "Strange" is used five times in this scene.

141 **You lack . . . sleep:** But Macbeth has murdered sleep. It is not without significance that Lady Macbeth's next appearance will be in the sleep-walking scene; **season:** that which preserves.

142 **self-abuse:** delusion. He seems to accept the idea that the Ghost was a figment of his imagination caused by fear (conscience).

143 **is the . . . use:** comes from the terror that is the result of too little experience.

144 **We are . . . deed:** a dark and dreadful thought. Granville-Barker says that it "looks to nethermost hell"; **in deed:** Theobald's emendation; F has *indeed*.

122-44 Dover Wilson says: "Perhaps the most terrible passage in *Macbeth*."

See also p. 175.

S.D. Hecate: See note on The Text, p. xxiv. Note the preceding references to her in II. i. 52 and III. ii. 41. The imagery seems altogether different from that of the earthy folk lore of the Weird Sisters.

1 **angerly:** angry.

2 **beldams:** old hags. It is ironic that originally the term was *belle dame*. 5 **riddles:** the prophecies.

7 **close contriver:** secret plotter. 10 **which:** what.

Macbeth. I hear it by the way: but I will send: 130
There's not a one of them but in his house
I keep a servant fee'd. I will to-morrow
(And betimes I will) to the weird sisters:
More shall they speak; for now I am bent to know,
By the worst means, the worst; for mine own good, 135
All causes shall give way: I am in blood
Stepp'd in so far, that should I wade no more,
Returning were as tedious as go o'er:
Strange things I have in head, that will to hand,
Which must be acted, ere they may be scann'd. 140
Lady Macbeth. You lack the season of all natures, sleep.
Macbeth. Come, we'll to sleep. My strange and self-abuse
Is the initiate fear, that wants hard use:
We are yet but young in deed. *Exeunt.*

Scene 5

THE HEATH.

Thunder. Enter the three Witches, meeting Hecate.

First Witch. Why, how now, Hecate? you look angerly.
Hecate. Have I not reason, beldams as you are,
Saucy, and over-bold? How did you dare
To trade and traffic with Macbeth
In riddles, and affairs of death; 5
And I, the mistress of your charms,
The close contriver of all harms,
Was never call'd to bear my part,
Or show the glory of our art?
And, which is worse, all you have done 10
Hath been but for a wayward son,
Spiteful, and wrathful, who (as others do)
Loves for his own ends, not for you.
But make amends now: get you gone,

15 **pit of Acheron:** Acheron, the Stream of Anguish, was one of the four rivers of Hades in classical mythology. Here, it refers to some gloomy spot where the Witches could be found, not far from Macbeth's castle.

16-17 **thither he . . . destiny:** Hecate is evidently aware of Macbeth's plans.

18-19 **Your vessels . . . beside:** The writer of these lines fits them into the Witches' sabbath in IV. i; this scene, though probably spurious, is well integrated.

23-24 **Upon the . . . drop:** It was believed that the moon, under magic influence, shed a foam on certain herbs and objects. "Corner" may refer to the horns of the new moon; **profound:** ready to fall.

26 **sleights:** arts.

27 **artificial sprites:** apparitions brought forth by art (IV. i. 68 ff.).

28 **illusion:** deceptiveness.

29 **confusion:** ruin, destruction.

30-31 An accurate forecast of Macbeth's behaviour.

32 **security:** carelessness resulting from over-confidence.

34-35 **Hark! I . . . me:** "A spectacular effect was achieved as a 'car' containing an attendant spirit was lowered and raised by a windlass through a trap-door in the 'heavens' above the stage. The car would be concealed in clouds of fluffy material and music would be needed to conceal the sound of the pulleys" (Dover Wilson); **A song:** See note on The Text, p. xxiv.

See also p. 177.

S.D. Lennox looks around cautiously and speaks in guarded tones. If the anonymous Old Man of II. iv. represented the common people, the "Lord" may represent the nobility. At that time Ross stood for the quiescent nobles; Lennox symbolizes those who are becoming restive and suspicious.

1-2 **My former . . . farther:** I have been implying more than I have actually said; now, you can draw your own conclusions.

3 **borne:** carried on.

4 **of:** by; **marry:** well, of course. (Macbeth could afford to pity him, seeing that he was dead. Lennox is heavily ironic throughout this speech.)

And at the pit of Acheron   15
Meet me i' the morning: thither he
Will come, to know his destiny:
Your vessels, and your spells provide,
Your charms, and every thing beside;
I am for the air; this night I'll spend   20
Unto a dismal and a fatal end.
Great business must be wrought ere noon:
Upon the corner of the moon
There hangs a vaporous drop profound,
I'll catch it ere it come to ground;   25
And that, distill'd by magic sleights,
Shall raise such artificial sprites,
As by the strength of their illusion
Shall draw him on to his confusion.
He shall spurn fate, scorn death, and bear   30
His hopes 'bove wisdom, grace, and fear:
And you all know, security
Is mortals' chiefest enemy.   *Music.*
Hark! I am call'd; my little spirit, see,
Sits in a foggy cloud, and stays for me.   *Exit.*   35
    A song within: "Come away, come away," etc.
First Witch.   Come, let's make haste; she'll soon be back again.
                                       Exeunt.

Scene 6

FORRES. THE PALACE.

Enter Lennox and another Lord.

Lennox.   My former speeches have but hit your thoughts,
   Which can interpret farther: only I say
   Things have been strangely borne. The gracious
     Duncan
   Was pitied of Macbeth: marry, he was dead:

5-7 And the . . . fled: No doubt this is the explanation offered by Macbeth.

8 who cannot . . . thought: who can fail to think; **monstrous:** inhuman.

10 fact: deed.

11-14 How it . . . done: We are reminded of Lennox's remark in II. iii. 101; **grieve:** verbal irony; **pious:** loyal; **tear:** We get the impression of butchery; **thralls:** slaves; **nobly:** verbal irony.

1-16 Of these lines, Harrison writes: "This is Shakespeare at his best."

17 borne: managed, manipulated.

19-20 they should . . . Fleance: Macbeth would certainly put them out of the way, supposedly in punishment for their "offences", but actually as protection for himself.

21 But, peace: He speaks in a whisper; **broad:** blunt, plain. Macduff's speeches (II. iii. and iv.) have been noticeably terse and trenchant.

22 tyrant's: For the first time, this term, used of a blood-thirsty monarch and usurper, is being applied to Macbeth.

24 bestows himself: is settled, has taken refuge.

25 holds the . . . birth: withholds the rightful crown.

27 the most pious Edward: Edward the Confessor, who reigned from 1042-66. A mild, religious, amiable man, he is remembered as the founder of Westminster Abbey, where his shrine is still to be seen. This reference helps to date the action of the play. There is a marked contrast between Edward and Macbeth.

28-29 malevolence of . . . respect: His ill-fortune in no way diminishes the high respect in which he is held.

30 upon his aid: on Malcolm's behalf.

31 wake: rouse; **Northumberland:** Siward's earldom of Northumbria. (See map, p. xliii.) **Siward:** According to Holinshed, Siward was Malcolm's grandfather, the father of Duncan's wife. As Earl of Northumberland (Northumbria), he performed yeoman service for King Edward in suppressing the rebellion of Earl Godwin and his sons in 1053.

33 ratify: confirm.

34-36 give to . . . honours: a picture of the lawless disorder from which Scotland is suffering. Hunger and fear are rampant; **free from . . . knives:** rid our feasts and banquets of bloody knives; **faithful:** *i.e.*, to the rightful king; **free:** honestly won and enjoyed in freedom.

And the right-valiant Banquo walk'd too late, 5
Whom you may say (if't please you) Fleance kill'd,
For Fleance fled: men must not walk too late.
Who cannot want the thought, how monstrous
It was for Malcolm and for Donalbain
To kill their gracious father? damned fact, 10
How it did grieve Macbeth! did he not straight, *irony*
In pious rage, the two delinquents tear,
That were the slaves of drink, and thralls of sleep?
Was not that nobly done? Ay, and wisely too;
For 'twould have anger'd any heart alive 15
To hear the men deny 't. So that I say,
He has borne all things well, and I do think
That, had he Duncan's sons under his key,
(As, an 't please heaven, he shall not) they should
     find
What 'twere to kill a father; so should Fleance. 20
But, peace! for from broad words, and 'cause he
     fail'd *apposem m*
His presence at the tyrant's feast, I hear
Macduff lives in disgrace: sir, can you tell
Where he bestows himself?
Lord.   The son of Duncan
(From whom this tyrant holds the due of birth) 25
Lives in the English court, and is receiv'd
Of the most pious Edward with such grace *R.n.G*
That the malevolence of fortune nothing *r 0*
Takes from his high respect. Thither Macduff is gone,
To pray the holy king, upon his aid 30
To wake Northumberland and warlike Siward,
That by the help of these (with Him above
To ratify the work) we may again
Give to our tables meat, sleep to our nights,
Free from our feasts and banquets bloody knives, 35
Do faithful homage, and receive free honours,
All which we pine for now. And this report

38 **the king:** F reads *their king*; *i.e.*, Edward. "The king" might refer to Macbeth; if so, it implies that Macbeth knew of Macduff's departure, a fact belied by his response to Lennox's announcement in IV. i. 141-2. If "the king" does mean Edward, there is a problem in regard to the pronoun "he" in line 38 which obviously refers to Macbeth.

40 **with:** and having received as an answer; **an absolute . . . I:** a curt refusal from Macduff. At the end of the banquet scene, Macbeth was about to "send to" Macduff. Holinshed connects this with Macduff's refusal to come in person to assist with the construction of Dunsinane Castle.

41 **cloudy:** surly, angry; **me:** ethic dative, or dative of interest, which calls attention to a person, other than the subject, interested in an action.

42-43 **hums:** mutters; **as who . . . answer:** like one who would say: "You'll regret the day when you burdened me with this answer." He does not relish the thought of reporting such a statement to Macbeth.

44-45 **to hold . . . provide:** to stay as far away as possible from Macbeth.

48 **suffering country:** country suffering.

49 **a hand accurs'd:** We are reminded of Macbeth's remark, II. ii. 61-63.

See also p. 177.

Acts IV and V show how "Fate, having cheated Macbeth, proceeds to destroy him" (Harrison). Act IV begins with the grisly rites of a witches' sabbath.

S.D. **A cavern:** The Witches are now "at home". The cauldron is set over the trap-door, and through or behind it the Apparitions rise.

1 **brinded:** brindled; brownish with streaks of another colour; hence, striped like a tiger. The reference is perhaps to Graymalkin.

2 **thrice, and once:** possibly so expressed to emphasize the number "three"; **hedge-pig:** hedgehog.

3 **Harpier:** the Third Witch's familiar spirit; this demon gives the signal to begin.

8 **venom:** It is said that the skin glands of a toad exude a poisonous substance sharp enough to be felt on the eyes and tongue; hence, perhaps, the superstition that toads cause warts. The poison is exuded while the toad sleeps.

Hath so exasperate the king that he
Prepares for some attempt of war.
Lennox.   Sent he to Macduff?
Lord.   He did: and with an absolute "Sir, not I,"   40
The cloudy messenger turns me his back,
And hums; as who should say "You'll rue the time
That clogs me with this answer."
Lennox.   And that well might
Advise him to a caution, to hold what distance
His wisdom can provide. Some holy angel   45
Fly to the court of England, and unfold
His message ere he come, that a swift blessing
May soon return to this our suffering country
Under a hand accurs'd!
Lord.   I'll send my prayers with him.
                                   Exeunt.

ACT IV

Scene 1

A CAVERN. IN THE MIDDLE, A BOILING CAULDRON.

Thunder. Enter the three Witches.

First Witch.   Thrice the brinded cat hath mew'd.
Second Witch.   Thrice, and once the hedge-pig whin'd.
Third Witch.   Harpier cries " 'Tis time, 'tis time."
First Witch.   Round about the cauldron go:
In the poison'd entrails throw;   5
Toad, that under cold stone
Days and nights has thirty one
Swelter'd venom sleeping got,
Boil thou first i' the charmed pot.

10-11 The well-known refrain imitates the sound of a thick brew boiling. The purpose of the concoction is to increase the hardships and misfortunes of men.

12 **fillet of . . . snake:** slice of a snake bred in fens or marshes.

14 **newt:** amphibian creature allied to the salamander, which is a lizard-like creature that is supposed to live in fire.

15 **wool:** down.

16 **fork:** forked tongue; **blind-worm:** slow-worm, a small, harmless reptile classified between the snake and the lizard.

17 **howlet:** owl or owlet.

23 **mummy:** a medicinal preparation, liquid or dry, made from mummified bodies. The latter type of this common drug was made from "the dried flesh of human bodies embalmed with myrrh and spice" (Johnson); **maw and gulf:** Both words mean *stomach*.

24 **ravin'd:** glutted. Some interpret it as *ravenous*. The former seems more repulsive and therefore more appropriate.

25 **root of . . . dark:** If dug up by night, the already poisonous plant would be still more deadly. Socrates drank a potion made from it.

26 **blaspheming:** uttering profanity. (Intolerant Elizabethans would so interpret his beliefs.)

27 **yew:** an evergreen tree planted in graveyards and used to make bows. It was said that birds eating the red berries either died or lost their feathers.

28 **sliver'd:** cut off; **moon's eclipse:** In such a time of darkness, black magic was most potent.

29 **Turk, Tartar:** Since Turks and Tartars were infidels, these items would be regarded as powerful for evil.

30 The babe would also be unchristened.

31 **drab:** prostitute.

32 **slab:** slimy; a most expressive word.

33 **chaudron:** entrails.

39-43 The contrast between the grisly, ghoulish incantation of the three Witches and Hecate's insipid speech makes it clear that Hecate is not Shakespeare's creation; S.D. **Black spirits:** The song is found in Middleton's *The Witch*; it begins: "Black spirits and white, red spirits and grey, / Mingle, mingle, mingle, you that mingle may!"

All. Double, double, toil and trouble;   10
  Fire burn, and cauldron bubble.
Second Witch. Fillet of a fenny snake,
  In the cauldron boil and bake;
  Eye of newt, and toe of frog,
  Wool of bat, and tongue of dog;   15
  Adder's fork, and blind-worm's sting,
  Lizard's leg, and howlet's wing;
  For a charm of powerful trouble,
  Like a hell-broth, boil and bubble.
All. Double, double, toil and trouble,   20
  Fire burn, and cauldron bubble.
Third Witch. Scale of dragon, tooth of wolf,
  Witches' mummy, maw and gulf
  Of the ravin'd salt-sea shark;
  Root of hemlock, digg'd i' the dark;   25
  Liver of blaspheming Jew,
  Gall of goat, and slips of yew
  Sliver'd in the moon's eclipse;
  Nose of Turk, and Tartar's lips;
  Finger of birth-strangled babe,   30
  Ditch-deliver'd by a drab,
  Make the gruel thick and slab:
  Add thereto a tiger's chaudron,
  For the ingredients of our cauldron.
All. Double, double, toil and trouble,   35
  Fire burn, and cauldron bubble.
Second Witch. Cool it with a baboon's blood,
  Then the charm is firm and good.
      Enter Hecate to the other three Witches.
Hecate. O, well done! I commend your pains,
  And every one shall share i' the gains: 40
  And now about the cauldron sing,
  Like elves and fairies in a ring,
  Enchanting all that you put in.
          Music and a song: "Black spirits," etc.

44 **pricking:** "Pins and needles" were a premonition of something to come.

48 **How now . . . hags:** Macbeth's entrance is violent and abrupt. Even though he has come to get help from the Witches, he is defiant and hostile. A harried modern executive would go to his psychiatrist.

49 **A deed . . . name:** It is the more hideous and horrible for being nameless.

50 **conjure:** charge; **by that . . . profess:** in the name of your black art.

52-54 **untie the winds:** In Greek mythology, Aeolus gave Odysseus a leather bag containing all the unfavourable winds; the latter's inquisitive companions "untied" it and released the gales. Shakespeare probably knew this story; **untie the . . . churches:** a vigorous aerial tournament. We picture the hurricanes charging the steeples as Don Quixote once attacked the windmills; **yesty:** foaming, frothy; **though the . . . up:** a vivid picture of a wild and surging sea; **confound:** destroy; **navigation:** ships.

55 **bladed corn:** unripe grain; **lodg'd:** beaten down.

56-58 **topple:** totter and fall; a very imitative word; **warders:** sentinels, keepers; **though castles . . . foundations:** the image of an earthquake; **slope:** bend.

59 **germins:** seeds, the creative power of the universe; **tumble all together:** Such a disaster would make nature barren or cause it to produce hideous deformities and mutations. We are reminded of the effect of atomic fallout and the results of certain modern drugs.

60 **sicken:** become surfeited and weary of its work of horror; **answer me:** The command is curt.

50-61 Macbeth's images of cosmic destruction show him pitting his puny will against the universe in stubborn defiance; nothing matters as long as he gets his own way.

63 **masters:** The Witches are "instruments of darkness"; **Call 'em . . . 'em:** Macbeth is scornful.

65-66 **nine farrow:** litter of nine. Unnatural behaviour such as this caused a sow to be stoned to death, according to the laws of the Scottish King, Kenneth II; **grease that's . . . gibbet:** This is the final and most revolting detail of the Witches' brew. We cannot but marvel at Shakespeare's fertile imagination.

67 **high or low:** of more or less importance in Satan's kingdom.

68 **office:** function; **deftly:** aptly; S.D. **an armed Head:** Macbeth's own head, cut off by Macduff. Since he does not recognize it, dramatic irony is created by the words. (Comment on the theory that the head is Macduff's.)

Second Witch.   By the pricking of my thumbs,
   Something wicked this way comes: 45
   Open locks,
   Whoever knocks!
      Enter Macbeth.
Macbeth.   How now, you secret, black, and midnight hags!
   What is't you do?
All.   A deed without a name.
Macbeth.   I conjure you, by that which you profess,   50
   (Howe'er you come to know it) answer me:
   Though you untie the winds, and let them fight
   Against the churches; though the yesty waves
   Confound and swallow navigation up;
   Though bladed corn be lodg'd, and trees blown down,   55
   Though castles topple on their warders' heads;
   Though palaces and pyramids do slope
   Their heads to their foundations; though the treasure
   Of nature's germins tumble all together,
   Even till destruction sicken; answer me   60
   To what I ask you.
First Witch.   Speak.
Second Witch.   Demand.
Third Witch.   We'll answer.
First Witch.   Say, if thou'dst rather hear it from our mouths,
   Or from our masters.
Macbeth.   Call 'em: let me see 'em.
First Witch.   Pour in sow's blood, that hath eaten
   Her nine farrow; grease that's sweaten   65
   From the murderer's gibbet throw
   Into the flame.
All.   Come high or low:
   Thyself and office deftly show!
      Thunder. First Apparition: an armed Head.
Macbeth.   Tell me, thou unknown power,—
First Witch.   He knows thy thought:
   Hear his speech, but say thou nought.   70

71 Note the triple salutation.
72 S.D. **Descends:** an indication that the trap-door was used.
73 **good caution:** timely word of warning.
74 **harp'd:** guessed.
76 **more potent:** more powerful, since it represents Macduff; S.D. **a bloody Child:** Macduff, who was "from his mother's womb/ Untimely ripp'd" (V. viii. 15-16).
78 **three ears:** a reference to the triple salutation; as we would say: "I am all ears"; *i.e.,* paying close attention.
83 **make assurance double sure:** take no chances.
84 **take a . . . fate:** By killing Macduff, he will make fate give him some security.
85 **that I . . . lies:** Macbeth will be able to dismiss his cowardly fears.
86 **thunder:** of his own conscience. He still has sleepless nights; S.D. **a Child . . . hand:** Malcolm, the rightful heir, is holding in his hand a branch such as he later in the play ordered his soldiers to carry before them to conceal the numbers of his army.
88-89 **round and top:** the crown, circular in shape and representing the summit—kingship. (Comment on the theory that the Child represents James I, bearing his "family tree".)
90 **Be lion-mettled:** Have the courage of the king of beasts. Macbeth's physical courage is never in question; **proud:** Macbeth's pride is one of his salient characteristics.
91 **chafes:** shows irritation, fumes.
93 **Birnam:** See map, p. xliii; a high hill north-west of Perth, about twelve miles from Dunsinane; it is thought that Birnam Wood extented to within four or five miles of Dunsinane; **Dunsinane:** See map, p. xliii; a hill about 1,012 feet in altitude, approximately seven miles north-east of Perth. On its summit are the remains of a hill-fort locally known as Macbeth's Castle.
94 **That will never be:** Macbeth is supremely confident.
95 **impress:** force into service, as if by means of a press-gang. The dramatic irony is evident: little does Macbeth realize what Malcolm, as the unconscious agent of destiny, will do.
96 **bodements:** prophecies, portents.

First Apparition.   Macbeth! Macbeth! Macbeth! beware
    Macduff,
   Beware the thane of Fife. Dismiss me: enough.
                                     Descends.
Macbeth.   Whate'er thou art, for thy good caution, thanks;
   Thou hast harp'd my fear aright: but one word more,—
First Witch.   He will not be commanded: here's another,   75
   More potent than the first.
           Thunder. Second Apparition: a bloody Child.
Second Apparition.   Macbeth! Macbeth! Macbeth!
Macbeth.   Had I three ears, I'ld hear thee.
Second Apparition.   Be bloody, bold, and resolute; laugh
   to scorn
   The power of man: for none of woman born   80
   Shall harm Macbeth.   *Descends.*
Macbeth.   Then live, Macduff: what need I fear of thee?
   But yet I'll make assurance double sure,
   And take a bond of fate: thou shalt not live,
   That I may tell pale-hearted fear it lies;   85
   And sleep in spite of thunder.
          Thunder. Third Apparition: a Child crowned,
          with a tree in his hand.
                           What is this,
   That rises like the issue of a king,
   And wears upon his baby-brow the round
   And top of sovereignty?
All.   Listen, but speak not to't.
Third Apparition.   Be lion-mettled, proud, and take no
   care   90
   Who chafes, who frets, or where conspirers are:
   Macbeth shall never vanquish'd be until
   Great Birnam wood to high Dunsinane hill
   Shall come against him.   *Descends.*
Macbeth.   That will never be:
   Who can impress the forest, bid the tree   95
   Unfix his earth-bound root? Sweet bodements! good!

97 **rebellious dead:** so F, in the sense of the troubled ghost of Banquo. Theobald's emendation was *rebellion's head.*

99 **lease of nature:** normal span of life.

100 **mortal custom:** natural death.

101 **throbs:** This word, at the beginning of the line, emphasizes the intensity of Macbeth's emotion.

104 **I will be satisfied:** Note the future of determination.

106 **sinks:** The cauldron disappears through the trap-door to provide a clear view of the procession; **noise:** music; to conceal the sound of the vanishing cauldron; S.D. **hautboys:** *haut bois,* "high wood" instruments, oboes.

107 **Show:** Reveal the future.

111 S.D. **A show of eight Kings:** These figures represent the Stewart dynasty: Robert II (son of Walter Steward, Banquo's descendant, who married the granddaughter of Robert Bruce), Robert III, and six Jameses. (James VI of Scotland became James I of England. His mother, Mary Queen of Scots, is not shown, since the prophecy referred only to kings.) **glass:** mirror.

113 **sear:** scorch. The sight is blinding.

114 **gold-bound:** circled with a crown.

116 **Why do . . . this:** It is ironic that what he insisted on seeing now fills him with fury; **Start:** Leap from your sockets. He has seen enough.

117 **crack of doom:** thunder-clap of the Day of Judgement.

119 **the eighth:** James I.

121 **two-fold balls:** twin orbs; this may refer to the double coronation of James at Scone and at Westminster; **treble sceptres:** usually interpreted to refer to Great Britain, France, and Ireland; some say they symbolize England (with Wales), Scotland, and Ireland.

122 **Horrible sight:** He sees Banquo.

123 **blood-bolter'd:** his hair matted with blood; **smiles:** With what emotion?

127 **sprites:** spirits.

Rebellious dead, rise never, till the wood
Of Birnam rise, and our high-plac'd Macbeth
Shall live the lease of nature, pay his breath
To time, and mortal custom. Yet my heart   100
Throbs to know one thing: tell me, if your art
Can tell so much: shall Banquo's issue ever
Reign in this kingdom?
All.   Seek to know no more.
Macbeth. I will be satisfied: deny me this,
And an eternal curse fall on you! Let me know: 105
Why sinks that cauldron? and what noise is this?
                                   Hautboys.

First Witch. Show!
Second Witch. Show!
Third Witch. Show!
All. Show his eyes, and grieve his heart,   110
Come like shadows, so depart!
          *A show of eight Kings, the last with a glass in
          his hand; Banquo's Ghost following.*
Macbeth. Thou art too like the spirit of Banquo: down!
Thy crown does sear mine eye-balls. And thy hair,
Thou other gold-bound brow, is like the first.
A third is like the former. Filthy hags!   115
Why do you show me this? A fourth? Start, eyes!
What, will the line stretch out to the crack of doom?
Another yet? A seventh? I'll see no more:
And yet the eighth appears, who bears a glass
Which shows me many more; and some I see   120
That two-fold balls and treble sceptres carry:
Horrible sight! Now I see 'tis true,
For the blood-bolter'd Banquo smiles upon me,
And points at them for his. What, is this so?
First Witch. Ay, sir, all this is so: but why   125
Stands Macbeth thus amazedly?
Come, sisters, cheer we up his sprites,
And show the best of our delights:

130 **antic round:** quaint round-dance, as opposed to a square-dance.

131-2 **that this . . . pay:** that Macbeth may say we have welcomed him respectfully. The lines are a bitter taunt.

125-32 These lines are regarded as spurious. See note on The Text, p. xxiv.

133 **pernicious:** deadly, fatal; a word that can be said with great vehemence.

134 **aye:** always.

135 S.D. Lennox presumably had been standing on guard outside the cavern.

138 **infected:** as with plague; **ride:** Witches are still thought of as riding through the air on broomsticks.

139 **damn'd all . . . them:** He pronounces a curse on himself.

142 **Fled to England?** Some editors prefer an exclamation mark to a question mark. Should Macbeth shout or whisper? Macbeth's faith in the prophecies will be strengthened as the first warning is validated. His amazement makes it difficult to explain the reference to "the king" in III. vi. 38.

144 **anticipat'st:** forestall'st; **dread exploits:** the murder of Macduff.

145-6 **flighty:** swift; **The flighty . . . it:** Unless one carries out his intentions immediately, his deeds can never keep pace with his plans. The image is of one bird overtaking another.

147-8 **The very . . . hand:** My first impulses will be translated immediately into action.

150-3 This ruthless plan is born of spite and frustration only.

153 **trace:** follow.

154 **deed, do:** The noun and the verb recur. What is their significance?

155 **sights:** Apparitions. From this moment, the link between Macbeth's conscience and his imagination appears to have snapped.

See also p. 180.

I'll charm the air to give a sound,
While you perform your antic round: 130
That this great king may kindly say,
Our duties did his welcome pay.

> *Music. The Witches dance, and then*
> *vanish, with Hecate.*

Macbeth.   Where are they? Gone? Let this pernicious hour
Stand aye accursed in the calendar!
Come in, without there!

> *Enter Lennox.*

Lennox.   What's your grace's will?   135
Macbeth.   Saw you the weird sisters?
Lennox.   No, my lord.
Macbeth.   Came they not by you?
Lennox.   No indeed, my lord.
Macbeth.   Infected be the air whereon they ride,
And damn'd all those that trust them! I did hear
The galloping of horse: who was 't came by?   140
Lennox.   'Tis two or three, my lord, that bring you word
Macduff is fled to England.
Macbeth.   Fled to England?
Lennox.   Ay, my good lord.
Macbeth (aside).   Time, thou anticipat'st my dread exploits:
The flighty purpose never is o'ertook   145
Unless the deed go with it: from this moment
The very firstlings of my heart shall be
The firstlings of my hand. And even now,
To crown my thoughts with acts, be it thought and
   done:
The castle of Macduff I will surprise,   150
Seize upon Fife; give to the edge o' the sword
His wife, his babes, and all unfortunate souls
That trace him in his line. No boasting like a fool;
This deed I'll do before this purpose cool,
But no more sights!—Where are these gentlemen?   155
Come, bring me where they are.   *Exeunt.*

S.D. Macduff's castle: Two quadrangular towers on the coast of Fife about three miles from Dysart are said to be the ruins of Macduff's castle.

1 Lady Macduff's question introduces an interrupted scene. What information is supplied in the question? What is her mood?

2 **patience:** self-control.   3 **His flight was madness:** Why?

4 **Our fears . . . traitors:** The fact that he fled lays him open to the charge of treason.

7 **titles:** possessions; those things to which he was "entitled".

9 **wants the natural touch:** lacks natural human affections; **wren:** Lady Macduff's indignation makes her exaggerate the characteristics of the wren.

12 **All is . . . love:** His fear for himself is greater than his love for his family.

14 **My dearest coz:** Ross's connection with the family makes it logical that he should once more be the bearer of news.

1-14 It is evident that Macduff left his family without discussing the reason for his going, without bidding them farewell, and without taking measures for their safety. In answer to the first, it may be argued that he did not wish to implicate them. In answer to the second, it may be stated that his affection would have triumphed over his patriotic purpose. Finally, he may have felt that Macbeth, villain though he knew the King to be, would be incapable of the savage behaviour illustrated in IV. ii. Like some of the men who escaped from occupied countries in World War II, Macduff may have had to face a conflict of loyalties and to choose between his country and his family.

15 **school:** control. 16 Note Ross's analysis of Macduff's character.

16-17 **knows the . . . season:** understands the violent disorders of the time. The metaphor is drawn from recurring bouts of fever; **I dare . . . further:** Ross looks around fearfully, as though the walls themselves had ears.

19-20 **and do . . . ourselves:** without realizing it. Under such tyranny, many men would be accused of treachery, as Macbeth willed that they should be; **when we . . . fear:** when our fears make us credit vague reports, even though our fears themselves are indefinable.

21-22 **but float . . . move:** We are like rudderless ships drifting this way and that at the mercy of the waves.

25 **My pretty cousin:** addressed to young Macduff. Small boys in Shakespeare are frequently precocious, and many came to tragic ends. In them Shakespeare may be portraying his own son Hamnet, who died in 1596 at the age of eleven.

Scene 2

FIFE. MACDUFF'S CASTLE.

Enter Lady Macduff, her Son, and Ross.

Lady Macduff.   What had he done, to make him fly the
    land?
Ross.   You must have patience, madam.
Lady Macduff.   He had none:
    His flight was madness: when our actions do not,
    Our fears do make us traitors.
Ross.   You know not
    Whether it was his wisdom, or his fear.   5
Lady Macduff.   Wisdom? to leave his wife, to leave his
        babes,
    His mansion, and his titles, in a place
    From whence himself does fly? He loves us not;
    He wants the natural touch. For the poor wren
    (The most diminutive of birds) will fight,   10
    Her young ones in her nest, against the owl.
    All is the fear, and nothing is the love;
    As little is the wisdom, where the flight
    So runs against all reason.
Ross.   My dearest coz,
    I pray you school yourself: but, for your husband,   15
    He is noble, wise, judicious, and best knows
    The fits o' the season. I dare not speak much further,
    But cruel are the times, when we are traitors
    And do not know ourselves; when we hold rumour
    From what we fear, yet know not what we fear,   20
    But float upon a wild and violent sea
    Each way and move. I take my leave of you:
    Shall not be long but I'll be here again:
    Things at the worst will cease, or else climb upward,
    To what they were before. My pretty cousin,   25

27 **Father'd he . . . fatherless:** Lady Macduff speaks bitterly in this paradox.

28-29 **I am . . . discomfort:** Ross is close to tears.

30 **Sirrah:** sometimes used by parents to children; **your father's dead:** Lady Macduff speaks out of the heaviness of her heart.

33 **with:** on.

34 **lime:** birdlime, a sticky substance spread on twigs to entangle birds that were eaten as food.

35 **pitfall:** a fowler's snare; **gin:** trap, snare.

36 **poor:** as opposed to rich. He is too insignificant to be bothered with. In view of his fate, this is dramatic irony.

40 **Why, I . . . market:** Lady Macduff speaks with wry humour.

41 **Then you'll . . . again:** a shrewd remark, which points up the fact that the boy knows that his father is not dead and that his mother really loves her husband.

42-43 Lady Macduff implies that her son has spoken truly.

44, 46, 48, 50, 52 The use of questions is characteristic of a child, but the logical succession indicates that this child is old for his years.

45 **that he was:** Lady Macduff means that he was a traitor to her.

49 **a traitor . . . hanged:** This is considered to be a reference to the Jesuit Garnet, the equivocator mentioned in II. iii. 8 by the Porter. This allusion may help to date the play, although some editors consider it a later interpolation.

Blessing upon you!
Lady Macduff.   Father'd he is, and yet he's fatherless.
Ross.   I am so much a fool, should I stay longer,
   It would be my disgrace and your discomfort:
   I take my leave at once.   *Exit.*
Lady Macduff.   Sirrah, your father's dead,   30
   And what will you do now? How will you live?
Son.   As birds do, mother.
Lady Macduff.   What, with worms and flies?
Son.   With what I get, I mean, and so do they.
Lady Macduff.   Poor bird, thou'ldst never fear the net
      nor lime,
   The pitfall, nor the gin.   35
Son.   Why should I, mother? Poor birds they are not
      set for.
   My father is not dead, for all your saying.
Lady Macduff.   Yes, he is dead: how wilt thou do for
      a father?
Son.   Nay, how will you do for a husband?
Lady Macduff.   Why, I can buy me twenty at any market.   40
Son.   Then you'll buy 'em to sell again.
Lady Macduff.   Thou speak'st with all thy wit, and yet,
      i' faith,
   With wit enough for thee.
Son.   Was my father a traitor, mother?
Lady Macduff.   Ay, that he was.   45
Son.   What is a traitor?
Lady Macduff.   Why, one that swears, and lies.
Son.   And be all traitors that do so?
Lady Macduff.   Every one that does so is a traitor, and
      must be hang'd.
Son.   And must they all be hang'd that swear and lie?   50
Lady Macduff.   Every one.
Son.   Who must hang them?
Lady Macduff.   Why, the honest men.
Son.   Then the liars and swearers are fools; for there are

54-56 Then the . . . them: so cynical and yet so young! But Young
Macduff falls victim to the evil forces he seems to be aware of.

57 monkey: a term of endearment.

59-61 If he . . . father: another precocious statement; this one
shows the child's use of inescapable logic, so realistic as to be
almost satirical.

62 S.D. Enter a messenger: Some editors believe him to be one
of the murderers who has managed to come in advance of his
companions in order to give a warning. Others support the
idea that he comes from Lady Macbeth. "He is a welcome reminder that all have not been corrupted by Macbeth's tyranny"
(Muir).

64 in your . . . perfect: I know well that you are Lady Macduff.

65 doubt: fear.

66 homely: simple, plain.

68-70 To fright . . . person: Even to frighten you like this is
brutal; to do worse would be sheer savagery, but this savagery
is already much too close to you.

73-75 I am . . . folly: a bitter comment on human depravity.
Shakespeare was well aware of the problem of human suffering, especially the suffering of the innocent; **sometime:** at times.

76 womanly: feminine.

78 S.D. Murderers: How likely is it that Macbeth would employ
the same murderers he had used before?

79 Where is your husband: What is the purpose of the question?

80-81 I hope . . . him: Lady Macduff's spirited defence of her
husband and brave rebuke of the Murderers win our anguished
pity and prove that fundamentally she loved and trusted
Macduff; **unsanctified:** unholy; *i.e.,* hell.

82 Thou liest . . . villain: This courageous defiance adds to the
tragic pathos; **shag-hair'd:** shaggy-haired, unkempt and vil-
lainous in appearance. F reads *shag-ear'd*; **you egg:** This type
of grim pun was also used in the murder of Banquo; viz., "Let
it come down."

liars and swearers enow to beat the honest men, and   55
hang up them.

Lady Macduff.   Now, God help thee, poor monkey!
But how wilt thou do for a father?

Son.   If he were dead, you'ld weep for him: if you
would not, it were a good sign that I should quickly   60
have a new father.

Lady Macduff.   Poor prattler, how thou talk'st!

      Enter a Messenger.

Messenger.   Bless you fair dame! I am not to you known,
Though in your state of honour I am perfect;
I doubt some danger does approach you nearly: 65
If you will take a homely man's advice,
Be not found here; hence, with your little ones.
To fright you thus, methinks I am too savage;
To do worse to you were fell cruelty,
Which is too nigh your person. Heaven preserve
   you!   70
I dare abide no longer.   *Exit.*

Lady Macduff.   Whither should I fly?
I have done no harm. But I remember now
I am in this earthly world, where to do harm
Is often laudable, to do good sometime
Accounted dangerous folly: why then, alas,   75
Do I put up that womanly defence,
To say I have done no harm?
—What are these faces?

      Enter Murderers.

First Murderer.   Where is your husband?

Lady Macduff.   I hope in no place so unsanctified   80
Where such as thou mayst find him.

First Murderer.   He's a traitor.

Son.   Thou liest, thou shag-hair'd villain!

First Murderer.   What, you egg!
               Stabbing him.

Young fry of treachery!

83-84 **fry:** offspring. "Small fry" is still used of little children; **He has . . . you:** The little boy knows he has received a fatal wound, but his unselfish last words are directed to his mother. See also p. 181.

S.D. The entrance of Macduff immediately on the heels of the murder of his wife and family creates dramatic irony of a very poignant type.

1-4 Malcolm's words have a peculiar appropriateness in the light of what has just occurred onstage; **Let us . . . birthdom:** The metaphor is drawn from the fighting of that time when one man would stand over a fallen comrade and fight to protect him. Here, Scotland is personified; **hold fast:** grasp firmly; **mortal:** death-dealing.

6-8 **strike heaven . . . dolour:** a rather unusual metaphor, meaning "slap the sky's face so that the smack echoes as if heaven shared Scotland's woes and uttered a similar cry of sorrow or distress".

10 **to friend:** favourable.

12 **sole:** mere.

13 **you have . . . well:** This fact makes Macbeth's behaviour the more reprehensible.

14 **He hath . . . yet:** another example of the dramatic irony in which the play abounds; **young:** hence, not a threat.

15 **deserve:** Theobald's emendation. F has *discern*; **wisdom:** Supply *it would be* in this elliptical phrase.

16-17 **lamb, god:** the image of sacrifice. Malcolm shrewdly hints that Macduff has offended Macbeth and Malcolm's death is the price of his return to favour.

8-17 Malcolm's evident caution gives the impression that some time has passed.

18 **I am not treacherous:** a characteristic example of Macduff's terseness of expression.

19-20 **A good . . . charge:** an image from gunnery. A man, noble in nature, may stoop to evil or fall back from what is good (recoil) if he is sent on a royal mission (charge).

21 **That which . . . transpose:** My thoughts cannot alter your character, whether it is good or bad.

Son.   He has kill'd me, mother:
  Run away, I pray you!   *Dies.*
                    Exit Lady Macduff, crying "Murder!"
                    Exeunt murderers, following her.

[Dramatic Irony]

Scene 3

ENGLAND. BEFORE THE
KING'S PALACE.

Enter Malcolm and Macduff.

Malcolm.   Let us seek out some desolate shade, and there
  Weep our sad bosoms empty.
Macduff.   Let us rather
  Hold fast the mortal sword, and like good men
  Bestride our down-fall'n birthdom: each new morn
  New widows howl, new orphans cry, new sorrows   5
  Strike heaven on the face, that it resounds
  As if it felt with Scotland, and yell'd out
  Like syllable of dolour.
Malcolm.   What I believe, I'll wail;
  What know, believe; and what I can redress,
  As I shall find the time to friend, I will.   10
  What you have spoke, it may be so perchance.
  This tyrant, whose sole name blisters our tongues,
  Was once thought honest: you have lov'd him well;
  He hath not touch'd you yet. I am young; but something *[Dramatic*
  You may deserve of him through me, and wisdom   15 *irony]*
  To offer up a weak, poor, innocent lamb
  To appease an angry god.
Macduff.   I am not treacherous.
Malcolm.   But Macbeth is.
  A good and virtuous nature may recoil
  In an imperial charge. But I shall crave your pardon: 20
  That which you are, my thoughts cannot transpose;

22 **Angels are . . . fell:** a reference to Lucifer who was cast out of heaven because of his rebellion against God. The brightest of angels, he became Satan. (The story is developed in Milton's "Paradise Lost" and is based on medieval tradition.) The line is one of the most memorable in the play, with its suggestion of brilliance in the repetition of "bright" and the imitative word "fell" at the end of the line to suggest the plunge from heaven to hell. It offers consolation for the crash of a fallen idol. Perhaps, there is an indirect reference to Macbeth, who is sometimes compared to Satan.

23-24 **Though all . . . so:** Even though an appearance of goodness may conceal inner wickedness, inner goodness still reveals itself in an outer appearance of goodness. (You look honourable; you may be so at heart.) The passage recalls Duncan's comment: "There's no art/To find the mind's construction in the face" (I. iv. 11-12); **hopes:** of succour for Scotland.

25-28 **Perchance even . . . leave-taking:** Your coming raised your hopes, but it has made me suspicious, since you have left your family unprotected. Knowing what he does of Macbeth, Malcolm cannot but assume that there is an understanding between Macduff and Macbeth; **rawness:** unprotected condition; **motives:** influences, objects or persons that can inspire love; **knots of love:** symbols of the strength of love.

29-30 **Let not . . . safeties:** Do not let my suspicions cast doubts upon your honour; I am only acting to preserve my own safety.

32 **tyranny:** personified as a tyrant, possibly Macbeth; **sure:** confidently.

33 **goodness dare . . . thee:** Malcolm will not call you to account; **wear thou thy wrongs:** possibly, the garment image. Enjoy your ill-gotten gains, as though they were a royal mantle.

34 **The title is affeer'd:** Your right is confirmed. Macduff ironically implies that Macbeth is not to be regarded as a usurper.

37 **the rich East:** The East India Company was founded in 1600, and the profits made by investors were fabulous; **to boot:** in addition. 38 **fear:** distrust.

39 **beneath the yoke:** symbolic of servitude and heavy burdens.

42 **my right:** what is rightfully mine, the throne.

43 **gracious England:** the saintly Edward (the Confessor).

45-46 **when I . . . sword:** a foreshadowing of Macbeth's fate at the hands, however, of Macduff; **wear:** bear.

49 **by:** at the hands of; **what should:** what sort of man could. Having tested Macduff's loyalty, Malcolm proceeds to test his moral standards.

Angels are bright still, though the brightest fell:
Though all things foul would wear the brows of grace,
Yet grace must still look so.
Macduff.   I have lost my hopes.
Malcolm.   Perchance even there where I did find my
    doubts.   25
Why in that rawness left you wife and child,
Those precious motives, those strong knots of love,
Without leave-taking? I pray you,
Let not my jealousies be your dishonours,
But mine own safeties. You may be rightly just,   30
Whatever I shall think.
Macduff.   Bleed, bleed, poor country:
Great tyranny, lay thou thy basis sure,
For goodness dare not check thee: wear thou thy
    wrongs;
The title is affeer'd. Fare thee well, lord:
I would not be the villain that thou think'st   35
For the whole space that's in the tyrant's grasp,
And the rich East to boot.
Malcolm.   Be not offended:
I speak not as in absolute fear of you:
I think our country sinks beneath the yoke,
It weeps, it bleeds, and each new day a gash   40
Is added to her wounds: I think withal
There would be hands uplifted in my right;
And here from gracious England have I offer
Of goodly thousands: but for all this,
When I shall tread upon the tyrant's head,   45
Or wear it on my sword, yet my poor country
Shall have more vices than it had before,
More suffer, and more sundry ways than ever,
By him that shall succeed.
Macduff.   What should he be?
Malcolm.   It is myself I mean: in whom I know   50
All the particulars of vice so grafted

51-52 **all the . . . open'd:** The metaphor is drawn from gardening. The special kinds of evil are so firmly incorporated (grafted) on the original stock that when they are fully revealed (opened, like buds); **black Macbeth:** a far cry indeed from the "brave", "noble" Macbeth of the opening act. Note the contrast between "black" (evil) and *snow, lamb* (purity and innocence).

55-57 **confineless harms:** unlimited vices; **Not in . . . Macbeth:** Macduff's vehemence emerges in the order of his words and the alliteration; **top:** surpass.

57-59 **luxurious:** lustful. We have not seen evidence of lechery or greed in Macbeth. Malcolm, however, is about to accuse himself of all the vicious evils he can think of. It has been suggested that James I would listen with interest to these negative charges. The philosophy of kingship was a subject that attracted him; **bloody, luxurious, malicious:** How many of these qualities has Macbeth exhibited? **sudden:** impetuously violent.

61 **voluptuousness:** love of sensual pleasures.

63 **cistern:** used by Shakespeare to suggest a cesspool.

64 **continent impediments:** restraining limitations; the picture is that of a river overflowing its banks. Shakespeare had no doubt observed the flooding of the Avon in his native Warwickshire. 65 **will:** desire.

60-66 **but there's . . . reign:** It has been suggested that Malcolm would play this part of the scene, including his later self-accusations, with his back turned to Macduff. Why?

66-67 **boundless intemperance in nature:** lack of control over natural appetites. This constitutes a form of tyranny in that a man cannot curb his inordinate desires any more than a slave can obtain his freedom. Both man and slave are under the control of a dominant power.

68 **untimely:** premature.

70 **what is yours:** the kingship. 71 **convey:** secretly manage.

72 **cold:** unemotional; **the time:** the world; **hoodwink:** deceive.

74 **vulture:** An insatiable appetite is compared to a bird of prey.

73-76 **There cannot . . . inclined:** As King he would have no difficulty obtaining mistresses. Macduff seems prepared to overlook this fault.

77 **ill-composed affection:** evil disposition. 78 **stanchless:** insatiable.

80 **his:** this man's. Note the type of possessions then considered desirable: lands, jewels, houses.

81-82 **And my . . . more:** The more I had, the more I would want, just as a sauce increases the appetite; **that:** so that; **forge:** invent, fabricate.

That, when they shall be open'd, black Macbeth
Will seem as pure as snow, and the poor state
Esteem him as a lamb, being compar'd
With my confineless harms.
Macduff.　　　　　　　Not in the legions　　　55
Of horrid hell can come a devil more damn'd
In evils, to top Macbeth.
Malcolm.　　　　　I grant him bloody,
Luxurious, avaricious, false, deceitful,
Sudden, malicious, smacking of every sin
That has a name: but there's no bottom, none,　　60
In my voluptuousness: your wives, your daughters,
Your matrons, and your maids, could not fill up
The cistern of my lust, and my desire
All continent impediments would o'erbear,
That did oppose my will: better Macbeth　　　65
Than such an one to reign.
Macduff.　　　　　　Boundless intemperance
In nature is a tyranny; it hath been
The untimely emptying of the happy throne,
And fall of many kings. But fear not yet
To take upon you what is yours: you may　　　70
Convey your pleasures in a spacious plenty,
And yet seem cold, the time you may so hoodwink:
We have willing dames enough; there cannot be
That vulture in you, to devour so many
As will to greatness dedicate themselves,　　　75
Finding it so inclined.
Malcolm.　　　　　With this there grows
In my most ill-compos'd affection, such
A stanchless avarice, that, were I king,
I should cut off the nobles for their lands,
Desire his jewels, and this other's house:　　　80
And my more-having would be as a sauce
To make me hunger more, that I should forge
Quarrels unjust against the good and loyal,

85 **sticks:** goes; **pernicious:** deadly, a word Shakespeare seemed to like. Cf. IV. i. 133.

86 **summer-seeming lust:** Lust seems like summer in that it too flames hotly and fades away; it is a passion associated with youth and thus with the summer of one's years on earth.

87 **sword:** a metaphor implying that the death of many a king has been caused by his greed for gain. 88 **foisons:** plenty.

89 **of your mere own:** of that which rightfully belongs to you, royal property; **portable:** bearable.

90 **graces weigh'd:** virtues counterbalanced.

84-90 Macduff is still hopeful that Malcolm will make a better king than Macbeth. Malcolm continues with the testing, piling vice on vice.

91 **the king-becoming graces:** Shakespeare's recipe for a good king.

92 **temperance:** self-control, moderation.

93 **perseverance:** Accent the second syllable. 94 **fortitude:** constancy.

91-94 Comment on the validity of these qualities in a sovereign. "The most nearly perfect picture in Shakespeare of the ideal king" (Goddard).

95 **relish:** hint, trace.

96 **division:** descant, variation; a metaphor drawn from music; **several:** separate. 97 **acting:** a metaphor drawn from the stage.

95-97 Malcolm asserts that he is guilty of all the permutations and combinations of evil.

98 **pour the . . . hell:** banish all kindliness from earth.

99 **uproar:** throw into confusion; **confound:** destroy.

97-100 **Nay, had . . . earth:** Malcolm ends with a horrific climax.

100 Macduff's first thoughts are for his country.

102-3 **Fit to . . . live:** Macduff's words would be music to Malcolm's ears.

104 **with an . . . bloody-scepter'd:** ruled by a usurper who won and retains his sceptre by bloodshed.

107 **interdiction:** exclusion; a term in Scottish law whereby a person may resign conduct of his affairs to another.

108-11 **blaspheme his breed:** slander his own parentage; **Thy royal . . . king:** Note the description of Duncan; Shakespeare developed this aspect of Duncan's character, which is not found in Holinshed; **the queen . . . liv'd:** Malcolm's mother died to sin daily in her prayers. This is the only reference to the late Queen of Scotland. 112 **repeat'st upon:** recit'st against.

114 **this noble passion:** righteous indignation. This proves what Malcolm has been trying to establish; namely, not merely that Macduff hates Macbeth, but that he hates evil.

115 **child of integrity:** born of uprightness.

Destroying them for wealth.
Macduff.   This avarice
  Sticks deeper, grows with more pernicious root   85
  Than summer-seeming lust, and it hath been
  The sword of our slain kings: yet do not fear;
  Scotland hath foisons to fill up your will
  Of your mere own: all these are portable,
  With other graces weigh'd.   90
Malcolm.   But I have none: the king-becoming graces,
  As justice, verity, temperance, stableness,
  Bounty, perseverance, mercy, lowliness,
  Devotion, patience, courage, fortitude,
  I have no relish of them, but abound   95
  In the division of each several crime,
  Acting it many ways. Nay, had I power, I should
  Pour the sweet milk of concord into hell,
  Uproar the universal peace, confound
  All unity on earth.
Macduff.   O Scotland, Scotland!   100
Malcolm.   If such a one be fit to govern, speak:
  I am as I have spoken.
Macduff.   Fit to govern?
  No, not to live. O nation miserable!
  With an untitled tyrant, bloody-scepter'd,
  When shalt thou see thy wholesome days again,   105
  Since that the truest issue of thy throne
  By his own interdiction stands accurs'd,
  And does blaspheme his breed? Thy royal father
  Was a most sainted king: the queen that bore thee,
  Oftener upon her knees than on her feet,   110
  Died every day she liv'd. Fare thee well!
  These evils thou repeat'st upon thyself
  Have banish'd me from Scotland. O my breast,
  Thy hope ends here!
Malcolm.   Macduff, this noble passion,
  Child of integrity, hath from my soul   115

116 **scruples:** suspicions.
118 **trains:** schemes, stratagems; a metaphor drawn from hawking or hunting, where the "train" is bait laid down to lure the prey. A negative quality of Macbeth's character is revealed here.
119 **modest wisdom:** restraining prudence.
121 **deal between . . . me:** control our dealings.
123 **unspeak mine own detraction:** take back the charges I made against myself.
125 **for:** as.
126 **was forsworn:** perjured myself.
129 **fellow:** comrade, equal.
132 **thine and . . . command:** at the service of Scotland, which is your country and mine.
125-32 **I am . . . command:** Note Malcolm's character sketch of himself. "He seems to have inherited the gentleness of his father along with a greater valour" (Goddard).
134 **Siward:** See III. vi. 31.
133-5 **before thy . . . forth:** Was Macduff's errand unnecessary? **at a point:** fully equipped and ready.
136-7 **the chance . . . quarrel:** May our prospects of success be in proportion to the justice of our dispute (in which case we shall be victorious); **Why are you silent:** It is easy to understand why Macduff would be dumbfounded by this sudden reversal. We cannot help feeling sorry for him; he has been so earnest and serious; nevertheless, Malcolm could not afford to take any chances.
139 S.D. **Enter a Doctor:** This episode is frequently omitted on the stage and seems to have been introduced as a compliment to King James. Some argue that it helps to date the play; others, that it is an interpolation.
140 **the king:** Edward the Confessor.
142-3 **stay:** await; **convinces the . . . art:** baffles the utmost efforts of medical skill; **at his touch:** The healing power was supposed to have come from the fact that the King's hands were anointed with holy oil at his coronation.
145 **presently amend:** immediately improve.
146 **the evil:** scrofula; a morbid constitutional condition with glandular swellings and a tendency to consumption.

Wip'd the black scruples, reconcil'd my thoughts
To thy good truth and honour. Devilish Macbeth
By many of these trains hath sought to win me
Into his power; and modest wisdom plucks me
From over-credulous haste: but God above   120
Deal between thee and me! for even now
I put myself to thy direction, and
Unspeak mine own detraction; here abjure
The taints and blames I laid upon myself,
For strangers to my nature. I am yet   125
Unknown to woman, never was forsworn,
Scarcely have coveted what was mine own,
At no time broke my faith, would not betray
The devil to his fellow, and delight
No less in truth than life: my first false speaking   130
Was this upon myself: what I am truly,
Is thine and my poor country's to command:
Whither indeed, before thy here-approach,
Old Siward, with ten thousand warlike men,
Already at a point, was setting forth.   135
Now we'll together, and the chance of goodness
Be like our warranted quarrel! Why are you silent?
Macduff.   Such welcome and unwelcome things at once
    'Tis hard to reconcile.
        Enter a Doctor.
Malcolm.   Well, more anon. Comes the king forth, I
    pray you?   140
Doctor.   Ay, sir; there are a crew of wretched souls
    That stay his cure: their malady convinces
    The great assay of art; but at his touch,
    Such sanctity hath heaven given his hand,
    They presently amend.
Malcolm.   I thank you, doctor. *Exit Doctor.*   145
Macduff.   What's the disease he means?
Malcolm.   'Tis call'd the evil:
    A most miraculous work in this good king,

149 **solicits:** prevails by petition. James I ascribed his powers to prayer; though he was sceptical of the process, he continued to practise it.

150 **strangely-visited:** sorely afflicted.

152 **mere:** utter; **surgery:** the physician's art.

153 **golden stamp:** Each person received a gold coin worth ten shillings. Later, a medal was substituted; the one used by Queen Anne to "touch" Dr. Johnson is still in the British Museum.

155-6 **To the . . . benediction:** a deft compliment; **healing benediction:** blessed gift of healing; **virtue:** healing power. In what sense is "strange" used?

146-59 Edward's activities are in marked contrast to those of Macbeth.

159 S.D. **Enter Ross:** once more, the messenger.

160 **My countryman:** It has been suggested that Ross was wearing a typically Scottish item of clothing, perhaps a blue bonnet.

162 **betimes:** early, soon.

163 **means:** cause; **amen:** Cf. note on II. ii. 26.

164 Note Macduff's first question.

169 **not mark'd:** not noticed, because very common.

170-1 **a modern ecstasy:** a commonplace emotion; **the dead . . . who:** So common is this sound that no one asks for whom the bell tolls.

172 **flowers in their caps:** It is said that Highlanders on the march would stick a sprig of heather in their bonnets.

173 **dying or . . . sicken:** indicative of violent death; **relation:** report.

174 **nice:** precise, exact.

175 **That of . . . speaker:** News an hour old is stale and causes the speaker to be hissed for giving it.

176 **teems:** brings forth, produces. Ross's monosyllabic utterances imply that all is not well.

Which often, since my here-remain in England,
I have seen him do. How he solicits heaven
Himself best knows: but strangely-visited people,   150
All swoln and ulcerous, pitiful to the eye,
The mere despair of surgery, he cures,
Hanging a golden stamp about their necks,
Put on with holy prayers, and 'tis spoken
To the succeeding royalty he leaves   155
The healing benediction. With this strange virtue
He hath a heavenly gift of prophecy,
And sundry blessings hang about his throne
That speak him full of grace.
     Enter Ross.
Macduff.   See, who comes here?
Malcolm.   My countryman; but yet I know him not.   160
Macduff.   My ever gentle cousin, welcome hither.
Malcolm.   I know him now: good God, betimes remove
   The means that makes us strangers!
Ross.   Sir, amen.
Macduff.   Stands Scotland where it did?
Ross.   Alas, poor country!
   Almost afraid to know itself! It cannot   165
   Be call'd our mother, but our grave: where nothing,
   But who knows nothing, is once seen to smile;
   Where sighs, and groans, and shrieks that rend the air,
   Are made, not mark'd; where violent sorrow seems
   A modern ecstasy: the dead man's knell   170
   Is there scarce ask'd for who, and good men's lives
   Expire before the flowers in their caps,
   Dying or ere they sicken.
Macduff.   O, relation
   Too nice, and yet too true!
Malcolm.   What's the newest grief?
Ross.   That of an hour's age doth hiss the speaker;   175
   Each minute teems a new one.
Macduff.   How does my wife?

178 **batter'd at:** attacked. Macduff appears suspicious.
179 **well at peace:** The grave is peaceful. There is great dramatic irony in the remark.
180 **a niggard:** a stingy person. Macduff asks Ross not to be so terse.
182 **heavily:** with a heavy heart.
183 **out:** up in arms, in the field.
185 **power:** army.
186 **your:** Malcolm's.
188 **doff:** cast off, as of a hat or another article of clothing. The "d" sound is dominant. Note the garment image.
181-8 Ross cannot bring himself to break the dreadful news.
191-2 **An older . . . out:** Christendom (the kingdoms that acknowledge Christ) has no older or better soldier to show.
194 **would:** ought to.
195 **latch:** catch.
196 **fee-grief:** a sorrow peculiar to one person, a metaphor drawn from law. An estate held in *fee simple* is private property.
197 **due to:** owned by.
201 **Let not . . . ever:** The bearer of bad news was often associated with the news he bore. Sometimes, he was even slain.
202-3 **possess:** put in possession of; **the heaviest . . . heard:** The sound is like the tolling of a bell; **Humh:** This expression is intended to represent a sound of inarticulate anguish, as he suspects the worst.

Ross. Why, well.

Macduff.   And all my children?

Ross.   Well too.

Macduff. The tyrant has not batter'd at their peace?

Ross. No, they were well at peace, when I did leave 'em. [*dramatic irony*]

Macduff. Be not a niggard of your speech: how goes 't? 180

Ross. When I came hither to transport the tidings,
  Which I have heavily borne, there ran a rumour
  Of many worthy fellows that were out,
  Which was to my belief witness'd the rather,
  For that I saw the tyrant's power a-foot: 185
  Now is the time of help; your eye in Scotland
  Would create soldiers, make our women fight,
  To doff their dire distresses.

Malcolm.   Be 't their comfort
  We are coming thither: gracious England hath
  Lent us good Siward, and ten thousand men; 190
  An older and a better soldier none
  That Christendom gives out.

Ross.   Would I could answer
  This comfort with the like! But I have words
  That would be howl'd out in the desert air,
  Where hearing should not latch them.

Macduff.   What concern they, 195
  The general cause, or is it a fee-grief
  Due to some single breast?

Ross.   No mind that's honest
  But in it shares some woe, though the main part
  Pertains to you alone.

Macduff.   If it be mine,
  Keep it not from me, quickly let me have it. 200

Ross. Let not your ears despise my tongue for ever,
  Which shall possess them with the heaviest sound
  That ever yet they heard.

Macduff.   Humh! I guess at it.

Ross. Your castle is surpris'd; your wife and babes,

205-7 **to relate . . . you:** To give the details would kill you and thus add your body to the heap of the slain creatures (quarry). The metaphor is drawn from hunting. Macduff's wife and children were as defenceless as deer.

208 Shakespeare sees Macduff as speechless and trying to hide his face to conceal his emotion.

209-10 **Give sorrow . . . break:** Malcolm is practising sound psychology. To give vent to grief is better than bottling it up inside; **o'erfraught:** over-burdened, overladen.

211-12 **My children too:** Macduff speaks in a strangled voice; **wife, children . . . found:** Once Ross has forced himself to break the news, he does so directly without glossing over the facts; **must be from thence:** had to be away. This might imply that there was some compulsion on Macduff that obliged him to leave Scotland.

214-15 **Let's make . . . revenge:** Let's make ourselves medicines out of our great revenge; **medicines, cure:** a medical metaphor. Shakespeare's son-in-law, John Hall, was a physician.

216 **He has no children:** "He" may refer to Malcolm, who, had he any children, would not speak of revenge to a man with a broken heart. It may refer to Macbeth, who, if he had children, could not have carried out such a slaughter. Again, it may refer to Macbeth, on whom, because he had no children, Macduff could not take revenge. This last interpretation is surely unworthy of Macduff.

217 **hell-kite:** Macduff compares Macbeth to a cruel, fiendish bird of prey.   218 **dam:** suggests a mother hen.

219 **At one fell swoop:** The hawk plunges down on its hapless prey in a single, fierce attack. The phrase has become part of our everyday speech partly because of its imitative harmony and partly because of the accuracy of its meaning.

220 **dispute it:** struggle against your grief.

211-20 The broken lines emphasize the intensity of Macduff's grief.

220-1 A man can show courage in facing grief, but if he is human, he must also suffer when grief-stricken.

225 **for:** on account of; **naught:** wicked, worthless.

228 **whetstone:** sharpener. The murder will make Macduff's sword more potent (sharper) when he seeks revenge.

229 **convert:** be changed; **blunt not . . . it:** Let grief inflame your feelings rather than making them dull and useless.

230-1 **play the . . . tongue:** shed tears as a woman would and utter loud-sounding threats as a boaster would.

232-3 **intermission:** delay; **front to . . . myself:** Note Macduff's prayer.

   Savagely slaughter'd: to relate the manner   205
   Were on the quarry of these murder'd deer
   To add the death of you.
Malcolm.   Merciful heaven!
   What, man, ne'er pull your hat upon your brows;
   Give sorrow words; the grief that does not speak
   Whispers the o'erfraught heart and bids it break.   210
Macduff.   My children too?
Ross.   Wife, children, servants, all
   That could be found.
Macduff.   And I must be from thence!
   My wife kill'd too?
Ross.   I have said.
Malcolm.   Be comforted.
   Let's make us medicines of our great revenge,
   To cure this deadly grief.   215
Macduff.   He has no children. All my pretty ones?
   Did you say all? O hell-kite! All?
   What, all my pretty chickens, and their dam
   At one fell swoop?
Malcolm.   Dispute it like a man.
Macduff.   I shall do so;   220
   But I must also feel it as a man:
   I cannot but remember such things were,
   That were most precious to me. Did heaven look on,
   And would not take their part? Sinful Macduff,
   They were all struck for thee! naught that I am,   225
   Not for their own demerits, but for mine,
   Fell slaughter on their souls: heaven rest them now!
Malcolm.   Be this the whetstone of your sword; let grief
   Convert to anger: blunt not the heart, enrage it.
Macduff.   O, I could play the woman with mine eyes,   230
   And braggart with my tongue! But, gentle heavens,
   Cut short all intermission; front to front
   Bring thou this fiend of Scotland and myself,
   Within my sword's length set him; if he 'scape,

234-5 **if he . . . too:** If he escapes from my sword, may God forgive him also (but neither of these things is likely to happen); **this tune:** Such a vigorous statement is music to Malcolm's ears; it has a martial sound; **goes manly:** is worthy of your manhood. "Manly" is an adjective form, but Shakespeare sometimes uses such forms adverbially.

236 **power:** army.

237 **Our lack . . . leave:** We have only to bid farewell to the King.

238-9 **ripe for shaking:** ready to fall like ripe fruit; the hour appointed for his doom is near; **the powers . . . instruments:** Providence encourages its agents, Malcolm, Macduff, and their followers, against the tyrant. Another interpretation is that angelic hosts are arming themselves as though to assist the earthly forces of righteousness.

240 The reference to night and day suggests evil and good; the forces of light are beginning to triumph. Malcolm, as the rightful heir, has the last speech of the scene and of the act.

See also p. 183.

Harrison writes: "In this brief scene, which is less than a hundred lines long, Shakespeare achieves his most concentrated example of dramatic irony."

S.D. Doctor of Physic: a physician.

1-3 Note how clearly the first speech suggests the situation and also creates the atmosphere of suspense.

4 **went into the field:** began to prepare for war. Later, he prepared to withstand a siege.

5-6 **nightgown:** dressing-gown; **closet:** place where valuables were kept.

7 **fold it:** perhaps to indicate a margin.

6-8 Lady Macbeth may be trying to write a letter to Macbeth in reply to the fateful missive she received in I. v. Possibly, she just wishes to keep in touch with him. It has also been suggested that this is a confession. In any case, it is not likely to be a lucid document.

10 **perturbation in nature:** constitutional disorder.

11-12 **do the . . . watching:** act like a person who is awake; **slumbery agitation:** walking in her sleep, somnambulism.

13 **actual performances:** physical actions.

15-16 **That, sir . . . her:** Why not? Is the Waiting-Gentlewoman's refusal to report what Lady Macbeth had said based on selfish fears or on consideration for her mistress?

Heaven forgive him too!

Malcolm.   This tune goes manly.   235
  Come, go we to the king; our power is ready,
  Our lack is nothing but our leave. Macbeth
  Is ripe for shaking, and the powers above
  Put on their instruments. Receive what cheer you
      may;
  The night is long that never finds the day.   *Exeunt.*   240

ACT V

Scene 1

DUNSINANE. ANTE-ROOM
IN THE CASTLE.

*Enter a Doctor of Physic and a Waiting-
Gentlewoman.*

Doctor. I have two nights watch'd with you, but can
  perceive no truth in your report. When was it she last
  walk'd?

Gentlewoman. Since his majesty went into the field, I
  have seen her rise from her bed, throw her night-   5
  gown upon her, unlock her closet, take forth paper,
  fold it, write upon 't, read it, afterwards seal it, and
  again return to bed; yet all this while in a most fast
  sleep.

Doctor. A great perturbation in nature, to receive at   10
  once the benefit of sleep, and do the effects of watching. In this slumbery agitation, besides her walking,
  and other actual performances, what (at any time)
  have you heard her say?

Gentlewoman. That, sir, which I will not report after   15
  her.

19   S.D. **Enter Lady . . . taper:** a most dramatic moment. How changed this broken pathetic woman is from the proud confident lady of I. v.! It would seem logical for her to set the candle down.

20   **guise:** practice, custom.   21   **close:** concealed, aside.

23-24   **she has . . . command:** an ironic comment on the invocation to darkness in I. v. Like a child, she fears the dark.

27-28   **Look how . . . hands:** Note the indirect stage direction. The verb seems to suggest desperate, anguished action.

32   **yet:** still; a far cry from: "A little water clears us of this deed."

33-34   **Hark! she . . . strongly:** This taking of notes makes us feel, somehow, that Lady Macbeth is being spied upon.

35   **one: two:** possibly a reference to the signal in II. i., which indicated that all was in readiness.

38   **hell is murky:** She seems to see before her the dark, yawning depths to which her soul is doomed; **Fie, my . . . afeard:** This may refer to her attempts to shame Macbeth during the banquet scene and thus restore him to sanity, or to her taunts during I. vii.; **What need . . . account:** A reigning monarch in those times was above the law. The speech then might refer to Banquo's death.

39-40   **Yet who . . . him:** a speech that shows what it cost Lady Macbeth to return the daggers; it may also be adduced as evidence of the genuineness of her faint. When we remember that Duncan resembled her father, we can begin to grasp the profound horror of her question. Bradley calls these "the most horrible lines in the whole tragedy".

35-40   Note the echoes of two crimes, her fear of damnation, and her desire to protect Macbeth. Out of the depths of her subconscious mind come her deepest emotions, which, in sleep, she cannot control.   41   **mark:** note.

42-45   **The thane . . . now:** a strange oblique reference to the third great crime. Though Lady Macbeth had no hand in this massacre, the report must have shaken her to the roots of her being; **No more . . . starting:** She speaks sternly, rebuking Macbeth for his conduct in the banquet scene; **mar:** ruin; **starting:** fits and starts, sudden convulsive movements.

46   **Go to:** an exclamation implying reproach.

50   **smell:** It has been pointed out that Macbeth's imagination is visual; Lady Macbeth's imagination is shown to be olfactory. Even if the stains could be washed off, they would still make their presence known in this insidious fashion.

51   **perfumes of Arabia:** Crusaders returning from Persia and Arabia helped to introduce perfume into western Europe.

Doctor. You may to me, and 'tis most meet you should.

Gentlewoman. Neither to you, nor any one, having no witness to confirm my speech.

> *Enter Lady Macbeth, with a taper.*

Lo you, here she comes! This is her very guise, and,   20
upon my life, fast asleep. Observe her, stand close.

Doctor. How came she by that light?

Gentlewoman. Why, it stood by her: she has light by ~~money~~
her continually, 'tis her command.

Doctor. You see her eyes are open.   25

Gentlewoman. Ay, but their sense is shut.

Doctor. What is it she does now? Look how she rubs her hands.

Gentlewoman. It is an accustom'd action with her, to seem thus washing her hands: I have known her con-   30
tinue in this a quarter of an hour.

Lady Macbeth. Yet here's a spot.

Doctor. Hark! she speaks. I will set down what comes from her, to satisfy my remembrance the more strongly.

Lady Macbeth. Out damned spot! out I say! One: two: 35
why then 'tis time to do't: hell is murky. Fie, my lord,
fie, a soldier, and afeard? What need we fear who
knows it, when none can call our power to account?
Yet who would have thought the old man to have had
so much blood in him?   40

Doctor. Do you mark that?

Lady Macbeth. The thane of Fife had a wife; where is
she now? What, will these hands ne'er be clean? No
more o' that, my lord, no more o' that; you mar all
with this starting.   45

Doctor. Go to, go to; you have known what you should
not.

Gentlewoman. She has spoke what she should not, I
am sure of that: heaven knows what she has known.

Lady Macbeth. Here's the smell of the blood still: all   50
the perfumes of Arabia will not sweeten this little

51-52   **this little hand:** This does not imply that Lady Macbeth was a small person, but rather provides a contrast between "all the perfumes" and "one hand"; **Oh, oh, oh:** a triple sigh from the depths of her being. It is reported that Mrs. Siddons uttered this sigh with a convulsive shudder.

53   **sorely charg'd:** heavily burdened.

55   **for the . . . body:** for all the honours in her possession.

57   **Pray God . . . sir:** Supply *well*. A pun is made on the two senses of the word "well".

58-60   **practice:** art; **yet I . . . beds:** The implication is that most come to violent ends.

61-63   **Wash your . . . grave:** Her thoughts move swiftly from the first murder to the second, as though they were confused in her mind. She relives the moments of greatest tension; **on's:** of his.

64   **Even so:** His suspicions are verified.

66   **give me your hand:** a plea or a command? This may be an echo of I. vi. 28.

67   **what's done . . . undone:** said with tragic finality; an echo of previous speeches; **to bed:** Lady Macbeth's last words in the play create pity for her, despite her evil deeds. Shakespeare's power to do this is one of the hallmarks of his genius.

70   **foul whisperings:** evil rumours.

72   **deaf pillows:** an odd personification.

73   **More needs . . . physician:** Her troubles are those that require the ministrations of a priest, not a doctor. Her immortal soul is in more danger than her physical body.

75   **annoyance:** injury to herself; possibly, a foreshadowing of suicide.

76   **still:** constantly.

77   **mated:** confounded, bewildered, confused.

See also p. 187.

hand. Oh, oh, oh!

Doctor.   What a sigh is there! The heart is sorely charg'd.

Gentlewoman.   I would not have such a heart in my
bosom for the dignity of the whole body.   55

Doctor.   Well, well, well,—

Gentlewoman.   Pray God it be, sir.

Doctor.   This disease is beyond my practice: yet I have
known those which have walk'd in their sleep, who
have died holily in their beds.   60

Lady Macbeth.   Wash your hands, put on your nightgown, look not so pale: I tell you yet again Banquo's
buried; he cannot come out on 's grave.

Doctor.   Even so?

Lady Macbeth.   To bed, to bed; there's knocking at the   65
gate: come, come, come, come, give me your hand:
what's done, cannot be undone: to bed, to bed, to bed.

                                                        Exit.

Doctor.   Will she go now to bed?

Gentlewoman.   Directly.

Doctor.   Foul whisperings are abroad: unnatural deeds   70
Do breed unnatural troubles: infected minds
To their deaf pillows will discharge their secrets:
More needs she the divine than the physician.
God, God forgive us all! Look after her,
Remove from her the means of all annoyance,   75
And still keep eyes upon her. So good night:
My mind she has mated and amaz'd my sight:
I think, but dare not speak.

Gentlewoman.   Good night, good doctor.

                                                      Exeunt.

S.D. **colours:** pennants and banners.

1 **power:** army.

2 **uncle:** According to Holinshed, Siward was Malcolm's grand-father. Why would Shakespeare make him Malcolm's uncle? **good:** the adjective most frequently applied to Macduff.

3 **dear causes:** the great wrongs they have suffered at Macbeth's hands.

4-5 **would to . . . man:** would rouse the dead to take part in battle; **alarm:** a summons to take up arms.

6 **well:** probably.

7 **Donalbain:** Apparently, he did not take part in Macbeth's overthrow. Shakespeare ties up a loose thread by this reference. We assume that Donalbain is still in Ireland.

8-9 **file of . . . gentry:** list of the nobility; **Siward's son:** This reference prepares us for the part he will play in V. vii.

10 **unrough:** smooth-faced, unbearded.

11 **protest their . . . manhood:** proclaim that they have reached man's estate.

12 **great Dunsinane . . . fortifies:** Why?

13-14 **Some say . . . fury:** Note the two opinions expressed. What do they imply about Macbeth?

15-16 **He cannot . . . rule:** Conditions in Scotland are beyond his control. The metaphor is that of a stout or dropsical man who can no longer fasten his belt around his middle; **distemper'd cause:** disorganized party.

17 **sticking on his hands:** a significant phrase in view of the pre-ceding scene and of II. ii. 60-61. The word "sticking" suggests in its homely simplicity something viscous that cannot be re-moved.

18 **minutely:** at intervals of a minute, though some take it as an adjective modifying "revolts", meaning *very frequent*; **upbraid his faith-breach:** reproach him for his own treason; as he proved false to his King, so others are proving false to him.

20-22 **now does . . . thief:** another example of the clothing image. Macbeth is not big enough for the job; he stole the royal mantle and now appears merely a grotesque travesty of a king.

23 **his pester'd . . . start:** ragged nerves for being jumpy (Dover Wilson).

Scene 2

THE COUNTRY
NEAR DUNSINANE.

*Drum and colours. Enter Menteith, Caithness,
Angus, Lennox, and Soldiers.*

Menteith. The English power is near, led on by Malcolm,
His uncle Siward, and the good Macduff:
Revenges burn in them; for their dear causes
Would to the bleeding and the grim alarm
Excite the mortified man.
Angus.   Near Birnam wood   5
Shall we well meet them; that way are they coming.
Caithness. Who knows if Donalbain be with his brother?
Lennox. For certain, sir, he is not: I have a file
Of all the gentry: there is Siward's son,
And many unrough youths, that even now   10
Protest their first of manhood.
Menteith.   What does the tyrant?
Caithness. Great Dunsinane he strongly fortifies:
Some say he's mad; others, that lesser hate him,
Do call it valiant fury, but, for certain,
He cannot buckle his distemper'd cause   15
Within the belt of rule.
Angus.   Now does he feel
His secret murders sticking on his hands;
Now minutely revolts upbraid his faith-breach;
Those he commands move only in command,
Nothing in love: now does he feel his title   20
Hang loose about him, like a giant's robe
Upon a dwarfish thief.
Menteith.   Who then shall blame
His pester'd senses to recoil, and start,
When all that is within him does condemn

24-25 **when all . . . there:** when all his mental powers are occupied in self-criticism and self-blame; said to be a specific reference to Macbeth's conscience. It is evidence of his tendency to introspection.

27-29 **medicine:** the doctor: Malcolm. The medical metaphor is continued in "sickly", "pour", "purge", "drop". There is some basis for believing that "medicine" means *drug*; Caithness implies that Scotland is to receive a good dose of castor oil, of which they are to form a part! Another interpretation is that "purge" refers to the remedy of *blood-letting*.

30 **to dew . . . weeds:** The action is to be like that of some ideal chemical that will preserve the desirable and destroy the undesirable; **sovereign flower:** Malcolm. "Sovereign" is a pun on *royal* and *remedial*, as in a *sovereign remedy*.

31 **Birnam:** The last word reminds us of the third prophecy in IV. i.

See also p. 189.

1 **them:** the Scottish Thanes.

3 **taint:** be infected; **boy:** used in contempt, but it emphasizes the youth of Malcolm in contrast with the (probable) middle age of Macbeth.

4 **born of woman:** If Macbeth and Duncan were first cousins, Macbeth would certainly have known Duncan's wife and the circumstances of Malcolm's birth; **spirits:** the Apparitions.

5 **all mortal consequences:** everything that will happen to human beings; **me:** in my case.

8 **epicures:** sybarites. The wealthy southerners were said to live in much greater luxury than the Scots, who were noted for their stern Spartan customs. Macbeth speaks in contempt.

9 **I sway by:** I direct my actions by.

10 **sag:** droop.

1-10 Macbeth's insistence on his lack of fear suggests a deep-seated fear. Note the way in which he flies into a passion in the next speech.

11-12 The fear displayed by the servant is a manifestation of Macbeth's own feelings; hence, he turns on him. Note the contrast between black and white; **loon:** rogue, worthless fellow, often applied to a lad; **goose:** often regarded as a symbol of cowardice.

13 **ten thousand:** The number mentioned by Malcolm in IV. iii. 134.

14 **Go prick . . . fear:** Drops of blood would cover the ghastly white cheeks.

Itself for being there?
Caithness.   Well, march we on,   25
   To give obedience where 'tis truly owed:
   Meet we the medicine of the sickly weal,
   And with him pour we, in our country's purge,
   Each drop of us.
Lennox.   Or so much as it needs,
   To dew the sovereign flower, and drown the weeds: 30
   Make we our march towards Birnam.

                              Exeunt, marching.

Scene 3

DUNSINANE.
A ROOM IN THE CASTLE.

Enter Macbeth, Doctor, and Attendants.

Macbeth.   Bring me no more reports, let them fly all:
   Till Birnam wood remove to Dunsinane,
   I cannot taint with fear. What's the boy Malcolm?
   Was he not born of woman? The spirits that know
   All mortal consequences have pronounc'd me thus: 5
   "Fear not, Macbeth, no man that's born of woman
   Shall e'er have power upon thee." Then fly, false
      thanes,
   And mingle with the English epicures:
   The mind I sway by, and the heart I bear,
   Shall never sag with doubt, nor shake with fear.   10
          Enter a Servant.
   The devil damn thee black, thou cream-fac'd loon!
   Where got'st thou that goose look?
Servant.   There is ten thousand—
Macbeth.   Geese, villain?
Servant.   Soldiers, sir.
Macbeth.   Go prick thy face, and over-red thy fear,

15 **lily-liver'd:** A white liver was regarded as a symbol of coward-ice; **patch:** fool, so called from his motley garb.

16-17 **those linen . . . fear:** Your white face creates cowardice in others; **whey-face:** another reference to white and to coward-ice. "Whey" is the liquid part of the milk that remains after the rest is clotted.

19-20 **Take thy face hence:** Macbeth thrusts him bodily out; **Seyton!—I . . . say:** The shouts punctuated by an incomplete sentence show Macbeth's distracted state of mind; **push:** attack by my opponents.

21 **cheer:** It has been conjectured that this should be *chair* (enthrone in honour), in which case there is a play on this word and "disseat". In any case, the attack will be decisive.

22 **I have . . . enough:** This statement suggests that many years have gone by and that Macbeth has grown old and weary. See also "old age". Historically, Macbeth reigned from 1040 to 1057; **way of life:** the course of my life. Dr. Johnson suggested *May* as a contrast with autumn, but *May* implies a much younger man than Macbeth appears to be.

23 **sear:** dry, withered. Some editors take "the sear" as a noun meaning *the withered state*; **the yellow leaf:** symbolic of autumn and approaching death.

22-23 **my way . . . leaf:** The expression has a descending cadence, "a dying fall"; the picture is clear and memorable.

24-27 **And that . . . have:** He sees very plainly what he has for-feited: "golden opinions from all sorts of people", on which he had once set such a high value; **as:** namely; **but, in . . . not:** a vivid picture of Macbeth's court, where he receives the hatred and the lip-service of those who fear him but dare not leave him; **curses, not . . . deep:** They are the more intense for being suppressed. 28 **would fain deny:** would gladly withhold.

22-28 These lines provide a summary of the tragedy of Macbeth. His triumph has turned to dust and ashes in his mouth. Though we do not condone his evil deeds, we pity the waste of his great power and promise.

29 **Seyton:** The Setons of Touch were (and still are) the hereditary armour-bearers of the kings of Scotland.

32 **hack'd:** an ugly and vicious word. The line shows Macbeth's feverish desperation. 35 **moe:** more; **skirr:** scour. Why?

36 **Hang those . . . fear:** a brutal order surely. What does it imply? **armour:** Shakespeare was probably thinking of the armour of an Elizabethan knight, not of Saxon ring-mail.

37-39 **Not so . . . rest:** To what extent does this imply that Lady Macbeth's condition has worsened? (See p. 138.)

Thou lily-liver'd boy. What soldiers, patch?   15
Death of thy soul! those linen cheeks of thine
Are counsellors to fear. What soldiers, whey-face?
Servant.   The English force, so please you.
Macbeth.   Take thy face hence.   *Exit Servant.*
                          Seyton!—I am sick at heart,
When I behold—Seyton, I say!—This push   20
Will cheer me ever, or disseat me now.
I have liv'd long enough: my way of life
Is fall'n into the sear, the yellow leaf,
And that which should accompany old age,
As honour, love, obedience, troops of friends,   25
I must not look to have; but, in their stead,
Curses, not loud but deep, mouth-honour, breath,
Which the poor heart would fain deny, and dare not.
Seyton!
          Enter Seyton.
Seyton.   What's your gracious pleasure?
Macbeth.   What news more?   30
Seyton.   All is confirm'd, my lord, which was reported.
Macbeth.   I'll fight, till from my bones my flesh be hack'd.
Give me my armour.
Seyton.   'Tis not needed yet.
Macbeth.   I'll put it on.
Send out moe horses, skirr the country round,   35
Hang those that talk of fear. Give me mine armour.
How does your patient, doctor?
Doctor.   Not so sick, my lord,
As she is troubled with thick-coming fancies
That keep her from her rest.
Macbeth.   Cure her of that.
Canst thou not minister to a mind diseas'd,   40
Pluck from the memory a rooted sorrow,
Raze out the written troubles of the brain,
And with some sweet oblivious antidote
Cleanse the stuff'd bosom of that perilous stuff

40-45 Although Macbeth is asking about his wife, we feel that he is describing his own symptoms here. The imagery of disease is prevalent in the last act. Why? **rooted:** firmly fixed, deeply embedded. What is the fixation referred to as far as Lady Macbeth is concerned? **Raze out . . . brain:** Erase what has been inscribed as one would erase marks from a slate or blackboard; **oblivious:** causing forgetfulness; **sweet oblivious antidote:** What modern drug(s) might be so called? **stuff'd:** overburdened. The repetition of "stuff'd" and "stuff" emphasizes the image of congestion.

45-46 **Therein the . . . himself:** Although "himself" is grammatically correct, one would have expected *herself*. The doctor realizes that Macbeth is speaking about himself. How can a patient suffering from the disorder referred to help himself? How valid is the doctor's reply by modern standards?

47 **Throw physic . . . it:** Macbeth's irritable impatience is illustrated here. Because the art of medicine cannot help *him*, it is of no value.

48 **staff:** baton; some say *lance*; **Come, put . . . staff:** This line, with "Come, sir, dispatch", "Pull't off, I say", and "Bring it after me", gives us a vivid picture of the scene on the stage. The commands also reveal Macbeth's distracted state of mind.

50-51 **cast the water:** perform a urinanalysis; **her:** Scotland's.

52 **purge:** cleanse by means of a purgative drug. See V. ii. 28; **pristine:** former.

54 **Pull't off:** Macbeth is impatient of Seyton's awkwardness; whereas, it is his own fidgetiness that is probably causing the difficulty. The reference is to some strap, belt, or other item of equipment.

55 **rhubarb:** purgative made from the root of a Chinese and Tibetan plant; **senna:** a cathartic drug. F has *cyme*, but the Fourth Folio gives "senna".

57-58 **Ay, my . . . something:** The doctor speaks dryly; **it:** the item of equipment referred to in line 54.

59 **bane:** destruction.

61-62 This odd couplet provides a touch of ironic humour. Some critics feel that it is out of place.

See also p. 190.

S.D. What is proved by the information given in the stage directions?

2 **that chambers . . . safe:** when we shall be able to sleep without fear of assassination. Malcolm is perhaps thinking of his father's fate; **nothing:** not at all.

Which weighs upon the heart?

Doctor.   Therein the patient   45
   Must minister to himself.

Macbeth.   Throw physic to the dogs, I'll none of it.
   Come, put mine armour on; give me my staff.
   Seyton, send out. Doctor, the thanes fly from me.
   Come, sir, dispatch. If thou couldst, doctor, cast   50
   The water of my land, find her disease,
   And purge it to a sound and pristine health,
   I would applaud thee to the very echo,
   That should applaud again. Pull 't off, I say.
   What rhubarb, senna, or what purgative drug,   55
   Would scour these English hence? Hear'st thou of them?

Doctor.   Ay, my good lord; your royal preparation
   Makes us hear something.

Macbeth.   Bring it after me.
   I will not be afraid of death and bane,
   Till Birnam forest come to Dunsinane.   60

Doctor (aside).   Were I from Dunsinane away and clear,
   Profit again should hardly draw me here.   *Exeunt.*

Scene 4

COUNTRY NEAR BIRNAM WOOD.

*Drum and colours. Enter Malcolm, old Siward
and his Son, Macduff, Menteith, Caithness,
Angus, Lennox, Ross, and Soldiers, marching.*

Malcolm.   Cousins, I hope the days are near at hand
   That chambers will be safe.

Menteith.   We doubt it nothing.

Siward.   What wood is this before us?

Menteith.   The wood of Birnam.

Malcolm.   Let every soldier hew him down a bough,
   And bear't before him; thereby shall we shadow   5

4-7 This example of camouflage is found in Holinshed. Malcolm thereby becomes the unconscious instrument of destiny. (It has been suggested that the moving forest is related to the myth of the coming of spring.) **shadow:** conceal; **discovery:** Macbeth's scouts.

8 **no other but:** nothing to alter the fact that; **confident:** Why would Siward believe him to be confident?

9-10 **will endure . . . before't:** is prepared to withstand a siege; **main hope:** He does not have sufficient men to force a battle; moreover, the castle appeared impregnable.

11 **advantage to be given:** a favourable opportunity open to them. Many editors consider "given" a transcriber's error in F and prefer a reading such as *gain'd.*

12 **more and less:** the more important and the less important; nearly everyone.

13-14 **constrained things . . . too:** only those who have been pressed unwillingly into his service; **things:** creatures.

10-14 Malcolm shows optimism.

14-16 Macduff, a more experienced soldier, hints that Malcolm should not count his chickens before they are hatched. We cannot judge events accurately until they have actually taken place; **censures:** opinions; **put we . . . soldiership:** Let us make sound military preparations and leave nothing to chance.

17 **due decision:** right amount of definiteness.

18 **have:** (if victorious); **owe:** have lost (if defeated).

19-20 **Thoughts speculative . . . arbitrate:** Guesses deal with uncertainties; only blows can really decide the outcome.

16-21 Siward also recommends a cautious attitude. Neither one wishes to rebuke Malcolm openly.

See also p. 191.

1 **Hang out . . . walls:** The line has a fine martial ring.

4 **the ague:** malarial fever, with cold, hot, and sweating stages; **eat them up:** Famine and the ague are thought of as birds of prey or perhaps fierce dogs.

5 **forc'd:** reinforced.

6 **dareful:** boldly; **beard to beard:** face to face. The picture suggested is one of warriors in single combat.

The numbers of our host, and make discovery
  Err in report of us.
Soldiers.   It shall be done.
Siward.   We learn no other but the confident tyrant
  Keeps still in Dunsinane, and will endure
  Our setting down before 't.
Malcolm.   'Tis his main hope: 10
  For where there is advantage to be given,
  Both more and less have given him the revolt,
  And none serve with him but constrained things
  Whose hearts are absent too.
Macduff.   Let our just censures
  Attend the true event, and put we on   15
  Industrious soldiership.
Siward.   The time approaches,
  That will with due decision make us know
  What we shall say we have, and what we owe.
  Thoughts speculative their unsure hopes relate,
  But certain issue strokes must arbitrate: 20
  Towards which advance the war.   *Exeunt, marching.*

Scene 5

DUNSINANE. WITHIN THE CASTLE.

*Enter Macbeth, Seyton, and Soldiers, with drum
and colours.*

Macbeth.   Hang out our banners on the outward walls;
  The cry is still "They come:" our castle's strength
  Will laugh a siege to scorn: here let them lie
  Till famine and the ague eat them up;
  Were they not forc'd with those that should be ours,   5
  We might have met them dareful, beard to beard,
  And beat them backward home.
          A cry within of women.

8 **cry of women:** Some editors interpret this as evidence that Lady Macbeth ended her own life.

9 **taste of fears:** as if fear were a type of food.

10 **the time has been:** once upon a time; **my senses . . . cool'd:** as we say: "My blood would have run cold."

11 **fell of hair:** scalp. 12 **dismal treatise:** tale of horror.

14 **direness:** horror. 15 **start:** startle.

9-15 Macbeth has become hardened in crime; no hallucinations (the product of his imagination and his conscience) torment him now. He appears drained of emotion.

16 **The queen . . . dead:** The line with its heavy monosyllables is like the slow tolling of a funeral knell. Its shortness allows for a pause at the end; the order creates emphasis.

17 **should:** The word can mean *would* or *ought*, and the line can be made to bear a sympathetic or unsympathetic interpretation. If the meaning *would* is taken, it is the comment of a weary mind, dulled and numb. Death would have come sooner or later. If the meaning *ought* is taken, it implies that if she had waited, he might have joined her or at least have found time to mourn for her.

19 **To-morrow, and . . . to-morrow:** The repetition creates monotony.

20 **creeps in . . . day:** (The future) is mean and trivial, perhaps like some crawling insect.

21 **to the . . . time:** to the final word in the book of time.

22-23 **yesterdays have . . . death:** The past has served merely to show foolish men the way to die; **dusty:** a reference to the service for the burial of the dead. Theobald suggested *dusky*; **candle:** stands for the flame of life, so easily snuffed out.

19-23 Both future and past seem to be symbols of futility.

24 **shadow:** suggests the insubstantial quality of life; **poor player:** wretched actor, not necessarily incompetent, but rather pitiful.

25 **struts and frets:** imitative verbs that suggest man's conceited, complaining nature; **his hour:** Life is brief.

26-28 **It is . . . nothing:** This image emphasizes life's empty noise and lack of meaning. Note the emphatic last word.

24-28 a series of metaphors suggesting the littleness of man.

17-28 This great speech is a supreme statement of Macbeth's tragedy. Because of his own wrong doing and because of his wife's death, life has ceased to have any meaning, and man is reduced to a cipher; such is the philosophy of pessimism. The imitative and imaginative qualities of the speech make for superb poetry.

33 **did stand my watch:** stood guard. 34 **anon:** presently, soon.

37 **this three mile:** these three miles.

What is that noise?

Seyton.   It is the cry of women, my good lord.   *Exit.*

Macbeth.   I have almost forgot the taste of fears:
The time has been, my senses would have cool'd   10
To hear a night-shriek, and my fell of hair
Would at a dismal treatise rouse and stir
As life were in't: I have supp'd full with horrors;
Direness, familiar to my slaughterous thoughts,
Cannot once start me.

      Re-enter Seyton.

              Wherefore was that cry?   15

Seyton.   The queen, my lord, is dead.

Macbeth.   She should have died hereafter;
There would have been a time for such a word.
To-morrow, and to-morrow, and to-morrow,
Creeps in this petty pace from day to day,   20
To the last syllable of recorded time;
And all our yesterdays have lighted fools
The way to dusty death. Out, out, brief candle!
Life's but a walking shadow, a poor player
That struts and frets his hour upon the stage,   25
And then is heard no more. It is a tale
Told by an idiot, full of sound and fury,
Signifying nothing.

      Enter a Messenger.

Thou com'st to use thy tongue; thy story quickly.

Messenger.   Gracious my lord,   30
I should report that which I say I saw,
But know not how to do it.

Macbeth.   Well, say, sir.

Messenger.   As I did stand my watch upon the hill,
I look'd toward Birnam, and anon methought
The wood began to move.

Macbeth.   Liar, and slave!   35

Messenger.   Let me endure your wrath, if't be not so:
Within this three mile may you see it coming;

40 **cling:** wither, shrink up; **sooth:** truth.
42 **pull in:** check, rein in, as one would a mettlesome horse; **resolution:** confidence and determination.
43 **doubt:** suspect; **equivocation:** double-dealing, ambiguity. Cf. II. iii. 11-12.
46 **Arm, arm, and out:** an abrupt change of plan. Why? How wise is this decision?
47 **avouches:** affirms, avers; **does appear:** is seen to be true.
50 **estate o' the world:** the universe.
51 **wrack:** wreck, ruin.
52 **harness:** armour.

See also p. 192.

2 **show like . . . are:** appear like your true selves.
4 **battle:** division of an army, possibly here, the vanguard.
6 **order:** plan.
1-6 Malcolm shows authoritative control of the situation, as he tells his uncle, his cousin, and Macduff what to do.
7 **do we:** if we.
10 **harbingers:** forerunners. See also I. iv. 45 for the use of the word in its true sense.
9-10 The couplet has a sonorous ring, as it heralds the combat.

See also p. 192.

I say, a moving grove.
Macbeth.   If thou speak'st false,
  Upon the next tree shalt thou hang alive
  Till famine cling thee: if thy speech be sooth,   40
  I care not if thou dost for me as much.
  I pull in resolution, and begin
  To doubt the equivocation of the fiend
  That lies like truth: "Fear not, till Birnam wood
  Do come to Dunsinane;" and now a wood   45
  Comes toward Dunsinane. Arm, arm, and out!
  If this which he avouches does appear,
  There is nor flying hence nor tarrying here.
  I 'gin to be a-weary of the sun,
  And wish the estate o' the world were now undone.   50
  Ring the alarum-bell! Blow, wind come, wrack!
  At least we'll die with harness on our back.   *Exeunt.*

Scene 6

DUNSINANE. BEFORE THE CASTLE.

*Drum and colours. Enter Malcolm, old Siward,
Macduff, and their Army, with boughs.*

Malcolm.   Now near enough; your leavy screens throw down,
  And show like those you are. You, worthy uncle,
  Shall, with my cousin, your right noble son,
  Lead our first battle: worthy Macduff and we
  Shall take upon's what else remains to do,   5
  According to our order.
Siward.   Fare you well.
  Do we but find the tyrant's power to-night,
  Let us be beaten, if we cannot fight.
Macduff.   Make all our trumpets speak; give them all breath,
  Those clamorous harbingers of blood and death.   10
                                                    Exeunt.
          Alarums continued.

1-3 **They have . . . course:** The metaphor is drawn from the popular Elizabethan sport of bear-baiting. The bear was fastened by means of a chain to a stake in the middle of a ring; it was then set upon by four to six mastiffs (or by bull dogs). Why is the metaphor appropriate? Though brought to bay, Macbeth is still formidable; **course:** the technical term for a single bout or round in a bear-baiting match; **What's he . . . woman:** Macbeth puts his trust in the second prophecy.

11 **I'll prove . . . speak'st:** I'll prove that what you say is a lie; S.D. **They fight . . . slain:** Shakespeare found this episode in Holinshed, but he emphasizes the youth of Siward in order to deepen the tragedy of his death.

5-11 The sharp exchange is expressed in short abrupt speeches.

11-13 **Thou wast . . . born:** Macbeth's confidence is increased and a certain element of suspense is created. The entrance of Macduff immediately on the heels of this statement is dramatically ironic; S.D. **Alarums:** The noise of fighting.

16 **still:** always.

17-18 **wretched kerns . . . staves:** miserable, poorly armed mercenaries, probably Irish; **staves:** the shafts of their spears; **either thou:** Add *must be my opponent.*

20 **undeeded:** unused.

21 **clatter:** dry, confused sound. Why is the word appropriate? **note:** importance.

22 **bruited:** announced.

24 **gently render'd:** surrendered without resistance.

Scene 7

Alarums. Enter Macbeth.

Macbeth. They have tied me to a stake; I cannot fly,
But bear-like I must fight the course. What's he
That was not born of woman? Such a one
Am I to fear, or none.
    Enter young Siward.
Young Siward. What is thy name?
Macbeth.   Thou'lt be afraid to hear it. 5
Young Siward. No; though thou call'st thyself a hotter name
Than any is in hell.
Macbeth.   My name's Macbeth.
Young Siward. The devil himself could not pronounce a title
More hateful to mine ear.
Macbeth.   No, nor more fearful.
Young Siward. Thou liest, abhorred tyrant; with my sword 10
I'll prove the lie thou speak'st.
    They fight, and young Siward is slain.
Macbeth.   Thou wast born of woman;
But swords I smile at, weapons laugh to scorn,
Brandish'd by man that's of a woman born.   *Exit.*
    Alarums. Enter Macduff.
Macduff. That way the noise is. Tyrant, show thy face!
If thou be'st slain and with no stroke of mine, 15
My wife and children's ghosts will haunt me still.
I cannot strike at wretched kerns, whose arms
Are hir'd to bear their staves: either thou, Macbeth,
Or else my sword with an unbatter'd edge
I sheathe again undeeded. There thou shouldst be; 20
By this great clatter, one of greatest note
Seems bruited: let me find him, fortune,
And more I beg not.   *Exit. Alarums.*
    Enter Malcolm and old Siward.
Siward. This way, my lord, the castle's gently render'd:

25 **on both sides:** Many of Macbeth's garrison have changed sides, or Macbeth's followers support him so half-heartedly that they might as well be fighting against him.

29 **that strike beside us:** Two interpretations are possible: either, that fight by our sides, or, that miss us on purpose.
See also p. 193.

1-2 **Why should . . . sword:** Macbeth refers contemptuously to men such as Cassius, Brutus, and Antony, who had committed suicide and of whom Shakespeare has written. It is almost impossible to deduce Shakespeare's own feelings in regard to suicide, although he makes Hamlet speak against it. What is Macbeth's attitude towards it? Why? What light does this throw on his character? **lives:** living men.

3 **Turn, hell-hound, turn:** Why does Shakespeare have Macduff enter while Macbeth's back is turned? What is shown by his command? Why are the words effective? **hell-hound:** fiend.

4-6 **Of all . . . already:** This has been referred to as: "the only real touch of remorse in Macbeth" (Chambers). Why does Shakespeare introduce it at this time?

8 **than terms . . . out:** than words can express.

9 **intrenchant:** invulnerable, incapable of being cut.

10 **impress:** try to make an imprint on.

11 **crests:** heads, wearing helmets with crests.

12 **must not:** is not destined to.

13 **despair:** give up your trust in.

14 **angel:** demon; **still:** always.

15-16 **Macduff was . . . ripp'd:** Macduff was not born in the normal way, but prematurely delivered, perhaps by Caesarean section, perhaps as the result of lacerations caused by horned cattle (Furness). A child so brought into the world was supposedly endowed with power and heroic strength; Macduff's speech expresses these qualities; **untimely:** prematurely.

18 **cow'd my . . . man:** intimidated my very soul. Dover Wilson interprets "my . . . man" as *courage*.

The tyrant's people on both sides do fight,   25
The noble thanes do bravely in the war,
The day almost itself professes yours,
And little is to do.
Malcolm.   We have met with foes
That strike beside us.
Siward.   Enter, sir, the castle.
                                    Exeunt. Alarum.

Scene 8

Enter Macbeth.

Macbeth.   Why should I play the Roman fool, and die
On mine own sword? whiles I see lives, the gashes
Do better upon them.
          Enter Macduff.
Macduff.   Turn, hell-hound, turn!
Macbeth.   Of all men else I have avoided thee:
But get thee back, my soul is too much charg'd   5
With blood of thine already.
Macduff.   I have no words,
My voice is in my sword, thou bloodier villain
Than terms can give thee out!   *They fight.*
Macbeth.   Thou losest labour;
As easy mayst thou the intrenchant air
With thy keen sword impress, as make me bleed: 10
Let fall thy blade on vulnerable crests;
I bear a charmed life, which must not yield
To one of woman born.
Macduff.   Despair thy charm,
And let the angel whom thou still hast serv'd
Tell thee, Macduff was from his mother's womb   15
Untimely ripp'd.
Macbeth.   Accursed be that tongue that tells me so;
For it hath cow'd my better part of man!

19 **juggling fiends:** deceitful Witches who have cheated him.
20 **palter:** quibble, equivocate. (Equivocation is also referred to in the Porter's speech, II. iii. and in Macbeth's lines V. v.)
22 **I'll not . . . thee:** Overcome by this revelation, Macbeth is panic-stricken.
19-22 Banquo's prediction is thus validated. (Cf. I. iii. 123-6); Macbeth realizes the bitter truth at last.
23 **Then yield thee, coward:** Macduff taunts him.
24 **the show . . . time:** the spectacle and exhibit of the day.
25-26 **We'll have . . . pole:** Freaks and monsters were painted on a board or cloth that was then hung on display outside a booth.
29 **baited:** tormented, as a bear was worried by dogs.
27-29 Macbeth's pride comes to his rescue.
32 **will try the last:** will make a final effort.
34 **him:** Although *he* would be more grammatical, "him" sounds better. *Let him be damned* may be what is meant.
32-34 Macbeth's last words in the play reveal courage, but it has been described as the courage of a cornered animal; S.D. The stage directions in F make it clear that Macbeth is killed on-stage. The problem of decapitation then arises. Dover Wilson suggests that Macbeth is killed on the inner stage, whence the body could be more easily removed. Granville-Barker thinks that the death of Macbeth would occur on the upper stage. Some editors omit the direction: "Enter fighting, and Macbeth slain."
35 **arriv'd:** in the castle.
36-37 **go off:** die; the expression suggests an actor's exit. There is dramatic irony in Siward's speech; **and yet . . . bought:** We do not seem to have paid too high a price for so great a victory.
41 **the which . . . confirm'd:** which his courage had no sooner proved.
42 **the unshrinking station:** the post from which he did not shrink. Siward receives the bad news stoically.
39-43 Ross brings a final piece of news.
46 **hath:** would have; **Had he . . . before:** The father is concerned, not as much about his son's death, as about his courage in facing death.

And be these juggling fiends no more believ'd,
That palter with us in a double sense,   20
That keep the word of promise to our ear,
And break it to our hope. I'll not fight with thee.
Macduff.   Then yield thee, coward,
And live to be the show and gaze o' the time:
We'll have thee, as our rarer monsters are,   25
Painted upon a pole, and underwrit,
"Here may you see the tyrant."
Macbeth.   I will not yield
To kiss the ground before young Malcolm's feet,
And to be baited with the rabble's curse.
Though Birnam wood be come to Dunsinane,   30
And thou oppos'd, being of no woman born,
Yet I will try the last: before my body
I throw my warlike shield: lay on, Macduff;
And damn'd be him that first cries "Hold, enough!"
                        Exeunt, fighting. Alarums.
       Enter fighting, and Macbeth slain.
       Retreat and flourish. Enter, with drum and
       colours, Malcolm, old Siward, Ross, the other
       Thanes, and Soldiers.
Malcolm.   I would the friends we miss were safe arriv'd.   35
Siward.   Some must go off: and yet by these I see
So great a day as this is cheaply bought.
Malcolm.   Macduff is missing, and your noble son.
Ross.   Your son, my lord, has paid a soldier's debt:
He but only liv'd but till he was a man,   40
The which no sooner had his prowess confirm'd
In the unshrinking station where he fought,
But like a man he died.
Siward.   Then he is dead?
Ross.   Ay, and brought off the field: your cause of sorrow
Must not be measur'd by his worth, for then   45
It hath no end.
Siward.   Had he his hurts before?

47   **God's soldier:** perhaps, one of the militant angels.
48   **sons as . . . hairs:** a pun on the idea of *sons and heirs*.
50   **knoll'd:** sounded.
52   **parted:** died; **score:** debt, reckoning (to nature).
51-53   To what extent is Siward's attitude admirable? Note also the contrast between the death of Young Siward and that of Macbeth.
54   **Hail, king:** Why is it fitting that Macduff should be the first so to salute Malcolm? **stands:** on a pole, as indicated in Holinshed. "Then cutting his head from his shoulders, he set it upon a pole and brought it unto Malcolme. This was the end of Makbeth after he had reigned 17 yeeres over the Scotishmen."
55   **the time is free:** The age has regained its freedom.
56   **compass'd:** encircled; **pearl:** nobility. The image may be that of a crown with a circlet of pearls.
59   **Hail, King of Scotland:** a triumphant shout.
60   **expense:** in the sense of *amount*.
61   **before we . . . loves:** before we figure out how much is owing to you for the love each of you has shown.
62   **make us . . . you:** reward you for the services you have performed. The image of payment takes us back to "paid his score".
63   **earls:** Malcolm had perhaps learned this term during his stay at the English court. Why would he introduce a new title at this time?
64   **what's more to do:** what more is to be done.
65   **planted newly:** The image suggests a new era; the idea of growth has been positively and negatively presented in the play. Of Banquo, Duncan said, "I have begun to plant thee" (I. iv. 28); Macbeth was ready to defy nature's creative principle (IV. i. 58-59).   66   **as:** for example.
67   **snares of watchful tyranny:** an apt metaphor to describe Macbeth's network of spies.
68   **producing forth:** rounding up, bringing to justice.
69   **dead butcher . . . queen:** How valid are Malcolm's summaries?
70   **self:** her own. How did Shakespeare prepare us for the possibility of Lady Macbeth's suicide? How likely is it that she took her own life?
72   **by the grace of Grace:** by God's divine favour.
73   **in measure:** in due proportion.
75   **crown'd at Scone:** "Malcolme Cammore thus recovering the relme . . . was crowned at Scone, the 25 day of Aprill, in the year of our Lord 1057" (Holinshed).

See also p. 194.

Ross.   Ay, on the front.
Siward.   Why then, God's soldier be he!
   Had I as many sons as I have hairs,
   I would not wish them to a fairer death:
   And so his knell is knoll'd.
Malcolm.   He's worth more sorrow,   50
   And that I'll spend for him.
Siward.   He's worth no more,
   They say he parted well, and paid his score:
   And so God be with him! Here comes newer comfort.
          Re-enter Macduff, with Macbeth's head.
Macduff.   Hail, king! for so thou art: behold where stands
   The usurper's cursed head: the time is free: 55
   I see thee compass'd with thy kingdom's pearl,
   That speak my salutation in their minds;
   Whose voices I desire aloud with mine:
   Hail, King of Scotland!
All.   Hail, King of Scotland!
                                        Flourish.
Malcolm.   We shall not spend a large expense of time   60
   Before we reckon with your several loves,
   And make us even with you. My thanes and kinsmen,
   Henceforth be earls, the first that ever Scotland
   In such an honour nam'd. What 's more to do,
   Which would be planted newly with the time,   65
   As calling home our exil'd friends abroad,
   That fled the snares of watchful tyranny,
   Producing forth the cruel ministers
   Of this dead butcher and his fiend-like queen,
   Who (as 'tis thought) by self and violent hands   70
   Took off her life; this, and what needful else
   That calls upon us, by the grace of Grace
   We will perform in measure, time, and place:
   So thanks to all at once, and to each one,
   Whom we invite to see us crown'd at Scone.   75
                              Flourish. Exeunt.

DRAMATIS PERSONAE

Questions

1. a) How many father-and-son combinations are there?
   b) What may this suggest about the age of the main characters?
2. Show that the play deals with the following subjects: the supernatural, warfare, illness, violent death.
3. Prove that the play deals with the nobility. Why is it that all of Shakespeare's major tragedies do so?

The names of the characters are drawn chiefly from Holinshed's *Chronicles* and were first listed by Nicholas Rowe, the earliest critical editor of Shakespeare's plays, whose edition appeared in 1709. The name "MacBeth" is said to mean "Son of Life"; he is referred to in an ancient chronicle as "the furious Red One". Lady Macbeth's name may have been "Gruach". Another chronicle, according to Masefield,[1] states that she was a widow when she married Macbeth, and was also the mother of a son known as Lulach the Simpleton.

ACT I, SCENE 1

Dramatic Importance

The opening scene of *Macbeth* is important for the creation of atmosphere; it strikes the keynote of the play, which is one of

[1]John Masefield, *A Macbeth Production* (New York, The Macmillan Company, and London, The Society of Authors and Dr. John Masefield, O.M., 1946), p. 5.

smouldering evil. The introduction of the supernatural sets the stage for a tragic conflict between right and wrong, fair and foul, as indicated in the final couplet; this recalls the perversion of Satan in "Paradise Lost": "Evil be thou my good!" Suspense is created by references to a battle and to a forthcoming meeting with Macbeth. "The first scene, every word of which will bear the closest scrutiny, strikes one dominant chord."[1] A. C. Bradley[2] writes: "The action bursts into wild life amidst the sounds of a thunderstorm and the echoes of a distant battle."

This scene can be played in forty seconds, its intensity varying directly with its brevity. (It has been calculated that the normal rate of delivery in a Shakespearian play in Elizabethan times was 140 words a minute. In a three-minute conversation, according to the statistics of the Bell Telephone Company, about 300 words are spoken.)

As John Masefield[3] points out, the Witches' costumes "are those of women", their figures "those of bearded men". "They are black, secret and skinny. They have bloody chaps or cracks upon their fingers. You must therefore create three figures, impressive, shrivelled, intense and awful, with arms which look like skin and bone, and hands used to working with the hangman and in the charnel house." The Witches in David Garrick's production (1748-68) wore plaited caps, laced aprons, red stomachers, ruffs, and mittens. In the Stratford, Ontario, version of 1962, they squatted on the stage like evil toads, grotesque and ominous. Much of the power of the scene depends on the voices of the speakers.

Questions

1. Show that the opening scene sets the atmosphere of physical and moral conflict.

[1]L. Knights, *Explorations* (London, Chatto & Windus Ltd., 1946), p. 18.
[2]A. C. Bradley, *Shakespearean Tragedy* (Toronto, The Macmillan Company of Canada Ltd.; London, Macmillan & Co. Ltd., 1958), p. 332.
[3]Masefield, *op. cit.*

2. How are the supernatural and evil powers of the Witches suggested?

3. How does this scene create suspense?

4. Analyse the importance and effectiveness of the final couplet in the scene.

5. "If it be true that all art aspires to the state of music, the opening of *Macbeth* approximates perfection."[1] How does this scene suggest an overture?

ACT I, SCENE 2

Dramatic Importance

In this scene, we meet Duncan, the kindly and generous King of Scotland, who is presented as an elderly man (V. i., the old man), but not as a warrior. Holinshed[2] refers to his soft and gentle nature and to his "slacknesse in punishing offendors". He had, it was said, "too much of clemencie". Malcolm is seen to be appreciative of services done him and to have a warm, democratic nature. In this scene, Ross performs the first of his many duties as messenger.

The main purpose of the scene, however, is to present a glowing picture of the military prowess of Macbeth: "brave", "noble", "Bellona's bridegroom". We are thus prepared for his appearance in the next scene. It is significant that he is granted a traitor's title.

Structurally, the scene falls into two parts: first, the Sergeant's

[1]H. C. Goddard, *The Meaning of Shakespeare*, Vol. 2 (Phoenix Books; Chicago, University of Chicago Press, 1951), p. 108.

[2]*Holinshed's Chronicle as Used in Shakespeare's Plays*, Allardyce and Josephine Nicoll, ed. (Everyman's Library; Toronto, J. M. Dent & Sons, (Canada) Limited, 1927), p. 208.

report of Macdonwald's revolt and his incomplete account of Sweno's invasion, and second, Ross's account of the final stages of the Norwegian affair and the Thane of Cawdor's treachery. Suspense and interest are created by these two reports, both of which stress the might and valour of Macbeth.

Shakespeare shows great skill in compressing history for the sake of dramatic intensity and for the purpose of building up his hero. In addition to telescoping the events of the various battles, he causes Macbeth to slay Macdonwald; actually, according to the *Chronicles*, the latter committed suicide. The purpose of this particular change is clear.

Questions

1. What qualities of a) Duncan's character, b) Malcolm's character, are brought out in their first appearance in the play?
2. a) Of what importance are the bleeding Sergeant and Ross?
   b) Why does Shakespeare introduce two messengers?
3. Outline the part played by Macbeth in the battles described.
4. a) What terms are used to describe Macbeth in this scene? b) By whom? c) Why?
5. Of what importance are a) Macdonwald? b) Sweno? c) the Thane of Cawdor?
6. a) How does Scene 2 resemble and differ from Scene 1? b) How are the two connected?
7. What would be a) the advantages, b) the disadvantages, of beginning the play with Scene 2?

ACT I, SCENE 3

Dramatic Importance

Our conception of the Witches as malevolent beings is reinforced at the beginning of this scene. Here, too, Macbeth, described earlier as "brave" and "noble", makes his first appearance, only to utter words that link him with "the instruments of darkness". Banquo also appears for the first time. The pronouncements made to the two men provide a basis for the action of the play, and suspense is created when Macbeth is named Thane of Cawdor by the King's messengers. Macbeth's first soliloquy gives us a certain insight into his character, and the contrast between the two men is brought out by Banquo's warning.

On his first appearance, in one production, "Macbeth wears a short brown leather tunic with long sleeves to wrist and round neck-opening. Over this he wears a steel armour coat from neck to waist with no sleeves. Green linen trousers to ankle with cross gartering of leather. Leather belt studded with metal buttons. Conical helmet of bronze. Heavy dark red cloak with brass clasp on right shoulder. Sword. Brown shoes."[1]

Questions

1. Of what importance are the Witches a) before, b) after, the appearance of Banquo and Macbeth?
2. Why would the salutations used by the Witches win Macbeth's confidence?
3. a) Which is the more desirable prophecy: to be a king or to be the father of a line of kings? b) Why?
4. What difference is there in the reaction of the two men to the prophecies?

[1]*French's Acting Edition of Macbeth* (Toronto, Samuel French (Canada) Limited, 1927).

160 · MACBETH

5. What examples are there of dramatic irony in this scene?
6. How does this scene set the stage for the main plot?
7. What qualities of Macbeth's character are brought out in his first soliloquy?
8. State the prophecies of the witches for macbeth + Banquo
9. How does this scene maintain the theme - a comparison between appearance + reality.

ACT I, SCENE 4

Dramatic Importance

The meeting of Macbeth and Duncan in this scene is full of dramatic irony because we know of the Witches' prophecy that Macbeth will be king. Hence, we are aware of an element of hypocrisy in Macbeth's behaviour towards Duncan that contrasts with Banquo's loyalty on the one hand and Duncan's whole-hearted generosity on the other. With the announcement that Malcolm is to be the King's heir, Macbeth realizes that if he wants the crown he must take steps to achieve it. By a strange coincidence, Duncan plans to visit Macbeth's castle at once, and by so doing plays into Macbeth's hands.

Questions

1. a) Find two examples of dramatic irony and show how they exhibit the qualities of this device. b) What do they add to the play?
2. Of what importance are a) Duncan's naming Malcolm his successor? b) Duncan's decision to visit Inverness?
3. What stage in the temptation of Macbeth is reached in this scene?
4. What justification is there for Mac. expecting that he may be named heir apparent

ACT I, SCENE 5

The introduction of Lady Macbeth is the most important feature of this scene. Her inflexible will, her great love for her husband, and her willingness to sacrifice her better self in order to fulfil his ambitions are brought out in her soliloquy and in her invocation to evil and to darkness.

Macbeth's character is analysed in her soliloquy; she sees him as ambitious, but insufficiently ruthless. Some critics have argued that if she had really understood her husband she would not have encouraged him to commit the crime that would lead to their ultimate destruction.

The bond between them is shown to be strong and deep; this is brought out in the letter, in their meeting, and especially in phrases used by Macbeth: "my dearest partner of greatness", "my dearest love". Although Macbeth jibs a little at the torrent of his wife's encouragement, we have the feeling that the murder will take place. His doubts tend merely to increase the suspense to a minor degree.

Questions

1. Of what importance is Macbeth's letter to his wife? (Consider plot, character, atmosphere.)

2. a) Analyse Lady Macbeth's soliloquy to bring out the qualities of Macbeth's character and the qualities of her own character.

   b) How well does she understand her husband?

3. What purpose is served by her invocation to the powers of evil and to darkness?

4. Why is Lady Macbeth determined that her husband shall commit the murder?

5. "We will speak further." Explain the importance of this speech.

ACT I, SCENE 6

Dramatic Importance

Duncan's arrival at Macbeth's castle means that he is at the mercy of his unscrupulous hostess and her ambitious husband. The scene is noteworthy for its quiet atmosphere, which provides a sharp contrast with that of the preceding scene, and for the cool, hypocritical courtesy of Lady Macbeth as she welcomes her unsuspicious guest.

Questions

1. a) How is a peaceful atmosphere created as the scene begins?
   b) How does this add pathos?
2. What qualities does Lady Macbeth illustrate in this scene?
3. Explain why Macbeth does not appear.
4. " the dramatic *irony* in this scene

ACT I, SCENE 7

Dramatic Importance

Macbeth's hesitation with regard to the murder is overcome by his wife's taunts and by her presentation of a plan that will, she insists, prevent them from being suspected. Macbeth allows himself to be persuaded and succumbs to temptation.

Questions

1. How does Macbeth's soliloquy "If it were done" (I. vii. 1-28) a) create sympathy for him? b) destroy sympathy for him?
2. Show that this soliloquy brings out his imagination, his ambition, his conscience, his honesty, and his cowardice.
3. What taunts are used by Lady Macbeth to spur him on to commit the crime?
4. a) What are the details of the plan she suggests? b) What is shown about Macbeth by his acceptance of it?
5. a) To what extent is her plan a good one? b) What are its weaknesses?
6. a) In what respects is Lady Macbeth both admirable and despicable in this scene? b) Why may she be compared to Eve?
7. How does Scene 7 bring Act I to a dramatic conclusion?

& Paraphrase Macbeth's soliloquy her.

ACT I

Dramatic Importance

In seven swift-moving scenes, Shakespeare presents the temptation of Macbeth and his decision to yield to it. At the very outset, the note of evil is struck, and the supernatural is introduced by means of the Witches. This is followed by an account of Macbeth's glorious victories on the field of battle, his reward from the King being, ironically, a traitor's title.

When we meet the hero, he seems already linked with evil, and the Witches' prophecies fall on receptive ears. To Banquo also comes a prophecy that may nullify the one pronounced to

Macbeth. Then, by a strange irony, the second prophecy is fulfilled, but any legitimate hopes Macbeth may have entertained
are dashed when the King names his son Malcolm his heir.
Duncan now announces his plan to visit the Macbeths at Inverness, and Macbeth hastens home with murder in his heart.
He has already informed his wife of the Witches' pronouncements, and she, prior to his arrival, has independently made up
her mind that he shall be king. Her great love for him increases
her determination. He demurs, and Lady Macbeth must greet
the King herself.

During the feast that evening, Macbeth leaves the company
and delivers his second important soliloquy; here, his doubts
and his weaknesses, as well as his more sympathetic qualities,
are revealed. His hesitation is soon overcome by his wife's taunts
of cowardice, fickleness, and faithlessness. When she offers a
practical, but callous, plan, he yields, and the die is cast.

Stages in the Temptation of Macbeth

1. Macbeth's "start" when he hears the pronouncements of
   the Witches indicates that he is not entirely innocent
   (I. iii. 51).

2. On receiving word that he has been named Thane of
   Cawdor, Macbeth, in a soliloquy, shows that he is con-
   templating murder to win the crown, but at this stage such
   an idea is abhorrent to him (I. iii. 135).

3. He is prepared to leave the matter to fate: "chance may
   crown me,/Without my stir" (I. iii. 143-4).

4. Nevertheless, he still wishes to talk the matter over with
   Banquo when time permits (I. iii. 153-5).

5. When Duncan names Malcolm his heir, Macbeth is determined to overcome the obstacle: "yet let that be,/
   Which the eye fears, when it is done, to see" (I. iv. 52-53).

6. When Lady Macbeth tries to urge him forward, however,
   he hesitates: "We will speak further" (I. v. 71).

7. In his soliloquy (I. vii. 1-28), he reveals that fear of the

consequences and a genuine respect for the King's good qualities are holding him back, but ambition pricks him on. Here, we see the inner conflict at its strongest.

8. With Lady Macbeth's entrance, the conflict becomes a clash of wills. Although Macbeth begins: "We will proceed no further in this business" (I. vii. 31) and answers her charge of cowardice with: "I dare do all that may become a man" (I. vii. 46), her strength of will begins to dominate as he asks "If we should fail?" (I. vii. 59).

9. When Lady Macbeth presents her plan, Macbeth's scruples and fears are overcome: "I am settled, and bend up/Each corporal agent to this terrible feat" (I. vii. 80-81).

Questions

1. Assess in terms of percentages the relative value of each of the following in Macbeth's decision to murder Duncan: the influence of the Witches, the influence of Lady Macbeth, Macbeth's own character, circumstances.

2. How does Lady Macbeth's description of Macbeth in her soliloquy "Glamis thou art" compare with the revelation of his character in his own soliloquy "If it were done"?

3. Estimate the importance of the Witches in Act I. (Consider plot, character, and atmosphere.)

4. How does Shakespeare build up the character of Macbeth in Act I?

5. Of what importance in Act I are the following: Ross, Malcolm, the Thane of Cawdor, Duncan's decision to visit Inverness, Macbeth's letter to his wife?

6. State the dramatic importance of each of the three soliloquies in Act I.

7. Define dramatic irony and give three effective examples from Act I. (Prove that each is an example of the device.)

8. The word "strange" occurs at least six times in Act I. Find these examples and suggest reasons for the emphasis on this word.

9. Find three examples of the clothing image, and show how each may be related to the theme of hypocrisy.

10. Why may Lady Macbeth be described as a "Super-witch" (Goethe)?

11. Describe Macbeth's first appearance in the play and explain how it is made dramatic.

12. On the basis of Act I, how valid is the Sergeant's comment: "brave Macbeth"?

ACT II, SCENE 1

Dramatic Importance

Banquo refuses to sleep because he is tempted in dreams by the Witches' prophecy to him; this contrasts sharply with the way in which Macbeth has yielded to evil. Banquo also appears to reject Macbeth's tentative overtures.

The dagger soliloquy heightens the tension and makes us realize that Macbeth has reached the point of no return; the murder is imminent. The dagger is the first of Macbeth's hallucinations; after it vanishes, he nerves himself for the ordeal ahead. The soliloquy is brilliant in its evocation of atmosphere.

Questions

1. What evidence is there in the text that a) Banquo has been tempted by the prophecy made to him? b) he is trying to resist the temptation?

2. How does the dagger soliloquy create atmosphere, advance the plot, and reveal character?

3. Refer to three details in this scene which show that Shakespeare visualised the action that was taking place onstage.

ACT II, SCENE 2

Dramatic Importance

From Lady Macbeth's first taut, half-whispered remarks to Macbeth's remorseful concluding cry, this scene is superb in its creation of the atmosphere that follows a murder. It presents a vivid contrast between Lady Macbeth's resourceful presence of mind (which springs from love for her husband) and Macbeth's shattered, conscience-stricken state of mind. Despite his wickedness, his awareness of the enormity of his crime creates sympathy for him, and Lady Macbeth's courage and practicality win our respect, if not our admiration. It is only thanks to her that Macbeth is not discovered by those whose knocking at the gate becomes more insistent as the scene ends.

Questions

1. How does Lady Macbeth save the situation in this scene?
2. Why does Shakespeare not show the murder of Duncan onstage?
3. Show that Macbeth's imagination and conscience are both active in this scene.
4. Show that Shakespeare makes use of a) a pun, b) metaphors, c) onomatopoeia, to create atmosphere.
5. Illustrate the use of a) irony, b) dramatic irony, c) suspense, d) effective timing, e) contrast, f) surprise, as found in this scene. (The same example may illustrate more than one device.)
6. What evidence is there in this scene of Shakespeare's profound understanding of human nature?
7. In the relevant passage from Holinshed, which describes the murder of King Duff, the deed was carried out by

four servants. Why has Shakespeare made Macbeth commit the crime himself?

8. How does this scene advance the plot?
9. What is its chief importance?

ACT II, SCENE 3

Dramatic Importance

The "Discovery Scene" begins with the interlude of the drunken
Porter. This serves two purposes: it gives the Macbeths time to
make themselves presentable, and it relieves the dramatic tension
with touches of humour, some of it rather bawdy.

Macduff, the symbol of nemesis, comes into the play with
clean hands and heart; he discovers the body of the murdered
King and rouses the household. When Malcolm asks who has
committed the crime, Lennox replies that apparently the grooms
of the chamber are responsible. At this point, Macbeth confesses
to the murder of the two chamberlains. Dead men tell no tales,
but Macbeth may have increased suspicion, rather than silenced
it, by this move. Macduff, at least, has his doubts about their
guilt.

Lady Macbeth's faint at this juncture may or may not be
genuine. If it is genuine, she elicits our sympathy because we
feel that she is not the steely, heartless creature she had striven
to be. If it is feigned, she inspires a certain admiration for her
attempt to shield Macbeth from further awkward questions.

Banquo takes the lead in suggesting an investigation, but he
makes no move to have Malcolm recognized in his father's
place. The King's sons determine to flee, a course of action that

will enable Macbeth to place the blame on them. Macbeth, as the scene ends, has weathered the first crisis, but we have less sympathy for him now than we did at the end of the preceding scene because of his surprising self-confidence and hypocrisy.

Questions

1. Show that humour in the drunken-Porter soliloquy springs from the following sources: topical allusions, dramatic irony, pun, euphemism, irony.

2. What purposes are served by the episode involving the Porter?

3. a) Why did Macbeth murder the grooms? b) In what respects was this wise? foolish?

4. Give reasons for thinking that Lady Macbeth's faint was a) genuine, b) feigned. c) What effect would each have on our opinion of her?

5. What part is played a) by Banquo, b) by Macduff, in this scene?

6. Of what importance is the intended flight of the King's sons?

7. As this scene ends, how close is Macbeth to the fulfilment of the third prophecy made to him by the Witches?

8. "This low soliloquy of the Porter and his few speeches afterwards, I believe to have been written for the mob by some other hand" (Coleridge). a) Give reasons for thinking that the Porter episode is genuine. b) Why would Coleridge dismiss it as spurious?

ACT II, SCENE 4

Dramatic Importance

This scene ties Act II neatly together. It provides a commentary on the murder that brings out its unnatural aspects and shows that Macbeth has achieved his ambition: "He is already nam'd, and gone to Scone/To be invested." Thanks to the flight of Malcolm and Donalbain, Macbeth is temporarily safe; yet, Macduff's decision to retire to his own castle is a premonitory hint that all is not well. "The good Macduff" refuses to compromise, as Ross is prepared to do. The nameless Old Man with his memories of the past shows how horrifying the murder of Duncan is and closes the act on a rather ominous note, despite the prayer in the final couplet.

Questions

1. What contrast between Macduff and Ross is presented in this scene?
2. How successful has Macbeth been in the achievement of his ambition?
3. What factors have contributed to his success?
4. What details are used to bring out the unnatural aspects of the murder?
5. What purpose is served by the Old Man in particular and the scene in general?
6. Show that the scene provides information about Macbeth, Macduff, Duncan, Malcolm and Donalbain, and Ross.

ACT II

Dramatic Importance

The central incident in Act II is the murder of Duncan. The first scene, which includes both a discussion with Banquo and the awesome dagger soliloquy, leads up to the deed. The murder is committed offstage so that in the second scene we may concentrate on Macbeth's tortured emotions of guilt and remorse. Only through Lady Macbeth's determination and will power do they escape discovery. In the third scene, after the drunken Porter interlude, the murder is discovered by Macduff. Macbeth kills the grooms, Lady Macbeth faints, and the King's sons prepare to flee, as Banquo suggests an immediate investigation.

In the final scene of Act II, the events of the preceding scenes are seen in perspective after an interval of a week or two. Macbeth has gone to Scone to be crowned, Duncan has been buried, and the youthful princes have fled. Macduff, the unconscious agent of nemesis, prepares to withdraw to his own castle. The third prophecy has apparently been fulfilled.

Questions

1. In what respects is each of the four scenes in Act II related to the murder of Duncan?
2. What part is played in Act II a) by Banquo? b) by Macduff?
3. Assuming that Lady Macbeth's faint in Act II, Scene 2 is feigned, show how she contributes in this act to her husband's safety and success.
4. Show that Macbeth's imagination and conscience create sympathy for him in Act II, whereas his hypocrisy destroys it.

5. What differences are there between the murder of Duncan and the murder of the grooms? (Consider motive, method, and effect in each case.)

ACT III, SCENE 1

Dramatic Importance

Macbeth is no sooner made King than he proceeds to plan his second great crime, the murder of Banquo and his son Fleance. After Banquo's departure, Macbeth delivers his third great soliloquy, in which he explains his motives. He feels that Banquo knows too much and may even be planning to murder him, but Banquo is to be removed chiefly because of the prophecy made to him. Macbeth is determined to establish a dynasty. Although he murdered Duncan to gain the throne, he murders Banquo in order to keep it.

The interview with the Murderers shows us that this time Macbeth is not going to risk the after-effects he suffered following the murder of Duncan. Nor does he confide in Lady Macbeth. He is becoming more callous, hard-hearted, and cold-blooded. •

Questions

1. What evidence is there in this scene that Banquo a) suspects Macbeth of the murder of Duncan? b) is planning to make the prophecy come true?
2. By referring to Macbeth's soliloquy (III. i. 48-72), summarize his reasons for wanting Banquo murdered.

3. Compare and contrast Macbeth's soliloquy about Banquo (III. i. 48-72) with his soliloquy about Duncan (I. vii. 1-28).

4. How do the plans for the second great crime differ from those made for the first one?

5. a) Analyse Macbeth's soliloquy (III. i. 48-72) to show that it deals entirely with Banquo. b) What is its purpose?

6. Why are the Murderers prepared to carry out Macbeth's wishes?

7. Select and explain two examples of dramatic irony.

ACT III, SCENE 2

Dramatic Importance

This scene fills in the lapse of time between Banquo's departure and his return. The murder, now fully planned, will be executed when darkness falls.

Lady Macbeth's growing disillusionment is apparent, paralleled by Macbeth's increasing ruthlessness. The husband-wife relationship deteriorates as Macbeth no longer confides in his lady. Some of Lady Macbeth's remarks might be interpreted as attempts to deter Macbeth from a course that she suspects, but she cannot hope to brake the wheel that now revolves faster and faster.

As the scene ends, the contrast between this and previous occasions on which they spoke together (I. v. and I. vii.) is striking.

Questions

1. What evidence may be gathered from this scene to support

the idea that Lady Macbeth's faint (II. iii. 126) was genuine?

2. Show by means of definite examples that the relationship between Macbeth and his wife has altered.

3. What indication is there in this scene of a) Macbeth's growing ruthlessness? b) his tormented conscience? c) his poetic imagination?

4. What is the main purpose served by this scene?

ACT III, SCENE 3

Dramatic Importance

In this scene, the crisis or turning point of the play occurs—the murder of Banquo and the escape of Fleance. Short, terse speeches culminating in sharp, violent action make the scene dramatically powerful. The identity of the Third Murderer can not be definitely established, although some critics believe that Macbeth, nervous and anxious about the outcome of his plans, has sent along Seyton, a trusted servant. (Oddly enough, if the usual scene division is accepted, this scene marks the mathematical centre of the play, the fourteenth of twenty-eight scenes.)

Questions

1. a) Give reasons to support the view that the murder of Banquo is the crisis of the play. b) In what respects is the escape of Fleance the turning point? c) Why should both be considered as part of one incident?

2. Why would the murder scene be more effective on the screen than on the stage?

3. How likely is it that Banquo had told Fleance of the prophecy made to him?

4. To what extent did Banquo deserve the death that befell him?

5. What differences and similarities are there between the murder of Duncan and that of Banquo?

6. Which do you regard as the greater crime, the murder of Duncan or the murder of Banquo? Give reasons for your answer.

7. "The 'third murderer' at Banquo's death is in all likelihood the hovering spirit of Macbeth."[1] Discuss.

8. Show how the speeches of the Third Murderer may be used to support the theory that Macbeth *was* the Third Murderer.

ACT III, SCENE 4

Dramatic Importance

The banquet has scarcely begun when Macbeth catches sight of the First Murderer, who reports that Banquo has been killed but that Fleance has escaped. The second piece of information is such a shock to Macbeth that it is hard to believe he was the Third Murderer. No sooner has the Murderer departed than the Ghost of Banquo presents itself to Macbeth. Although it actually appears onstage as indicated by the stage directions, it is likely that it is a figment of Macbeth's imagination. As Macbeth raves wildly, Lady Macbeth makes a valiant effort to prevent him

[1] J. T. Shipley, *Guide to Great Plays* (Washington, Public Affairs Press, 1950), p. 652.

from revealing his full guilt, but after the Ghost has appeared a second time, she dismisses the guests before Macbeth can answer their suspicious questions. It has been argued that the appearance of Banquo's Ghost is the turning point of the play, since now Macbeth has virtually established his guilt before the Scottish nobles.

Lady Macbeth is exhausted after her superhuman effort, but Macbeth shows a feverish energy. His thoughts turn to Macduff as a possible enemy, now that Banquo has been murdered. He plans to visit the Witches to find out what the future holds for him. We sense the deterioration of his character in his grim concluding remark: "We are yet but young in deed."

Questions

1. What arguments can be used to support the idea that the appearance of Banquo's Ghost is the crisis or turning point of the play?

2. How does this scene indicate a) that Macbeth was probably not the Third Murderer? b) that he might have been?

3. What methods and arguments are used by Lady Macbeth to restore Macbeth to normality?

4. How successful is Lady Macbeth in her attempts to save her husband from giving himself away?

5. Compare the part played by Lady Macbeth in Act II, Scene 2 following the murder of Duncan with the part she plays in the banquet scene when the Ghost appears.

6. Comment on the repeated use of the word "strange" in this scene by finding examples of its use and telling why it is effective in each case.

7. It has been suggested that the first ghost to appear in this scene is that of Duncan, the second that of Banquo. What evidence is there to support the idea that on both occasions it is Banquo's Ghost?

8. a) What proof is there that Shakespeare intended a "real" ghost to appear on the stage?

b) What indication is there that the Ghost was another visual hallucination?

9. Of what importance is it that a) Macbeth's thoughts turn at this time to Macduff? b) he is determined to seek out the Weird Sisters?

ACT III, SCENE 5

Dramatic Importance

"Hecate's Harangue" adds nothing to the plot of the play, but gives an opportunity for music and spectacle; it is generally conceded to be spurious.

Questions

1. Show that the metre and the subject matter of Hecate's Harangue differ from the speeches of the Witches in Act I, Scene 1 and Act I, Scene 3.
2. What details in the scene link it with what has gone before and what comes later in the play?
✓ 3. Why is this scene usually omitted from productions of *Macbeth*?

ACT III, SCENE 6

Dramatic Importance

This scene, which concludes Act III, resembles Act II, Scene 4 in being a summary of the action to date. References are made to both of Macbeth's great crimes and to the unhappy plight of Scotland. Lennox and "another Lord" represent the suspicious nobility, and from them we learn of Malcolm's whereabouts and Macduff's departure for England. The purpose of Macduff's errand is also given.

Although the scene looks back over the play, it also looks forward, since we wonder what the result of Macduff's flight will be. Thus, it creates suspense as well as providing information.

Questions

1. By specific reference to the text, show how this scene resembles Act II, Scene 4.
2. What reference is made to the two great crimes of Macbeth?
3. What information are we given about Malcolm, Macduff, Edward the Confessor, and Siward?
4. How does the scene provide an effective conclusion to Act III?
5. By means of at least three examples show that Lennox's speech, lines 1-24, is heavily ironic.

ACT III

Dramatic Importance

As Act II was dominated by Duncan, so Act III is dominated by Banquo. Plans for his murder are made in the first scene; in the second, Macbeth yearns for nightfall, the appointed time for the murder. The murder is carried out in the third scene. Fleance, Banquo's son and heir, escapes; this escape, along with the murder of Banquo, marks the turning point of the play. The banquet scene is centred around the appearance of the Ghost of Banquo and its effect on Macbeth. Another reason for considering that Scene 5 may not be Shakespearian is the fact that it contains no reference to Banquo; in Scene 6, Lennox comments ironically on Banquo's death.

Although we find Macbeth speaking magnificent poetry, and see him tormented by pangs of conscience (without repentance), we also observe his character degenerating into ruthlessness. He plans the murders cold bloodedly, without assistance from Lady Macbeth; after giving himself away before his nobles in the banquet scene, he plans to visit the Witches and to investigate Macduff's behaviour.

Lady Macbeth is no longer the dominating partner; although her ambition, the crowning of her husband, has been achieved, she is bitterly disillusioned. She is no longer Macbeth's confidante, and after making a gallantly heroic effort to save him in the banquet scene, she appears utterly spent and exhausted.

Although Macduff does not appear in Act III, Shakespeare does not permit us to forget him. Macbeth's thoughts turn towards him as a possible enemy, and as Act III ends we learn that Macduff has departed for England in the hope of winning support for an attack against Macbeth. We are also reminded of Malcolm's presence in the English court.

The chief action in Act III centres about Macbeth's second great crime and its immediate consequences. We see how one crime leads to another, and we watch with horror and pity as Macbeth writhes in the meshes of the web he himself has woven.

Questions

1. Prove that Banquo dominates Act III.
2. Consider the second great crime under the following headings: a) the motive, b) the plans, c) the deed, d) the results.

3. What evidence is there in Act III to support the theory that Lady Macbeth's faint was genuine?

4. Illustrate the importance in Act III of a) Fleance, b) Lennox, c) Macduff.

5. What qualities of Lady Macbeth's character are brought out by her appearances in Act III?

6. What indication is there in Act III of the following qualities of Macbeth's character: a) poetic imagination? b) vestiges of conscience? c) increasing ruthlessness?

7. To what degree have the prophecies made by the Witches been fulfilled as Act III ends?

8. Show that references to darkness or night may be found in at least five of the six scenes.

9. Comment on the significance of the following hallucinations: a) the airdrawn dagger, b) the voice that cried: "Sleep no more", c) the Ghost of Banquo (assuming that it, too, is a figment of Macbeth's imagination). What points of similarity or difference are there among them?

10. "The murder of Banquo was a dismal failure." Comment.

ACT IV, SCENE 1

Dramatic Importance

The gruesome details of the Witches' incantation create an appropriate atmosphere of horror for this, their last appearance in the play. Into this evil, murky air comes Macbeth, who thus associates himself with the dark powers. The predictions of the Apparitions create confidence in him, but his sense of security is shaken by the appearance of Banquo and his royal descendants. Macbeth's rage is augmented by the news that Macduff has slipped through his fingers, and in his fury, he conceives a spiteful plan for revenge. The scene is filled with foreshadowings of future events, but dominating all is the grim picture of the degeneration of Macbeth's character.

Questions

1. a) What does each of the Apparitions represent? b) State the prediction given by each.
2. a) In what respects can these predictions be considered a manifestation of Macbeth's own thoughts? b) In what respects may they not be so considered?
3. a) Describe "Banquo's revenge". b) What is its effect on Macbeth?
4. How do the prophecies of Act IV, Scene 1 differ from or resemble those made in Act I, Scene 3?
5. How will Macbeth's confidence in the second set of prophecies be increased as the scene ends?
6. What difference is there between the plans for the third great crime and those that preceded the other two?
7. What evidence is there of the degeneration of Macbeth's character in this scene?
8. By giving at least two examples of each, show that Shakespeare uses sound, rhythm, and detail to create the atmosphere of horror in lines 1-38.

ACT IV, SCENE 2

Dramatic Importance

The main purpose of this brief, tense scene is to show the deterioration of Macbeth's character into savagery. The third great crime has neither motive nor justification; it is merely a senseless slaughter befitting a madman. The deliberate murder of defenceless women and children has always been regarded as one of the most heinous crimes known to civilization.

We meet two new characters in this scene: Lady Macduff and her son. Both make a great impact on us; we are struck by their courage and appalled by their fate. The suffering of the innocent endured with fortitude is one of the ingredients of high tragedy; their nobility in misfortune wrings our hearts.

Suspense is created by the use of two messengers: Ross and the kindly but nameless individual who came to offer a futile warning. The precocity of young Macduff adds a pitiful humour to the scene; his mother is depicted as a very human and loyal wife, who deeply loves her husband despite his apparent desertion. The note of domesticity in the scene provides a contrast with the formality of the court and the machinations of Macbeth.

It has been said that this is the deed which finally turned Ross against Macbeth. It also brings closer the hounds of nemesis that are pursuing Macbeth.

Questions

1. What dramatic purpose is served a) by Ross? b) by the nameless messenger?
2. a) Discuss the possible identity of the nameless messenger. b) What other examples are there in the play of characters unidentified by name?
3. How does the execution of the third great crime differ from and resemble the two preceding murders?
4. a) Why may the third great crime be considered the worst? b) What does it prove about Macbeth?
5. Illustrate the following devices as they are exemplified in this scene: suspense, dramatic irony, pathos, humour, contrast (within the scene and with other scenes).
6. What evidence is there of the following qualities in young Macduff's character: precocious logic, loyalty, courage?

7. Prove that despite his precocity he is still comparatively young.
8. a) Give examples of young Macduff's cynical observations. b) How do these add to the pathos of the situation?
9. a) Distinguish between pathos and tragedy. b) Which is shown in this scene?
10. What qualities does Lady Macduff share with her son?
11. Some critics argue that the scene is too harrowing to have been written by Shakespeare. Present arguments for and against this thesis.
12. "The slaughter of the innocent wife and child is final testimony to the public horrors of Macbeth's lawless reign."[1] What further evidence is there that Macbeth's personal disintegration is having its effect on life and conditions in Scotland? (See also Act II, Scene 4; Act III, Scene 6; and Act IV, Scene 3.)

ACT IV, SCENE 3

Dramatic Importance

Although this is only one of the twenty-eight scenes in the play, it is longer than any other and takes up approximately one-eighth of the total number of lines. It is closer to Holinshed than any other scene in the play; and the verbal similarities are many and marked.

The scene falls into three main parts: the testing of Macduff, the section dealing with the King's Evil, and the breaking of the news to Macduff. The testing of Macduff is divided into two parts: Malcolm first tests Macduff's loyalty and then his moral

[1]W. Rosen, *Shakespeare and the Craft of Tragedy* (Cambridge, Harvard University Press, 1960), p. 99.

standards. Only when satisfied on both counts does he tell Macduff of the projected plan to invade Scotland with Siward's help
and accept Macduff as a partner in the enterprise: "Now we'll
together." This section with its comment and discussion about
the character of an ideal monarch would be of great interest to
Shakespeare's patron, King James, as would the second episode
in the scene.

Nominally in praise of Edward the Confessor's power to heal
and to prophesy, this second interlude was doubtless intended to
flatter the King, a descendant of Edward's. It also provides a
sharp contrast between a bad king who trusts in the black magic
of the Witches and a good king who practises "white magic".
Apart from these aspects, this episode does not add to the
development of the plot.

In the final section, Shakespeare presents a scene of powerful
intensity as Ross gives Macbeth the news of the slaughter of his
wife and children. Prior to the actual announcement, the dramatic irony is unbearably sharp, and Macduff's response to the
news shows Shakespeare's deep insight into human nature. The
scene ends with Macduff's vow of vengeance and Malcolm's
decision to leave at once for Scotland with his army.

The scene offers ample opportunity for character analysis.
Malcolm appears to have become more mature, and we are
given the impression that some time has passed since the murder
of Duncan. The young Prince has become cautious and prudent;
he does not judge by appearances as his father was inclined to
do. Some editors are critical of his deliberate falsification of his
own character and of the way he deceives Macduff, but he
shows in this a practical realism that will stand him in good
stead as king. The episode brings out his concept of the high
moral standards a monarch should have; he mentions particularly his puritanical attitude towards sex, his lack of avarice, his
loyalty, and his love of truth.

H. C. Goddard[1] makes the following comment about the
passage in which Malcolm tests Macduff: "In it Malcolm reveals

[1]Goddard, *op. cit.*, p. 131.

on a smaller scale some of the most engaging traits of Hamlet: something of the same modesty, wisdom, circumspection, and poetic insight, the same tendency to dramatize himself, to pass himself off for less than he is, to lie low and play psychological games on others but without a trace of Hamlet's antic disposition. He speaks in this scene mainly about evil, but in doing so his vocabulary manages to be full of such words as angels, grace, child, snow, lamb, milk. If we know Shakespeare, we know what this means. The man's imagination is contradicting his intellect. His metaphors are giving away the deeper truth."

Macduff's dominant quality as revealed in this scene is his love of Scotland. We see also his high moral standards and his courage; he tells Malcolm that such a scoundrel as Malcolm asserted himself to be is not fit to live. That he is a man of deep and tender feelings is revealed by his reception of the shattering news brought by Ross. His strength of character emerges as he controls his grief and swears vengeance on the tyrant. His manner of speaking, blunt and direct, serves to emphasize the straightforward honesty of his character.

Macbeth's third great crime has caused Ross to turn against him at last, and his sympathy with Macduff is brought out as he first hesitates, and then blurts out the unhappy news he has come to deliver.

Questions

1. From this scene, give evidence of Malcolm's prudence and high moral standards.
2. a) Of what vices does he accuse himself? b) Why?
3. What qualities does he eventually state that he possesses?
4. Outline and comment on his recipe for an ideal king.
5. Of what dramatic importance is the testing of Macduff?
6. What contrasts are implied between Macbeth and Edward the Confessor?
7. Illustrate the following characteristics of Macduff: patriotism, moral standards, honesty, deep human affections, determination to secure revenge, blunt manner of speaking.

8. Why does Shakespeare choose to make Macduff rather than Malcolm the agent of nemesis?
9. By giving at least three examples of its use, show that dramatic irony dominates this scene.

ACT IV

Dramatic Importance

Although Macduff appears in only one of the scenes, he dominates Act IV. In the first scene, two of the prophecies have to do with him, and the announcement of his departure for England causes Macbeth to seek a spiteful revenge by slaughtering Macduff's household. This vicious deed takes place in the second scene. In the third scene, Macduff is tested by Malcolm; he is also informed by Ross of the tragedy that has befallen his family. As this scene and this act end, Macduff swears his oath of vengeance.

Malcolm is also important in Act IV. The third prophecy refers to him, and in the last scene we meet him at the court of Edward the Confessor, where he is planning an invasion of Scotland in which he will be assisted by Macduff and Old Siward. We notice his growing maturity and sense that he will be a better, because a more realistic, king than his father. What Banquo and Duncan are to the rising action of the play, Macduff and Malcolm are to the falling action.

Ross is the bearer of news in Act IV; he brings to Lady Macduff word of her husband's departure and to Macduff the news of the tragedy.

Macbeth appears only in the first scene. Since he has sought out the Witches, we feel that he has committed his soul to evil. The three prophecies give him confidence, but he is infuriated by "Banquo's revenge" and the announcement that Macduff has escaped his clutches. His third great crime follows.

Macbeth's third great crime is the central fact of Act IV, and events are now moving swiftly to bring about his doom and downfall.

Questions

1. a) How does Macduff help to unify Act IV? b) Show that Malcolm also contributes to its unity.
2. Of what importance is Ross in Act IV?
3. To what extent have the prophecies made in Act IV, Scene 1 already come true as the act ends?
4. How are we reminded in Act IV of the first series of prophecies made by the Witches?
5. How likely is it that Macbeth would employ the same murderers in Act III, Scene 3 and Act IV, Scene 2?
6. Of what importance is the supernatural in Act IV?
7. Comment on the following aspects of the third great crime: cause, method, result, what it proves about Macbeth.

ACT V, SCENE 1

Dramatic Importance

The incomparable sleep-walking scene shows the results of Lady Macbeth's surrender to evil at the beginning of the play. It reveals the suffering of a tormented soul on the verge of a complete breakdown. We cannot help noticing the contrast between the woman of iron will whom we met in Act I, Scene 5 and this broken, pitiable being with her fear of the darkness that she herself had invoked.

The scene provides us with a deeper insight into the true character of Lady Macbeth and makes us more sympathetic towards her, although we know that she brought disaster upon herself and is a victim of nemesis. Her isolation is emphasized, and we see her for the last time as she seeks in her bed the refuge of peace and untroubled sleep, both of which are denied her.

The scene also has certain practical values. It enables Shakespeare to concentrate fully on Macbeth and his plight, since we do not meet Lady Macbeth again. Her references to the three great crimes serve as a kind of recapitulation of the action.

Above all, however, the scene is charged with emotional tension and is one of the most dramatic in the play. Although Lady Macbeth speaks in prose, as befits a disordered state of mind, her words are deeply moving and utterly unforgettable.

Questions

1. The four main features of Lady Macbeth's delirium have been characterized as: a) the mere reproduction of the horrible scenes she has passed through, b) the struggle to keep her husband from betraying himself, c) the uprising of her feminine nature against the foulness of the deed, d) her fear of the after-death.[1] Illustrate accurately each of these features.
2. How does Shakespeare seek to create sympathy for Lady Macbeth?
3. Of what importance in the scene are the Doctor and the Waiting-Gentlewoman?

[1]*Macbeth*, A. W. Verity, ed. (Cambridge, Cambridge University Press, 1911), p. 148.

4. How does this scene support (or disprove) the validity of Lady Macbeth's faint?
5. Compare Lady Macbeth's first appearance in the play with her last.
6. Describe the symptoms of Lady Macbeth's disorder.
7. a) What is the Doctor's "prescription"? b) How valid is it? c) What would a modern psychiatrist advise?
8. a) Analyse the meaning of Lady Macbeth's action of washing her hands. b) What does it symbolize? c) Why does it seem ironic?
9. What would a person unfamiliar with the play (for example, the Doctor) deduce about Lady Macbeth's activities prior to this scene?
10. Why do great actresses regard the scene a) as a challenge? b) as an opportunity?

ACT V, SCENE 2

Dramatic Importance

Act V, Scene 2 might be entitled "The Defection of the Scottish Thanes". Their desertion emphasizes the isolation of Macbeth, who, in view of this and the third prophecy (IV. i.), has retired to his stronghold at Dunsinane. We learn, too, of the advance of the English force and the prospective rendezvous near Birnam Wood.

The Scottish Thanes are not very sharply characterized, since they symbolize a group, but what they stand for is unmistakable. Shakespeare is at pains to mention Donalbain's absence (although we do not learn where he is) and to introduce the name of Young Siward in preparation for the part he will play later.

The atmosphere is one of resolution; the forces of good are now inexorably gathering to bring about the destruction of evil.

Questions

1. In some of the more famous productions of the past; *e.g.*, those of Sir Henry Irving and Sir Johnston Forbes-Robertson, this scene was omitted. Give reasons for such an omission.
2. It has been remarked that it would be very difficult to "spot" passages from this scene. Why is this?
3. What do we learn of Macbeth and his plans?
4. Why does Shakespeare mention a) Donalbain, b) Young Siward, in this scene?
5. How does this scene suggest a) the growing isolation of Macbeth? b) the growing solidarity of the forces in opposition to him?

ACT V, SCENE 3

Dramatic Importance

Macbeth learns of the desertion of the Scottish Thanes, the approach of the English force, and the deteriorating condition of his wife. His insecurity is shown by his impatience and his irritability in his speeches to the Servant, the Doctor, and Seyton. He bolsters his courage by expressing his confidence in the prophecies of the Apparitions. And yet this blood-stained tyrant sums up the tragedy of his existence in sheer poetry; it is part of Shakespeare's genius that even his villains have redeeming qualities.

The main purpose of this scene is to provide us with a picture of Macbeth's situation in contrast to that of his opponents. Macbeth symbolizes disintegration, whereas his foes represent integration.

Questions

1. What is the effect on Macbeth of each of the items of news he receives in this scene?
2. How does Macbeth reveal his basic insecurity? Give specific references.
3. Show that he is apparently placing his trust in the second and third prophecies of the Apparitions.
4. What evidence is there in this scene that Shakespeare visualized the action which was taking place onstage? (Give three examples.)
5. Compare Macbeth's state of mind in this scene with that of Lady Macbeth in Act V, Scene 1.

ACT V, SCENE 4

Dramatic Importance

The English and Scottish forces have met at the appointed rendezvous. Malcolm's order to his army foreshadows the fulfilment of the prophecy of the Third Apparition and creates dramatic irony, since he is unaware of the significance of his action.

The scene presents an atmosphere of confidence and strength; the optimism of youth is balanced by the experience of age. Suspense is created as we wonder what the result of Malcolm's command will be.

Questions

1. a) Show that Malcolm is the unconscious agent of destiny.
   b) How does his command create dramatic irony?
2. What do we learn of Macbeth's plans?
3. How are optimism and restraint balanced in this scene?
4. How does Scene 4 provide a contrast with Scene 3?

ACT V, SCENE 5

Dramatic Importance

Macbeth receives two blows in this scene: he learns of the death of Lady Macbeth and of the approach of Birnam Wood. Although he had determined to remain within the castle, at the end of the scene we find him preparing to rush forth in a frenzy.

Questions

1. Compare Macbeth's reception of the news of his wife's death with the way Macduff reacted to Ross's announcement concerning the death of Lady Macduff and her children.
2. a) Of the two announcements made to Macbeth in this scene, which affects him more deeply? b) Why?
3. Account for Macbeth's change of plan as this scene ends.
4. With regard to Macbeth's speech, lines 17-28, a) state the theme, b) comment on the prevailing emotion, c) illustrate onomatopoeia, d) select three metaphors.

ACT V, SCENE 6

Dramatic Importance

In reverting to the attacking force, Shakespeare provides us with a contrast; solidarity and confidence are opposed to rage and desperation.

Questions

1. How does Malcolm show his qualities of leadership in this scene?
2. How does the scene indicate that battle is about to be joined?

ACT V, SCENE 7

Dramatic Importance

The death of Young Siward gives Macbeth confidence in the prophecy made by the Second Apparition so that the shock he later receives comes with more force. Pity is created by the death of this youth at the hands of a practised, able fighter. The incident serves to delay the climax and thus to create suspense. Suspense is also created as Macduff, thirsting for vengeance, enters on the heels of the encounter. Only a meeting of Macbeth and Macduff remains, for as the scene ends we learn of the surrender of Dunsinane Castle to Malcolm's forces.

Questions

1. What purposes are served by the encounter between Macbeth and Young Siward?
2. How do the following create suspense: a) the death of Young Siward? b) the speech of Macduff?
3. Of what importance is the surrender of the castle?

ACT V, SCENE 8

Dramatic Importance

The death of Macbeth at the hands of the avenging Macduff marks the catastrophe of the play; the meeting of these two also provides the emotional climax of the tragedy. The forces of good, as represented by the rightful heir Malcolm, are now triumphant, and it is only fitting that Macduff, who has sacrificed so much for his country, should be the first to hail the new King of Scotland. The only sad note struck is that of Ross's announcement to Siward that his son is dead; the old man's courage and strength fill us with respect and admiration. Malcolm's final speech restores us to the C major of life and we feel that the kingdom is in good hands.

Questions

1. And be these juggling fiends no more believ'd,
   That palter with us in a double sense.
   Why has Macbeth come to this conclusion about the Witches?
2. Show that Macbeth's pride and physical courage come to his rescue.
3. Some theatre-goers and students of the play have felt that the presentation of Macbeth's head on a pole is too ignominious and grotesque an end for a once-valiant warrior. Comment.
4. Show that Ross is once more the bearer of news.
5. a) How is the death of Young Siward turned from a matter for mourning into a cause of pride? b) Why does Shakespeare do this?
6. Discuss Malcolm's summary of Macbeth and Lady Macbeth: "this dead butcher and his fiend-like queen".

7. How likely is it that Lady Macbeth committed suicide?
8. How does Malcolm's speech bring the play to a satisfactory conclusion?
9. How does this scene satisfy the demands of justice with regard to a) Macbeth? b) Macduff? c) Malcolm?
10. To what extent is Macbeth entitled to our sympathy?
11. In what sense is the death of Macbeth a) tragic? b) not tragic?

ACT V

Dramatic Importance

Act V begins with the sleep-walking scene, but thereafter scenes connected with battle predominate. The principle of alternation is illustrated as we move back and forth from Macbeth's castle to scenes involving his enemies; the sense of disintegration and desperation contrasts with that of solidarity and optimism.

Lady Macbeth's death is reported, and one by one the prophecies made by the Apparitions are fulfilled. Birnam Wood comes to Dunsinane by means of branch-bearing soldiers; the unnatural circumstances surrounding Macduff's premature birth are made known to Macbeth.

Meanwhile battle has been joined, the only significant casualty in Malcolm's army being Young Siward. The play reaches its climax in the dramatic, long-awaited meeting of Macduff and Macbeth, and justice triumphs as the latter is slain. To Macduff goes the honour of hailing Malcolm as King of Scotland, and the play ends on a note of stability as the young King takes firm control of his rejoicing realm.

Questions

1. Show that nemesis overtakes Macbeth and Lady Macbeth in an appropriate way.
2. a) Account for the large number of short scenes in Act V.
   b) What effect is produced by this multiplicity?
3. How does Shakespeare build up the suspense in Act V, from Scene 2 to Scene 8?
4. Compare the death of Young Siward with the death of Macbeth. Consider the circumstances surrounding each and the effect of each.
5. Summarize the part played a) by Macduff, b) by Malcolm, in Act V.
6. What dramatic purpose is served in Act V by a) the Scottish nobles? b) Ross? c) Old Siward?
7. Show how the prophecies made by the Apparitions come true in Act V.
8. What evidence is there that Malcolm will make a good king?
9. Why do we acquiesce in the deaths of Macbeth and Lady Macbeth?

GENERAL QUESTIONS ON THE WHOLE PLAY

PART A   The following questions on the tragic aspect of the play are based on Bradley's *Shakespearean Tragedy*.[1]

1. A Shakespearean tragedy is a story of human actions producing exceptional calamity and ending in the death of a man in high estate. To what extent does Bradley's definition apply to *Macbeth*?

[1]Bradley, *op. cit., passim.*

2. Conflict is indispensable to drama. In *Macbeth*, there is an outward conflict of persons and groups, and also a conflict of forces in the hero's soul. Give examples of this double conflict.

3. The central feeling in a great tragedy is, according to Bradley, one of waste. How is this illustrated in *Macbeth*?

4. "The main source of the convulsion which produces suffering and death is never good . . . it is in almost every case . . . plain moral evil." Comment on this statement as applied to *Macbeth*.

5. Bradley implies that the ultimate power in the tragic world is a moral order. How does good triumph over evil as *Macbeth* ends?

6. "The hero [in a Shakespearian play] . . . always contributes in some measure to the disaster in which he perishes." Apply this statement to Macbeth.

7. "Character is destiny." How is this idea illustrated in *Macbeth*?

8. Show that Shakespeare makes use in *Macbeth* of a) abnormal conditions of mind, b) the supernatural, c) chance.

9. "The whole tragedy is sublime." Explain the meaning of this statement as applied to *Macbeth*.

10. *Macbeth* is "the most vehement, the most concentrated, perhaps we may say the most tremendous, of the tragedies". Discuss this estimate of *Macbeth*.

PART B   General Questions

11. "*Macbeth* is incomparably brilliant as it stands and within its limits perfect."[1] Why can the play be called brilliant?

12. "*Macbeth* has been extravagantly over-praised. It is the weakest of Shakespeare's great tragedies and so full of

[1]Mark Van Doren, *Shakespeare* (Doubleday Anchor Books; Garden City, Doubleday & Company Inc., 1954), p. 217.

blemishes that it is hard to believe that one man wrote it."[1] What are some of the blemishes that Harrison is referring to?

13. "*Macbeth*, like *Crime and Punishment*, is a study of evil through a study of murder. Each is its author's most rapid, concentrated, terrific and possibly sublime work. Each is a prolonged nightmare lifted into the realm of art."[2] How is the idea of a nightmare illustrated in the play?

14. "The interest in the tragedy of *Macbeth* is the perpetration of a crime by a man whose magnificent qualities of mind, extreme courage, and poetic imagination raise the villainies above common meanness and give occasion for a superhuman conflict of images and ideas."[3]

    a) Illustrate the characteristics of Macbeth that are referred to here.

    b) In what sense are his villainies raised above common meanness?

15. "In no other of Shakespeare's tragedies is such sustained power of poetry combined with such surging emotion and such unremitting force of action."[4] Select a scene in which poetry, emotion, and action are combined to a marked degree and illustrate each quality.

16. Show that *Macbeth* is a play of fathers and sons.

17. If nemesis is "the principle of avenging justice", bringing rewards as well as punishment, show how it operates with regard to Duncan, Banquo, Macbeth, Lady Macbeth, Malcolm, and Macduff.

18. In what respects would *Macbeth* make a) a good film? b) a good opera?

[1]G. B. Harrison, *Shakespeare's Tragedies* (London, Routledge & Kegan Paul, Ltd., 1952), p. 184.
[2]Goddard, *op. cit.*, p. 108.
[3]Robert Bridges, *The Influence of the Audience in Shakespeare* (The New Adelphi, Dec. 1927), p. 77.
[4]Shipley, *op. cit.*, p. 656.

19. Macbeth's crimes are regicide, murder, usurpation, and tyranny. By reference to the play, show that he is guilty of each.

20. " 'Macbeth' is indeed the tragedy of unchecked will destroying itself, as 'Hamlet' is the tragedy of unready will wasting itself."[1]

   a) What evidence is there in the play of the "unchecked will destroying itself"?

   b) In what ways does this quotation sum up the tragedy of Macbeth himself?

21. "Tragedy has to do with men possessing the capacity to become gods who, momentarily at least, become devils."[2] How does this statement apply to Macbeth?

22. Show that the substance of the play might be summed up in the words "war, murder, and tyranny".

Structure and Plot

23. "*Macbeth* falls naturally into three parts. The first shows how Macbeth murdered Duncan but allowed the ultimate avenger to escape. . . . The second part of the play tells how Macbeth tried to defeat Fate by murdering Banquo and his son Fleance so that there should be no chance that any son of Banquo's would become king. . . . The third and last section of the play . . . shows how Fate having cheated Macbeth, proceeds to destroy him."[3] Comment on the validity of these divisions.

24. According to Harley Granville-Barker,[4] *Macbeth* falls into three parts: the achievement of Macbeth's ambition (Acts I and II); his wielding of power (Act III and Act IV, Scenes 1 and 2); the process of retribution (Act IV,

[1]J. Drinkwater, *The Outline of Literature* (Revised by Horace Shipp; London, George Newnes Limited, 1962), p. 302.

[2]Goddard, *op. cit.*, p. 115.

[3]Harrison, *op. cit.*, pp. 198-9.

[4]H. Granville-Barker, Introduction to *The Players' Shakespeare: The Tragedie of Macbeth* (London, Field Roscoe & Co., 1923), p. xxxiii.

Scene 3 to end). Compare these divisions with those suggested in Question 23.

25. "The play of *Macbeth* falls naturally into two parts: the first part being concerned with the rise of Macbeth, the second with his fall. The turning point of the action is the murder of Banquo."[1] Justify (or challenge) this comment.

26. Apply the terms exposition, complication, crisis, falling action (sometimes called resolution), catastrophe (climax), and outcome to the play.

27. Select the crisis or turning point of the action and give reasons for your choice. (Suggested crises include the murder of Duncan, the murder of Banquo, the escape of Fleance, the appearance of Banquo's Ghost.)

28. *Macbeth* has been praised for its symmetry. Show how this quality is reflected in its structure.

29. Show that the play begins and ends with a battle and that each of the remaining acts deals with a great crime.

30. "Probably in no play of Shakespeare are so many questions asked."[2]
    a) How many scenes in Act I begin with questions?
    b) What is the value of this technique?
    c) Refer to at least five other questions asked in the play and state their importance.

Theme

31. "*Macbeth* is Shakespeare's most profound and mature vision of evil."[3] In what respects is the conflict of good and evil basic to the play?

32. How is the theme of revenge illustrated in *Macbeth*?

33. a) Show that the symbol of the blood-stained hand is central to the play. b) What does it symbolize?

[1]*Macbeth*, S. Wood, ed. (London, George Gill & Sons, 1902).
[2]G. Wilson Knight, *The Wheel of Fire* (London, Methuen & Co. Ltd., 1960), p. 141.
[3]*Ibid*, p. 140.

34. How is the reversal of the moral and social order illustrated in *Macbeth*?

35. The theme of the play is the eternal conflict between good and evil. a) What evidence is there of each in the play? b) Prove that good triumphs.

36. Equivocation plays an important part in *Macbeth*. Define and give three examples of this theme from the play.

Setting

37. What incidents in the play are associated with a) a desert place? b) a camp near Forres? c) Macbeth's castle at Inverness? d) the palace at Forres? e) Fife? f) Dunsinane?

38. a) Which is the only scene that takes place outside of Scotland? b) How is the atmosphere of Scotland retained in this scene?

39. What use is made of outdoor scenes in the play?

40. a) How important is the Scottish background? b) How is it suggested?

Time

41. a) In what historical period is the play supposedly set? b) What evidence is there of this in the text?

42. a) What examples of anachronism are found in the play? b) How can these be explained?

43. How much time appears to elapse between the beginning and the end of the play? Refer to incidents that suggest the passage of time.

44. a) Find three examples of topical allusions. b) What do they add to the play?

Atmosphere, Emotion, Dramatic Devices

45. "Darkness, we may even say blackness, broods over this tragedy."[1]

[1]Bradley, *op. cit.*, p. 333.

    a) In what sense is this darkness symbolic?

    b) Refer to at least four important scenes that take place at night.

46. Despite the darkness, "*Macbeth* leaves a decided impression of colour; it is really the impression of a black night broken by flashes of light and colour, sometimes vivid and even glaring."[1] a) Show that lightning, torches, a candle, and a blazing cauldron contribute to this effect. b) In what other sense can this statement be interpreted and illustrated?

47. "This world, which is at once without and within Macbeth, can be most easily described as 'strange'. The word, like the Witches, is always somewhere doing its work."[2]
    a) Find at least four examples of the use of the word.
    b) What effect is secured by the emphasis on it?

48. "Fear is the primary emotion of the *Macbeth* universe; fear is at the root of Macbeth's crime"[3] (the murder of Duncan). What evidence is there to support Professor Knight's theory?

49. a) Show that references to blood are prevalent in the play. b) What is the significance of the repeated references?

50. How does Act I, Scene 1 set the atmosphere of the play?

51. Only two humorous episodes are found in *Macbeth*: the Porter episode (II. iii.) and the conversation of Lady Macduff and her son (IV. ii. 30 ff.).
    a) What are the main differences between them?
    b) What purpose does each serve?

52. a) Define the term "dramatic irony". b) What is its dramatic value? c) What purpose does it serve in *Macbeth*? d) Refer to four particularly effective examples.

53. *Macbeth* is noted for antithesis. Give examples of con-

[1]Bradley, *op. cit.*, p. 334.
[2]Van Doren, *op. cit.*, p. 217.
[3]Knight, *op. cit.*, p. 150.

trast a) in the atmosphere, b) within single characters, c) between scenes or episodes, d) between characters.

54. a) Define "suspense". b) Find an effective example of this quality in each act. c) At what point in the play is suspense at its height?

55. Illustrate the following dramatic devices: surprise, effective timing, foreshadowing of events, coincidence, pathetic fallacy.

56. Find examples of the following: pathos, satire, verbal irony, parallelism.

57. Analyse the dramatic importance of a) the Witches, b) the Ghost of Banquo, c) the Apparitions.

58. Of what importance is the number "three" in the play?

Characters and Characterization

MACBETH

59. Using the three main methods of characterization; that is, what a character says, what a character does, what others say about him, show that Macbeth is ambitious.

60. Show that Macbeth is both the hero and the villain of the play.

61. *Macbeth* has been compared to *Hamlet* in certain respects. What similarities are there between Macbeth and a) Hamlet? b) Claudius?

62. "So long as Macbeth's imagination is active, we watch him fascinated; we feel suspense, horror, awe; in which are latent, also, admiration and sympathy. But so soon as it is quiescent, these feelings vanish. He is no longer 'infirm of purpose': he becomes domineering, even brutal, or he becomes a cool pitiless hypocrite."[1]

a) Refer to at least three occasions when Macbeth's imagination reveals his better qualities.

b) Show that once his imagination is inoperative, his conscience, too, appears dead.

[1]Bradley, *op. cit.*, p. 356.

63. The history of Macbeth after the murder of Duncan "is an engrossing spectacle, and psychologically it is perhaps the most remarkable exhibition of the *development* of a character to be found in Shakespeare's tragedies".[1] Illustrate the progressive deterioration of Macbeth's character.

64. "The murderer of Duncan inherits Hamlet's sensibility, his nervous irritability, his hysterical passion, his extraordinary gifts of visualization and imaginative expression."[2] By means of specific reference to the play, show that Macbeth possesses the qualities referred to. (Note that "sensibility" here means "over-sensitiveness" or "exceptional openness to emotional impressions".)

65. "Of all Shakespeare's tragic figures, Macbeth is the most isolated."[3] What evidence illustrates the increasing isolation of Macbeth as the tragedy unfolds?

OTHER CHARACTERS IN THE PLAY

66. "In the opening Act at least, Lady Macbeth is the most commanding and perhaps the most awe-inspiring figure that Shakespeare drew."[4] At what points in Act I does Lady Macbeth show that she is a) awe-inspiring? b) commanding?

67. Lady Macbeth is "clearly distinguished from Macbeth by an inflexibility of will, which appears to hold imagination, feeling, and conscience completely in check".[5] What evidence is there in Acts I and II that Lady Macbeth possesses inflexibility of will?

68. "The greatness of Lady Macbeth lies almost wholly in courage and force of will." Illustrate these two qualities by giving two examples of each from the play.

[1]Bradley, *op. cit.*, p. 359.
[2]Goddard, *op. cit.*, p. 111.
[3]Rosen, *op. cit.*, p. 84.
[4]Bradley, *op cit.*, p. 366.
[5]*Ibid.*

69. "Lady Macbeth is merely detested" (Dr. Johnson). How valid is this statement?

70. "The salient thing, perhaps, about Lady Macbeth . . . even more than her fixity of purpose, is her clarity of vision."[1]

    a) What evidence is there of Lady Macbeth's (i) fixity of purpose? (ii) clarity of vision?

    b) What evidence is there in the play that she lacked clarity of vision?

71. Nicolo Machiavelli (1469-1527), a Florentine politician, was the author of the influential book *The Prince*, in which he advocated unscrupulous statecraft. His name has become a symbol for the use of amoral principles in achieving political power. By direct reference to the play, show that Lady Macbeth in Act I can be considered a Machiavellian figure.

72. "O tiger's heart, wrapped in a woman's hide." How does this line, originally used of Henry VI's Queen Margaret in *Henry VI, Part III*, fit Lady Macbeth?

73. "Banquo in fact may be described much more truly than Macbeth as the victim of the Witches."[2] What evidence is there to support this statement?

74. What are the main points of contrast a) between Macduff and Banquo? b) between Malcolm and Duncan?

75. Estimate the importance of the Witches in *Macbeth*.

76. To what extent may the Witches be regarded as responsible for Macbeth's actions?

A MULTIPLE CHOICE QUIZ

1. William Shakespeare was born in a) Bread Street, London; b) Henley Street, Stratford-on-Avon; c) Castle Street, Hereford;

[1]Drinkwater, *op. cit.*, p. 302.
[2]Bradley, *op. cit.*, p. 379.

probably on a) May 18, 1600; b) December 11, 1592; c) April 23, 1564.

2. His father a) wrote English fluently; b) knew French and Italian; c) made his mark with a pair of glovers' compasses.

3. Shakespeare received his education at a) Eton; b) Winchester; c) Stratford Grammar School.
   He was familiar with the poetry of a) Horace; b) Vergil; c) Ovid.
   Tradition states that he left school at the age of a) 13; b) 16; c) 21.

4. In 1582, Shakespeare married a) Mary Arden; b) Anne Hathaway; c) Elizabeth Cecil;
   who was a) ten years younger than; b) the same age as; c) eight years older than, he was.

5. The Shakespeares had a) three; b) two; c) no, children and a) four; b) two; c) no, grandchildren.

6. Tradition also states that Shakespeare left Stratford in the late 1580's because he was accused of a) forgery; b) poaching; c) murder.

7. He is also said to have been in his early days a) a wool merchant; b) a fletcher; c) a schoolmaster in the country.

8. Still another legend has it that his first employment in London was a) selling papers; b) acting; c) holding the horses at the playhouse door.

9. In 1599, Shakespeare's father received a coat of arms, the motto of which was a) *Ich dien*; b) *Semper fidelis*; c) *Non sans droit*.

10. In 1597, Shakespeare purchased the largest house in Stratford, which was called a) New Place; b) Holmedon House; c) Sunninghill Park;
    for a) £100; b) £60; c) £500.

11. There is a legend that in the garden of this house Shakespeare a) wrote *Hamlet*; b) walked in the rain; c) planted a mulberry tree.

12. Shakespeare died on a) April 23, 1616; b) March 23, 1603; c) December 9, 1608.
    He is buried in a) Westminster Abbey; b) Canterbury Cathedral; c) the chancel of Holy Trinity Church at Stratford.

13. His epitaph is a) Exit Shakespeare; b) Here lies one whose name is writ in water; c) Good friend for Jesus' sake forbear/To dig the dust enclosed here;/Blest be the man that spares these stones/And curs'd be he that moves my bones.

14. In an elaborate will, he left his wife a) his manuscripts; b) a house in Blackfriars; c) the second-best bed with the furniture.

15. Judging by references in his plays, Caroline Spurgeon deduces that Shakespeare's favourite sport was a) archery; b) tennis; c) bowling.

16. The only book we know to have been owned by Shakespeare (for it bears his signature) is a copy of a) North's translation of Plutarch; b) Florio's translation of Montaigne; c) Holinshed's *Chronicles*. (The signature may be a forgery.)

17. Altogether Shakespeare is now credited with a) 25; b) 18; c) 37, plays
    and a) 50; b) 73; c) 154, sonnets
    as well as a) 2; b) 3; c) 4, long poems.

18. Most of his plays were acted in a) the Globe; b) the Swan; c) the Rose, Theatre,
    which was a) torn down; b) burned; c) destroyed by enemy action
    in a) 1600; b) 1605; c) 1613.

19. Although a) a few; b) none; c) about half, of the plays appeared in quarto during his lifetime,
    the collected edition or First Folio was not published until a) two years before his death; b) the year of his death; c) seven years after his death.

20. The longest of the plays is a) *Romeo and Juliet*; b) *Hamlet*; c) *Henry V*.
    The shortest of the tragedies is a) *Othello*; b) *Macbeth*; c) *King Lear*.
21. Some critics believe that his last play was a) *Henry VIII*; b) *The Tempest*; c) *A Winter's Tale*. During a production of this play, the theatre burned down; there were no casualties, although "one man had his breeches set on fire"; however, this minor blaze was doused with a bottle of ale.
22. Some scholars, chiefly American, believe that an Elizabethan lawyer and statesman called a) Lamb; b) Bacon; c) Veau, wrote these plays.
23. The structure of a Shakespearian play is often compared to a) a circle; b) an isosceles triangle; c) a rectangle, and the prevailing metre is a) trochaic tetrameter; b) iambic pentameter; c) anapaestic hexameter.

ACKNOWLEDGEMENTS

The editor is grateful to the publishers who have permitted her to quote from the following works:

Daemonologie in Forme of a Dialogue ed. by G. B. Harrison. Reprinted by permission of The Bodley Head Ltd. and David Higham Associates, London.

The Discoverie of Witchcraft by Reginald Scot. Reprinted by permission of Random House, Inc., New York.

Explorations by L. C. Knights. Reprinted by permission of Chatto and Windus Ltd., London.

Guide to Great Plays by J. T. Shipley. Reprinted by permission of Public Affairs Press, Washington.

Holinshed's Chronicle As Used in Shakespeare's Plays ed. by Allardyce and Josephine Nicoll, Everyman's Library. Reprinted by permission of J. M. Dent & Sons (Canada) Limited, Toronto.

The Influence of the Audience in Shakespeare by Robert Bridges. Reprinted by permission of the New Adelphi Press.

Macbeth ed. by Stanley Wood. Reprinted by permission of George Gill & Sons, London.

Macbeth, The Arden Shakespeare Edition ed. by Kenneth Muir. Reprinted by permission of Methuen & Co. Ltd., London.

Macbeth, French's Acting Edition. Reprinted by permission of Samuel French (Canada) Limited, Toronto.

Macbeth, The New Shakespeare Edition ed. by Dover Wilson. Reprinted by permission of Cambridge University Press, London.

Macbeth, A New Variorum Edition ed. by Horace Howard Furness. Reprinted by permission of Dover Publications, Inc., New York 14, New York.

A Macbeth Production by John Masefield. Reprinted by permission of The Macmillan Company, New York, and The Society of Authors and Dr. John Masefield O.M., London.

The Meaning of Shakespeare, Vol. 2, by H. C. Goddard. Reprinted by permission of The University of Chicago Press, Chicago.

On the Design of Shakespearean Tragedy by Harold S. Wilson. Reprinted by permission of University of Toronto Press, Toronto.

The Outline of Literature ed. by John Drinkwater, revised by

Horace Shipp, 1962. Reprinted by permission of George Newnes Limited, London.

The Players' Shakespeare: *The Tragedie of Macbeth* by Harley Granville-Barker. Reprinted by permission of Field Roscoe & Co., London.

Prince of Players, Edwin Booth by Eleanor Ruggles. Copyright, 1953, by W. W. Norton & Company, Inc., New York, N.Y. Reprinted by permission of the publisher.

The Rainbow Bridge and Other Essays on Education by R. W. Livingstone. Reprinted by permission of Clarke, Irwin & Company Limited, Toronto.

Samuel Johnson on Shakespeare ed. by W. K. Wimsatt, Jr., Dramabook. Reprinted by permission of Hill and Wang, Inc., New York.

Shakespeare by Mark Van Doren. Reprinted by permission of Doubleday & Company Inc., Garden City.

Shakespeare and the Craft of Tragedy by W. Rosen. Reprinted by permission of Harvard University Press, Cambridge.

Shakespearean Tragedy by A. C. Bradley. Reprinted by permission of The Macmillan Company of Canada Limited, Toronto, and Macmillan & Co. Ltd., London.

Shakespearian Tragedy by H. G. Charlton. Reprinted by permission of Cambridge University Press, London.

Shakespeare's Imagery by Caroline Spurgeon. Reprinted by permission of Cambridge University Press, London.

Shakespeare's Tragedies by G. B. Harrison. Reprinted by permission of Routledge & Kegan Paul Ltd., London.

Shakespeare's Tragic Justice by C. J. Sisson. Reprinted by permission of W. J. Gage Limited, Toronto.

The Wheel of Fire by G. Wilson Knight. Reprinted by permission of Methuen & Co. Ltd., London.

William Shakespeare by A. L. Rowse. Reprinted by permission of The Macmillan Company of Canada Limited, Toronto, and Macmillan & Co. Ltd., London.

The Works of William Shakespeare, Vol. X. Reprinted by permission of Basil Blackwell, Publisher, Oxford.

Every step has been taken to make the list of acknowledgements comprehensive, but in one case at least, all efforts to trace the owners of copyright failed. It is hoped that any such omissions will be pardoned.

The editor also wishes to express her gratitude to the staff of Longmans Canada Limited, in particular Mr. Robert Kilpatrick and Miss Janice Rogerson for their unfailing courtesy and co-operation.

David Garrick
1717-1779

Sir Henry Irving
1838-1905